The Helsinki Process and the Reintegration of Europe, 1986–1991

Analysis and Documentation

Vojtech Mastny

An Institute for East-West Security Studies Book

NEW YORK UNIVERSITY PRESS
Washington Square, New York

NEW YORK UNIVERSITY PRESS
New York and London

Library of Congress Cataloging-in-Publication Data
Mastny, Vojtech, 1936–
The Helsinki process and the reintegration of Europe 1986–1991 : analysis and
documentation / Vojtech Mastny
p.   cm.
"An Institute for East-West Security Studies book."
Includes bibliographical references and index.
ISBN 0–8147–5476–7   —ISBN 0–8147–5477–5 (pbk.)
1. Conference on Security and Cooperation in Europe (1972 : Helsinki, Finland)
2. Europe—Foreign relations—1989–
I. Institute for East-West Security Studies.   II. Title.
JX1393.C65M383   1992
327.1′7′094—dc20   91–46492
                                  CIP

New York University Press books are printed on acid-free paper,
and their binding materials are chosen for strength and durability.

Manufactured in the United States of America

c 10 9 8 7 6 5 4 3 2 1
p 10 9 8 7 6 5 4 3 2 1

23/2/06
27/4/06

University of Plymouth Library

Subject to status this item may be renewed
via your Voyager account

http://voyager.plymouth.ac.uk

Exeter tel: (01392) 475049
Exmouth tel: (01395) 255331
Plymouth tel: (01752) 232323

Also by Vojtech Mastny

The Czechs Under Nazi Rule: The Failure of
  National Resistance, 1939–42

Russia's Road to the Cold War: Diplomacy, Warfare,
  and the Politics of Communism, 1941–45

Helsinki, Human Rights, and European Security:
  Analysis and Documentation

CONTENTS

LIST OF DOCUMENTS

Part I: The CSCE in Transition

HELSINKI: FOR AND AGAINST

1. *from* US Congress, Commission on Security and Cooperation in Europe, *The Long, Hard Road from Helsinki to Vienna* (Washington, DC: US GPO, 1986).

BERN: A MEETING OF LOST OPPORTUNITIES?

2. *from* Speech by Michael Novak, head of the US delegation. CSCE Meeting of Experts on Human Contacts, Bern, May 1, 1986. In Michael Novak, "Toward an Open Soviet Union," chap. 14 in *Taking Glasnost Seriously* (Washington, DC: American Enterprise Institute for Public Policy Research, 1988)

3. *from* Roland Eggleston, "Neutral Compromise Effort in Bern." Report by Radio Free Europe/Radio Liberty correspondent, Bern, May 26, 1986. Radio Free Europe/Radio Liberty B-Wire, FF054.

4. *from* Roland Eggleston, "Summing up the Bern Conference." Report by RFE/RL correspondent, Bern, May 30, 1986. RFE/RL B-Wire, FF095.

5. *from* Michael Novak, "The Endgame," chap. 32 in *Taking Glasnost Seriously.*

6. *from* Speech by Michael Novak, head of the US delegation. CSCE Meeting of Experts on Human Contacts, Bern, May 27, 1986. In Michael Novak, "Words versus Compliance: Concluding Plenary Address," chap. 31 in *Taking Glasnost Seriously.*

7. *from* Speech by Iurii Kashlev, head of the Soviet delegation. CSCE Meeting of Experts on Human Contacts, Bern, May 27, 1986. RFE/RL B-Wire, CN104. Translated from German by Roger Malone and Jeannet Frössinger.

THE BREAKTHROUGH AT STOCKHOLM

8. *from* Speech by Hans-Dietrich Genscher, FRG minister of foreign affairs. CSCE Conference on Confidence- and Security-Building Measures and Disarmament in Europe, Stockholm, January 28, 1986. RFE/RL B-Wire, CN063.

9. *from* Speech by Marshal Sergei Akhromeev, Soviet chief of general staff. CSCE Conference on Confidence- and Security-Building Measures and Disarmament in Europe, Stockholm, August 29, 1986. RFE/RL B-Wire, FW 147.

10. *from* Richard Wallis, "Triumphant Mood in Western Camp at Stockholm Talks." Report by Reuters correspondent, Stockholm, September 11, 1986. RFE/RL B-Wire, FF020.

11. *from* Document of the Stockholm Conference on Confidence- and Security-Building Measures and Disarmament in Europe. Stockholm, September

THE ROAD TO THE SUMMIT

(Circolo di Studi Diplomatici, Rome) 22, no. 631 (November 12, 1990). Translated from Italian by Luigi Giovine and Roger Malone.

89. *from* Tom Heneghan, "Instead of Sealing German Spilt, CSCE Helped to Overcome It." Report by Reuters correspondent, Bonn, November 15, 1990. RFE/RL B-Wire, FF097.

90. *from* Sonia Winter, "Baltic States Press for Rights in Baker, Helsinki Meetings." Report by RFE/RL correspondent, New York, October 3, 1990. RFE/RL B-Wire, FF064.

91. *from* Colin McIntyre, " 'Swords-to-Plowshares' Accord Set to be Signed in Paris." Report by Reuters correspondent, Vienna, November 14, 1990. RFE/RL B-Wire, FF056.

92. *from* "CSCE Countries Adopt Document on Security-Building Measures." Agence France-Presse report, Vienna, November 18, 1990. RFE/RL B-Wire, FF002.

Part V: Clouds Over the New CSCE, 1990–1991

THE DIFFERENT KINDS OF CHALLENGES

93. *from* "A CSCE Club For All Europe," *The Economist,* November 17, 1990.

94. *from* Annika Savill, "The Russians Are Coming, But We Won't Talk About It," *The Independent* [London], November 15, 1990.

95. *from* Alan Riding, "Eastern Leaders Warn Against New Socioeconomic Division." *New York Times* report, Paris, November 21, 1990. RFE/RL B-Wire, FF005.

96. *from* Joel Blocker, "Council of Europe Asks for Major Role in Future CSCE Process." Report by RFE/RL correspondent, Paris, November 20, 1990. RFE/RL B-Wire, FF136.

97. *from* Statement from the Supreme Council of the Republic of Lithuania to the CSCE, Munich, November 22, 1990.

98. *from* Charter of Paris for a New Europe, Paris, November 21, 1990.

99. *from* Supplementary Document to Give Effect to Certain Provisions Contained in the Charter of Paris for a New Europe, Paris, November 21, 1990.

100. *from* Fred Kaplan, "Europe Choreographs New World Order, But Bush is Out of Step." Commentary in *The Boston Globe,* Paris, November 21, 1990. RFE/RL B-Wire, FF137.

101. *from* "Gorbachev, While Praised, Cuts a Lonely Figure at Summit." Reuters News Analysis report, Paris, November 21, 1990. RFE/RL B-Wire, FF055.

102. *from* "Stabilizing Europe," *The Times* [London], November 22, 1990.

SLOWDOWN AFTER EUPHORIA

TESTING THE NEW INSTITUTIONS

THE CSCE IN ANOTHER WORLD

FOREWORD

Looking back over the seismic shifts in the European landscape that have occurred since 1989, observers will see the profound impact of the Helsinki process as a force for change. The Conference on Security and Cooperation in Europe, as it is formally known, originated in Soviet proposals that were intended to legitimize the communist giant's position on the continent. But the term "Helsinki" has ironically come to symbolize the liberalizing political, economic, and security trends that eventually freed East Central Europe and indeed led to the devolution of Soviet authority within the former USSR itself.

In this book, Vojtech Mastny looks at the years between 1986 and 1991, a critical period for the Helsinki process. Through the use of 122 original documents, the Czech-born scholar illuminates both the internal dynamics of the process and the external policy considerations brought to it by many of the players. The central thesis of *The Helsinki Process and the Reintegration of Europe, 1986–1991: Analysis and Documentation* is that the issue of human rights has become an increasingly important element in the evolving definition of European security. Professor Mastny in essence argues that progress in the area of human rights in the late 1980s, no less than in the area of military confidence-building measures during earlier periods of the Helsinki process, has propelled the CSCE forward, bringing the participants ever closer to a secure Europe. And as Europe becomes more secure, more free of the divisions that have handicapped it, the Helsinki process must evolve and adapt, developing a new mission and instruments aimed at preserving the newly-won security and cooperation.

This book builds on the considerable insights the author displayed in his earlier work, *Helsinki, Human Rights, and European Security*. Policy makers and scholars alike will find that the author, a Professor of International Relations and Director of the Research Institute at the Paul H. Nitze School of Advanced International Studies of the Johns Hopkins University in Bologna, Italy, has an unrivalled grasp of the details and nuances that are important to an understanding of the history of the Helsinki process.

Professor Mastny concluded this work while an adjunct scholar with the Institute for East-West Security Studies. The Institute would like to express special appreciation to the Ford Foundation and the John D. and Catherine T. MacArthur Foundation for their comprehensive support for IEWSS programs. In addition, the Institute wishes to thank the William and Flora Hewlett Foundation and the Rocke-feller Brothers Fund for their support, and the W. Alton Jones Foundation, which underwrites the Institute's CSCE project.

John Edwin Mroz
President
Institute for East-West Security Studies
December 1991

PREFACE

After more than 15 years of existence, the "Helsinki process" (officially, the Conference on Security and Cooperation in Europe, or CSCE) still remains elusive even to Europeans and Americans otherwise well-versed in international affairs. This is regrettable, in view of the high hopes that many have entertained about the CSCE as the possible new structure of European security. Yet the elusiveness of the process is inherent in its complexity, which has grown rather than diminished over time. The CSCE has changed more than ever before during the last three years, when it was transformed from a pure process into a process with institutions; given the changes in Europe, this metamorphosis was warranted.

This book aims at explaining the CSCE's transformation—its achievements, prospects, and limitations—to both the specialist and the layperson. Chronologically a sequel to my *Helsinki, Human Rights, and European Security: Analysis and Documentation* (Durham, NC: Duke University Press, 1986), which covered the ten-year period from the onset of the Helsinki process in 1975 to the Budapest Cultural Forum of 1985, this new volume follows the same format. As suggested by the difference in titles, the thrust of this work is the CSCE's transition from a conference concerned overwhelmingly with human rights to one claiming a major role in the reintegration of post–Cold War Europe.

The analytical and interpretive introduction is to be read in close conjunction with the documents that follow. Not only does it frequently refer to them, but the documents are also structured to parallel the main themes of the introductory essay. So, too, are my headings before the individual documents, intended to highlight the dynamics of the CSCE's development. To facilitate the reader's orientation through the often bewildering array of the conference's numerous meetings, all of these along with their dates are listed in the Appendix.

Reflecting the diversification of the Helsinki process, the documentation draws on many diverse sources. There are the official products of the conference—proposals, concluding statements—but also speeches and working papers, or "non-papers" without official status, which are usually more illustrative of the issues underlying the CSCE's difficult process of consensus-building. The immediacy of the controversy involved is often best captured in reports by correspondents and other observers on the spot. Increasingly also views from a distance—by knowledgeable or not so knowledgeable but influential outsiders—are part of the Helsinki process, because of the expectations invested in it.

To help capture the essentials, most of the documents printed below have been edited for clarity and conciseness. In each case, however, the editing has entailed only deletion, marked in the text by ellipses, rather than any alteration by paraphrasing or adding to the text. Wherever necessary for comprehension of the text, I have made brief interpolations in square brackets, and when longer explanations or cross-references to other documents may be helpful I have provided them in notes following the document.

Each document is preceded by a heading providing the basic references. Rather than including exact bibliographical information, which is in any case impossible because most of the items are neither publications nor organized archival material, the main purpose is to give the reader a practical way of checking the original sources, if desired. Following the title or, in the absence of a title, another technical description, are the date and place of origin, and any further information that may be helpful in locating the document.

Official CSCE documents are recognizable by acronyms and numbers referring to the particular meetings (for example, WT, i.e., Wiener Treffen, the Vienna follow-up meeting). The originals were usually duplicated for distribution at the conference; most of the final documents were also printed either there or later by different governments, for example, by the Commission on Security and Co-operation in Europe of the US Congress. Only some of the correspondents' reports have been subsequently published in the press; the others are available in the raw telex copies supplied by the wire services. In the text below, reports by Reuters, Associated Press (AP), and Radio Free Europe/Radio Liberty (RFE/RL) correspondents are most commonly used.

Many of the documents printed here can be found in their entirety in the offices of the Commission on Security and Cooperation in Europe in Washington, DC, or in the Central News Room of Radio Free Europe/Radio Liberty in Munich. All of them are available in the CSCE Collection in the Library of the Paul H. Nitze School of Advanced International Studies of the Johns Hopkins University in Bologna, Italy. The only specialized research collection on the subject, it contains approximately 30,000 pages of documents on the CSCE's development since its inception in 1975 and is open to outside scholars.

The research for the book was made possible by a generous

grant from the US Institute of Peace in Washington, DC; its publication has been sponsored by the Institute for East-West Security Studies in New York. I gratefully acknowledge the support I have received as an adjunct of the Institute; the friendship of its Senior Vice President for Programs and Policy Peter Volten, and its Director of Publications Richard Levitt have been additional benefits.

Besides my own school, The Paul H. Nitze School of Advanced International Studies of the Johns Hopkins University in Bologna, the staff of several other institutions helped in providing research facilities, documentation, and an environment for discussion: the Commission on Security and Cooperation in Europe in Washington, DC (Sam Wise, Robert Hand), the Research Institute of Radio Free Europe/Radio Liberty in Munich (Vladimir Socor), the Netherlands Institute for Advanced Study in the Humanities and Social Sciences in Wassenaar (Dirk van de Kaa), and the Research Institute of the German Society for Foreign Policy in Bonn (Eberhard Schulz).

Many individuals shared their valuable opinions and expertise at different stages of the project. They include my closest friend and colleague at the Bologna Center, its director Stephen Low; Michael Novak, US representative to the CSCE conference in Bern; Michael Guhin, US representative at the Vienna Negotiation on Conventional Armed Forces in Europe; Rudolf Perina, US representative at the London Information Forum and later the Negotiations on Confidence- and Security-Building Measures in Vienna; Pertti Torstila, head of the Finnish Delegation to the CSCE in Vienna; Krister Wahlbäck, Director of Security Affairs at the Swedish Foreign Ministry in Stockholm; William Korey, former director of research of B'nai B'rith International in New York; Godfried van Benthem van den Bergh, head of the Peace and Security Advisory Council at the Netherlands Ministry of Foreign Affairs at the Hague.

For efficient and dedicated help in the editing of the book, I am grateful to Roger Malone, my research assistant at the Bologna Center, as well as to several other graduate students there, who lent their linguistic skills for the translation of documents: Jeannet Frössinger, Martine Gilbert, and Luigi Giovine. More of my special thanks belong to those extraordinarily conscientious copy editors, Amy E. Houpt and Rosalie Morales Kearns, both at the Institute for East-West Security Studies, the former subsequently at the Bologna Center as well.

Finally, my thanks to my editors at New York University Press, and to Pinter Publishers in London.

The Helsinki Process
and the Reintegration of Europe

The New Framework of European Security

Ever since the signing of the landmark Helsinki agreement in 1975, the Conference on Security and Cooperation in Europe (CSCE) has been a prism of the changing perspectives on a new European order. Originally a Soviet design to make the order more stable on Soviet terms, the CSCE unexpectedly turned the tables on Moscow by becoming a vehicle of change in the eastern part of the continent. Yet for many years, the meager results caused doubts in the West about the relevance and, indeed, the desirability of the whole "Helsinki process" as a harbinger of a better Europe.

The pluralization of the Soviet Union under Gorbachev and the collapse of its East European empire that ended the continent's division finally laid those doubts to rest. In turn, the demise of the familiar bipolar international order, on which, for better or for worse, Europe's stability had been resting for 40 years, gave rise to new expectations about the CSCE as the future security framework safeguarding both peace and justice. How well did the previous 15 years of the Helsinki process justify these lofty expectations?

THE INNOVATIONS OF HELSINKI

Launched in 1975 after three years of intensive negotiations involving the United States, Canada, and all the European states except Albania, the CSCE subsequently established itself as a distinct novelty on the international scene. Not all of its innovations could immediately be seen as practical and productive. Yet they were all peculiarly attuned to some of the key ingredients of the European security environment, ingredients that initially did not seem to matter very much, but were increasingly significant with the passage of time.

Of the military dimensions of security, the conference originally tackled only those that pertained to international trust because of their bearing on the intentions rather than the capabilities of potential belligerents. Unlike the assorted arms control negotiations that had been making headlines but little progress so long as the fundamental mistrust between East and West persisted, the CSCE addressed primarily the nonmilitary aspects of security—the underlying causes of the mistrust. At issue were the crucial intangibles that make nations and their leaders feel more secure or insecure for political, economic, cultural, and other reasons.

The most spectacular innovation of the Helsinki process was the inclusion in its "Basket Three" of a growing number of provisions for the protection of "human rights"—a shorthand for those diverse dimensions of security that impel insecure governments to repress their citizens. The 35 CSCE members unanimously accepted the principle that the manner in which sovereign states treat their own citizens is a legitimate concern of other sovereign states; because of its implications for international security, this acceptance was nothing short of revolutionary.

The practical effects of this innovation were often misjudged—particularly early in the process—because of the nature of the Helsinki accords as a statement of intentions rather than a legally binding international treaty. Yet this apparent weakness was more a strength, because it made adherence to stated intentions a test of political credibility rather than an invitation to search for legal loopholes. A product of the East-West détente of the 1970s, the CSCE has always been first and foremost about politics and trust. As such, it involved not only governments and their representatives talking behind closed doors but also citizens and their organizations hammering on those doors.

Nor was the Helsinki principle of consensus, which required the participating states to make all their decisions unanimously, the prescription for impotence it seemed to its critics. In a Europe divided against its will, consensus was a device through which a common will to overcome the division could gradually be forged. Aided by the practice of proceeding by stages, which made agreement on one set of issues the precondition for tackling the next, the consensus principle produced results. True, its workings were cumbersome and excruciatingly slow, but these qualities underscored only too well the magnitude of the task that needed to be accomplished.

Vast enough at its beginning, the CSCE's mandate kept expanding. That expansion, too, proved more an asset than a liability, because it allowed the conference to address almost anything as a security issue. Appropriately, the expansion conveyed the notion that security is changeable rather than fixed and that its different dimensions are interrelated. It created linkages that could facilitate agreements. Connecting the seemingly disconnected, Helsinki made a fine art of "mixing apples and oranges."

The conference established itself as an eminently useful forum for discussion about fundamentals. Its innovative system of follow-up meetings, where the implementation of previous agreements was reviewed and new proposals were discussed, allowed wide-ranging concepts of security to be formulated, tested, and clarified in the crossfire of adversary opinion. And, in the end, it was precisely a change in the Soviet Union's perception and definition of security that crumbled the walls dividing Europe.

THE FIRST TEN YEARS

Born of the hopes and illusions rooted in the détente of the Brezhnev-Nixon years, the Helsinki process reflected the ambivalencies toward détente; the term meant different things to different people. For Brezhnev and his acolytes, détente meant a transitional condition conducive to producing a gradual but irreversible shift of the global "correlation of forces" in the Soviet Union's favor, in an atmosphere of low tension despite high levels of armaments. If properly managed from Moscow, the CSCE could then assist movement in that direction by convincing other states that the shift was inevitable. As an added benefit, détente gave the promise of access to the bounties of Western technology and consumer goods on Soviet terms, without a political price to pay.

For the United States, which held the bounties, détente promised to enmesh the Soviet adversary in a web of interdependence that would gradually and irreversibly help terminate the arms race and stabilize the military relationship between the superpowers. There was little room or need for the CSCE in this scheme of things.

For most Europeans, in contrast, détente meant, above all, the prospect of overcoming the division of their continent by de-emphasizing the military ingredients of the East-West rivalry. This was the key concept animating their dedication to the Helsinki process.

It was the Soviet and European, rather than the US, thinking about détente that underlay the initial trade-off that launched the process in 1975. Linking political security with "human rights," the deal entailed Western recognition of the political status quo that

Moscow imposed in Eastern Europe as a result of World War II. In return, the Soviet Union and its allies subscribed to the Basket Three principles, which, if put into effect, threatened to undermine the repressive policies they deemed indispensable to maintain the status quo. The Soviet gain concerned the past—confirmation on paper of something Moscow already had in reality; the Western gain pointed to the future—the possibility of altering that reality by giving the paper undertakings on human rights a political substance.

The United States government, guided by Secretary of State Henry Kissinger to scorn such wishful thinking, exacted from the Soviet Union a concession Kissinger judged more pertinent to the hard realities of power: the commitment to start negotiating a mutual and balanced reduction of conventional forces in Europe (MBFR). However, in a twist suggestive of the limitations of *Realpolitik,* the MBFR negotiations promptly degenerated into sterile routine, while Basket Three emerged as the centerpiece of a vibrant Helsinki process.

This happened because dissidents throughout the Soviet bloc instilled political substance into the Helsinki Final Act by invoking its human rights provisions in their campaigns. Only then did the United States, under pressure from Congress, begin to take a prominent part in the CSCE as a vigorous advocate of human rights. US participation gave the Helsinki process the added dimension of public diplomacy by also involving, on a larger scale than other countries, individual citizens and their organizations.

The process evolved at a time when, for reasons extraneous to it, the peak of détente had already passed. Later in the 1970s, much to the chagrin of most Europeans, the two superpowers resumed their confrontational course. At the CSCE, the Soviet Union resisted Western pressure for compliance with its Helsinki commitments on human rights by invoking the clause from the Final Act that prohibited interference in the internal affairs of member states. At the same time, the USSR signaled that it might change its practices if the West responded favorably to its economic demands. Herein was a second Helsinki linkage—between trade and human rights.

In trying to exploit that linkage, the United States enacted legislation that made trade with the Soviet Union and other countries dependent on their human rights record, particularly on their willingness to allow free emigration of their citizens. Moscow proved not totally impervious to this pressure, allowing substantial Jewish emigration to continue briefly even after the enactment of the US legislation. However, nothing came of the second Helsinki linkage, as the paucity of Soviet concessions failed to satisfy Washington, and détente finally crumbled with the Soviet invasion of Afghanistan in 1979.

Indeed, the CSCE's very survival was uncertain as the new linkage between military security and human rights gained prominence during the apparent relapse into the Cold War in the early 1980s. Insisting that there could be no "political détente" without "military détente," the Soviet Union pressed for a CSCE conference on disarmament in Europe, hinting that its cooperation in human rights matters depended on the acceptance of the proposal. This was out of the question at a time when the United States was presiding over NATO's massive rearmament program.

Yet, while the United States resisted any "militarization" of the Helsinki process at the expense of human rights, a consensus was eventually reached at the end of the acrimonious second CSCE follow-up meeting in Madrid in 1983. The compromise entailed modest improvements in the human rights provisions of the Helsinki Final Act in return for Western acceptance of a "disarmament" conference to be held in Stockholm, concentrating on confidence-building measures. The outcome proved that there was a common interest in preserving the Helsinki process, even during high East-West tension —or precisely then.

The Soviet acceptance of the Madrid document in September 1983 promised to strengthen the hand of the Western opponents of the NATO "Euromissile" deployment in the great public debate that was reaching its climax at that time. Eight weeks later, however, a favorable vote in the West German parliament opened the way for the deployment, thus frustrating high Soviet hopes for the opposite outcome and compelling Moscow to honor its threat to break off the pending strategic arms negotiations in Geneva. Indeed, by 1984, all East-West military negotiations had been suspended—except those conducted in Stockholm under the auspices of the CSCE.

SECURITY AND HUMAN RIGHTS

The initial Soviet conduct at Stockholm hardly suggested that Moscow regarded the conference, which opened in January 1984, as anything but an additional forum in its public campaign against NATO rearmament. With scant regard for the mandate of the conference, which concerned confidence-building measures, Soviet representatives tried to put totally unpromising proposals on the Stockholm agenda. Included were the prohibition against the first use of nuclear weapons, which NATO was certain to veto, and such catchy but meaningless items as a mutual nonaggression pledge. For their part, Western delegates harped on how much Soviet observance of the Helsinki human rights provisions would foster an atmosphere of mutual confidence. There was little reason to expect a meeting of minds when East-West negotiations had been failing everywhere else.

By this time, to be sure, pressures were already building for both superpowers to wind down their increasingly costly arms race; the pressures, however, bore more heavily on the internally faltering Soviet Union than on the United States, seemingly reinvigorated under the Reagan administration. Moscow could still hope to mitigate the discrepancy by appealing to the West European opposition to NATO rearmament while trying to keep human rights off the CSCE agenda. But the longer the rearmament proceeded, while the Soviet internal crisis remained aggravated by uncertainty about the leadership succession, the shorter also was the time for negotiating favorable arms control agreements. Hence Moscow's sense of urgency, as well as its inability to act upon it.

At CSCE meetings, US representatives sought to impress upon the Soviet Union the linkage between the arms control agreements it wanted and the human rights commitments it continued to evade. They alluded to the fact of political life that the majority of the US Senate, necessary for the ratification of those agreements, came to regard Moscow's readiness to honor its voluntarily assumed Helsinki commitments as an acid test of its readiness to honor arms control treaties as well.

The Soviets had always been acutely sensitive to the security implications of their human rights policies, and for that very reason they were reluctant to change them under pressure. While under fire at the CSCE, they usually preferred to take shelter behind the noninterference clause of the Helsinki Final Act. At the 1977–1978 Belgrade review meeting, the Soviets at least implicitly acknowledged the legitimacy of interference by raising allegations of Western human rights abuses. In 1985, at the CSCE experts meeting in Ottawa, they went a step further by positing the supremacy of so-called social rights, supposedly safeguarded only under their brand of socialism. As the missile buildup mounted, they finally advanced the outrageous notion that the only human right that mattered was the "right" to survive.[1]

In 1985, the Soviet Union did return to the Geneva strategic arms talks, even though NATO had ignored the Soviet precondition that all Euromissiles be removed first. But this signal reversal of Moscow's arms control policy had no visible influence on its human rights practices. Neither did it have a favorable impact on the two main Helsinki meetings held in 1985—the Ottawa meeting and the Budapest cultural forum—both of which ended without consensus. Indeed, as the new Soviet leadership of Mikhail S. Gorbachev called for discarding the Brezhnev legacy, there were reasons to wonder whether the CSCE might be discarded as well. Nor was there a shortage of influential US supporters of the Reagan administration who insisted that the Helsinki "charade" should stop.[2]

THE FAILURE AT BERN

Accordingly, the United States anticipated without illusions the meeting of experts on human contacts convened in Bern in April 1986. Rather than aim at negotiating a concluding document, which had eluded the two previous CSCE gatherings, the administration instructed its ambassador, Michael Novak, to use the occasion mainly for pressing the Soviet Union and its allies to expedite the resolution of specific human rights cases listed on the US agenda.[3] This seemed to make more sense than additional verbal commitments beyond those already made at Helsinki and Madrid, whose implementation left so much to be desired anyway.

Novak, a noted Roman Catholic theologian and philosopher of East European descent, spoke eloquently about the pathetic predicament of a superpower whose security required putting priests and poets behind bars while keeping children of defectors as hostages for the transgressions of their parents. He looked forward to a time when the Soviet Union would be ready to open itself to the rest of the world, although he hardly believed the time to be coming soon.[4]

In this, the US delegate found himself out of step with many of his West European colleagues, who sensed that Moscow might be trying to get out of its predicament and deserved to be tested. Encouraged by Gorbachev's tribute to human rights in a speech on February 25, 1986, the British, in particular, saw the time propitious for insisting on technical improvements that would make contacts among people easier.[5] They viewed this course as more promising than a further elaboration of principles.

The Soviet representatives at Bern, however, offered little encouragement. They kept delivering speeches that their Western counterparts, wondering whom they were trying to impress, classified as "worn-out propaganda."[6] Moscow's envoys contested, as usual, all the sensitive and potentially operative words in the draft of the final document prepared by the group of neutral and nonaligned (NNA) countries.[7] Yet in the end, they accepted tangible, if modest, improvements in human contacts, while ensuring that loopholes would remain open as well. Whether the glass was half full or half empty depended upon an accurate judgment of Soviet intentions and the effect that unprecedented pressures would have on them.

The Bern conference convened under the fresh impact of the Chernobyl nuclear power plant disaster—a tragedy highlighting both the pitfalls of the regimented Soviet system and the plight of the ordinary people under it. Toward the end of the gathering, Moscow unexpectedly agreed to give exit visas to an unprecedented number of emigration applicants included on the US wish list.[8] The gesture came too late to prevent the United States representative from casting the lonely veto against the final document, shocking nearly everyone present. Yet even prompter Soviet action would hardly have made a difference, for Novak and his Washington superiors had in any case been set to cast the veto. They acted on the premise that the Gorbachev regime intended to continue the policy of human rights violations.

The subsequent course of events proved them wrong. Although the Soviet ambassador at Bern, Iurii Kashlev, exploited to the utmost the godsent opportunity to berate "those from far away across the ocean" who arrogate to themselves the role of "world policemen,"[9] Gorbachev proclaimed, on July 8, his country's readiness to abide by the provisions of the vetoed Bern document anyway. And, indeed, effective and substantive improvements followed in the very areas where Novak had suspected Soviet loophole-building—family reunification, short-term travel for urgent family matters, and publication of laws and regulations.

Thus, apart from the setback the United States suffered because of its diplomatic timidity, Bern was not the "meeting of lost opportunities" that the Polish representative Jerzy Nowak pronounced it to be.[10] It did not discourage the Soviets from trying to bring their human rights practices closer to the Helsinki standards. Indeed, regardless of its outcome, the conference was apt to impress on them the necessity to do so if, as Gorbachev evidently desired, they were to be accepted as bona fide inhabitants of the "common European house." In retrospect, the seemingly sinister Soviet maneuvers at Bern may be understood better as desperate and clumsy attempts to convince the incredulous that the intention to adapt was at last serious—but without losing too much face in the process.

THE SUCCESS AT STOCKHOLM

The watershed was reached at Stockholm, rather than at Bern. On November 21, 1985, Reagan and Gorbachev affirmed at their first summit in Geneva their intention to conclude the negotiations on confidence- and security-building measures (CSBMs), conducted in the Swedish capital since 1984, in time for the opening in November 1986 of the third CSCE follow-up meeting in Vienna. Also, other Western leaders perceived the Stockholm conference as an opportunity to move ahead. In a dramatic joint appearance before the conference participants, French Foreign Minister Roland Dumas and his West German counterpart Hans-Dietrich Genscher praised the talks, predicting correctly that they could eventually result in negotiations bringing about reductions of conventional forces in Europe.[11]

So far, the professed Soviet interest in conventional disarmament could plausibly be suspected as a ploy to weaken NATO by symmetrical reductions more painful to the Western alliance than to the Warsaw Pact, thus further increasing Moscow's lopsided advantage. Otherwise, given the "zero sum" competition that the Soviet leaders had traditionally seen themselves to be waging, there would have been no logic in wanting to negotiate away their superiority in conventional armaments. Indeed, this was their last indisputable asset —after nearly all the political, economic, ideological, and other assets had withered away, tilting the "correlation of forces" in the West's favor.

Conversely, if the new Kremlin leadership, having discarded the rigid concept of correlation of forces, decided to abandon the hostile competition, its willingness to give up the oversized conventional forces the West found so threatening was the single most convincing proof that the decision was genuine. In building upon mutual trust a détente more lasting than the previous fake one, the Stockholm talks were, indeed, the "acid test of Soviet intentions, sincerity, and credibility in arms control."[12]

Given the fundamental importance of secrecy in the Soviet system, the key issue was that of on-the-spot inspection and verification. On January 15, 1986, Gorbachev declared for the first time Moscow's readiness to allow on-site inspection of its nuclear test facilities; however, in Stockholm the Soviet delegation showed no willingness to apply the same principle to conventional forces. Perhaps its superiors were awaiting the outcome of the Bern conference, where the seriousness of Soviet intentions was also being tested. If so, then the US diplomatic fiasco at Bern may have reduced Moscow's incentive to make reassuring concessions elsewhere. Most probably, the whole idea of making concessions to reassure the West was intensely controversial in the Kremlin councils.

The approaching November 1986 deadline for the conclusion of the Stockholm conference, however, added pressure for accommodation. By August, the Soviet Union showed the will to achieve an agreement. Not only did it accept in principle on-site inspections of military exercises, but it did so without reserving the right of refusal envisaged in the proposal drafted by the neutral and nonaligned states. On August 29, 1986, the appearance in the Swedish capital of no less than Soviet Chief of General Staff Marshal Sergei Akhromeev, who announced the turnabout to the assembled diplomats as if no policy change had taken place, was an event of historic proportions.[13]

The sense of triumph felt by most of the Western delegates at the signing of the Stockholm final document on September 22, 1986 was amply justified by Moscow's acceptance of specific measures that for the first time materially reduced the threat posed by its conventional forces in Europe.[14] The possibility of outside monitoring of the movements of troops and other military activities appreciably increased the warning time of any attack. Nor were the statements in the document mere empty words, as subsequent developments proved.

The statements included the prohibition of the use of force even against allies—a thinly veiled allusion to the "Brezhnev Doctrine" Moscow had used to justify its invasion of Czechoslovakia in 1968. Also, the affirmation of a search for methods of peaceful solution of disputes that would be compulsory rather than optional marked a reversal of a Soviet position that had frustrated two previous CSCE conferences on this subject. Finally, the specific reference to human rights as one of the indispensable ingredients of security indicated how much closer the East had come to the West—at least in theory, if not yet in practice.

VIENNA BETWEEN NEW THINKING AND OLD

The persisting obstacles to a convergence between East and West reemerged at the Vienna follow-up meeting, which opened on November 4, 1986 under the shadow of the abortive Reykjavik summit, where trust was the casualty. This trust was what Gorbachev had put in jeopardy by overplaying his hand with his bid for complete nuclear disarmament—a prescription for Western military inferiority. Nor had Reagan's clumsy acceptance and subsequent rejection of the bid succeeded in breeding trust, not to mention confidence in his judgment. As a result, it became more difficult again to believe either in the novelty of Soviet thinking about security or in Washington's readiness to give Moscow the necessary benefit of the doubt—the two issues that proved critical at Vienna as well.

Soviet Foreign Minister Eduard Shevardnadze set the tone in his opening speech on November 5. After bitterly charging the US with responsibility for wasting a great opportunity at Reykjavik, Gorbachev's aide turned more pertinently to the new meaning of security. He reminded his audience that

> The concept of security . . . is acquiring new dimensions. It is increasingly seen as a task of creating, through joint efforts, political, material, institutional and other safeguards for preserving peace that would rule out the very possibility of war breaking out.[15]

In a new display of sensitivity to the ramifications of security, Shevardnadze then astounded the world by proposing to hold the next CSCE meeting on human rights in—of all places—Moscow. It was as if a meeting about chickens were to be held in a fox den, *Die Presse* of Vienna later commented wryly.[16]

The subsequent conduct of Soviet negotiators in Vienna was hardly revealing of the true motives of the proposal. On the one hand, Soviet First Deputy Foreign Minister Anatolii G. Kovalev insisted: "I want to convince this audience, I want you to believe, that great efforts are being made on humanitarian contacts."[17] On the other hand, however, he and his colleagues rarely missed an opportunity to answer Western charges of Soviet abuses by shopworn countercharges—from Britain's "Ulster killings" to the US threat to humanity's "right to life."[18] Hence the quality of dialogue in Vienna did not advance much above the previous CSCE meetings.

Meanwhile, the human rights situation in the Soviet Union, and still more so in Eastern Europe, presented a similarly mixed picture.[19] This lent credibility to later explanations by Soviet diplomats in Vienna, who said that Shevardnadze's conference proposal, as well as the whole notion of bringing Soviet human rights practices into line with the Helsinki standards, encountered strong opposition within the increasingly divided Moscow establishment. In any case, the foreign minister's initiative appeared to have been shelved.

It was not only on the Soviet side that the habits of old thinking persisted. The United States came to Vienna determined to apply much the same strategy as before, and for a good reason: its old strategy, unlike the old Soviet one, had been working, as Moscow's greater respect for the Helsinki principles seemed to indicate. Washington therefore continued to press for the resolution of specific human rights cases, while resisting Soviet efforts to redirect the CSCE toward military security.[20]

There was an air of confrontation on December 12, 1986, when US Ambassador Warren Zimmermann called upon the conference to observe a minute of silence in memory of Ukrainian dissident Anatolii Marchenko, who had recently died in a labor camp. The Soviet delegation, dutifully followed by those of Czechoslovakia and Bulgaria, stormed out of the hall. What was unprecedented, however, was the follow-up, calculated to overcome by deeds the effects and also the causes of the shameful episode.

On December 19, 11 days after Marchenko's death, the Soviet Union announced that its most famous dissident, the Nobel Prize winner Andrei Sakharov, had been freed from internal exile. This was followed by news of other political offenders released from prisons and additional emigration applicants released from the prison-state. Whether the more enlightened policy was the result of pressure from abroad or, as Soviet spokespersons insisted, of the evolving new thinking, was less important for the future than the readiness of the Gorbachev government to move forward in ways it had not contemplated before.

This readiness did not preclude (and may even have necessitated) efforts by Soviet diplomats in Vienna to cover up by aggressive posturing the concessions and retreats that their government had been trying to avoid but now considered inevitable and even desirable. Throughout 1987 and much of 1988, therefore, little progress was achieved in drafting the final document. The conferees spent—or, as many thought, wasted—much of their time fighting verbal battles, the fiercest one of which concerned the freedom of movement across national boundaries.

Reluctant to acknowledge the principle of free emigration, the Soviets seemingly improved their administrative practice instead. Decisions previously dependent on the whim of secretive officials were made subject to regulation by publicly announced laws. To critics, however, the new laws appeared to be more restrictive than the old arbitrary practices, whose rigor could often be mitigated by corruption. To counter the criticism, Moscow went so far as to dispatch to Vienna high-ranking judicial officials ready to answer questions. Despite progress in the opening of the closed Soviet society, however, agreement about the final document remained elusive.

THE EMERGING LINKAGES

On the US side, the new thinking evolved more slowly than on the Soviet side, where it had been more overdue. But once the change came, it had a greater effect on the Helsinki process. It took the United States six months—and pressure from its NATO allies disappointed by the outcome of Reykjavik—to act on the proposal that had been issued by the Warsaw Pact countries in Budapest in June 1986. The proposal envisaged incorporating in the Helsinki process negotiations for a reduction of conventional forces in Europe. In mid-December 1986, NATO agreed in principle.

By then, signs that Moscow might be serious about negotiating away its military advantages made the talks eminently attractive to the West. However, in view of the Soviet eagerness to get them started, it made tactical sense to hold out and bargain for the best deal. The United States insisted that the new negotiation must be different from the moribund conference on Mutual and Balanced Force Reduction of conventional forces in Europe that was still marking time in the Austrian capital after more than a decade of fruitless debating. Washington also wanted the new talks to remain separate from the Helsinki process, lest the latter's primary human rights content be diluted and an agreement on conventional arms be held hostage to the CSCE rule of consensus.

In contrast, the Soviet Union wanted the conventional arms talks to be part of the Helsinki process, and so did France, for its own reasons. While finally ready to substantially cut its military forces, Moscow still sought to do so at the lowest possible political price; that could be better accomplished within the political milieu of the CSCE than at specialized meetings of arms control professionals. For their part, the French favored the CSCE framework to avoid having the talks dominated by the superpowers. Unlike Moscow, however, Paris was in no hurry to start the talks any time soon, thus allowing for extensive bargaining to take place beforehand.

Acting on the Soviets' behalf, Poland suggested that the new conference be organized as an extension of the successful Stockholm negotiations. Although Austria was inclined to agree, other neutral countries were wary about a conference that would mandate disarmament. The Swiss, who maintained a large militia-type army threatening no one, feared an infringement of their special concept of sovereignty expressive of the free will of the people. They wished to be consulted during the negotiations but not necessarily bound by the resulting decisions.

Gone were the times when the neutral and nonaligned countries as a group often served as mediators between the two hostile blocs at the CSCE agreements. Now the superpowers and their alliances were moving toward accommodation, thus making the very concepts of neutrality and nonalignment increasingly questionable. The ingenious solution finally adopted to get preparations for the conventional arms talks started was NATO's initiative. It provided for representatives of the two alliances to meet in Vienna but to keep their premises separate from those of the CSCE.

As a *demandeur,* the Soviet Union negotiated from a position of weakness. It did not succeed in persuading NATO to accept its longstanding demand that a reduction of the air and naval forces be included on the agenda. Those were the forces in which, unlike in the ground forces, the West appeared to enjoy a margin of superiority. Moreover, Western diplomats in Vienna concluded that, since "the Soviet Union is anxious to have a new conference on military security [it] should be made to pay for it with concessions in the humanitarian fields."[21]

Sensitive to the linkage, the Soviet Union tried to limit the necessary concessions. Together with its allies, it flooded the Vienna conference with propagandistic proposals that could easily be withdrawn, while demanding substantive Western concessions in return.[22] For its part, the West also placed proposals on the agenda—ones that required from the Soviet bloc substantive rather than sham concessions on human rights.

In particular, the member states of the European Community (EC) and NATO proposed in February 1987 the introduction into the Helsinki process of a "human dimension" mechanism that would make the enforcement of human rights easier.[23] Envisaged were three stages: First, upon request, governments would be required to supply information about suspected violations. If the response proved unsatisfactory, bilateral consultations were to be held. As a last resort, a special CSCE meeting could be convened to address the situation.

So intrusive was the projected mechanism that the proposal was never expected to obtain the necessary consensus. Yet the Soviet delegation did not reject it out of hand. For several months it blocked discussion on a compromise Austrian-Swiss draft that incorporated the human dimension as well as provisions enhancing freedom of travel and freedom of information. In the end, however, Moscow accepted the draft after a face-saving maneuver; it insisted that the document be redrafted by another neutral country, and when Sweden did so in a perfunctory way, businesslike discussion followed. Now, weaponry and human rights were to be traded as they had never been before.

TRADING APPLES AND ORANGES

Connecting the seemingly disconnected had always been the forte of the Helsinki process. The wider and more entangling the ramifications of security grew, the greater also became the opportunities for "trading apples and oranges" to achieve an agreement—provided, to be sure, there was a will to agree. That will now depended not only on what was happening in Vienna, but also on the momentous developments beyond—the dramatically changing relations between the two superpowers and, especially, the great transformation of the Soviet Union and Eastern Europe.[24] Its relentless but difficult progress was the main reason why the Vienna conference lasted well over two years, much longer than originally anticipated.

In December 1987, the conclusion of the Intermediate-Range Nuclear Forces (INF) agreement during the US-Soviet summit in Washington also provided benchmarks for other arms control negotiations. The benchmarks consisted of asymmetrical cuts, reductions of substance rather than merely of growth rate, and, most importantly, verification on the spot—the principle that cut to the very heart of the Soviet concept of a closed society. Starting in the spring of 1988, in the discussions about the Vienna concluding document, Moscow's representatives showed a willingness to accept concessions that, if implemented, would make their society more transparent than ever before. Moreover, an unprecedented will to implement was now evident in the establishment of joint US-Soviet working groups designed to expedite the rectification of *Soviet* human rights deficiencies.

Just how distasteful this must have been to those vast segments of the Soviet establishment that habitually disregarded human rights can only be guessed from the tortuous course of Shevardnadze's project of holding a CSCE conference in Moscow in 1991.[25] By that time, the country's record was presumably to meet the Helsinki standards. After the project had been all but forgotten, the Soviet delegates in Vienna tentatively revived it in April 1988. Yet they seemed to drop the idea again until July, when Moscow suddenly reaffirmed its interest and began to press vigorously for acceptance of the proposal.

Sensing a new bargaining lever, the United States responded by presenting a set of conditions that would have to be fulfilled before its consent could be forthcoming.[26] The conditions amounted to measures facilitating further opening of Soviet society—something that Moscow's diplomats in Vienna had been grudgingly conceding during the laborious drafting of the concluding document. Now they not only indignantly rejected the US demands, but they also, together with four of their Warsaw Pact allies, introduced amendments that backtracked on the already agreed-upon draft. Yet two other Soviet allies, Poland and Hungary, accepted the text as it was—a breach of solidarity never before seen at the CSCE.

Romania, to be sure, had been deviating for some time from the Soviet line by resisting, for its own reasons, provisions that even Moscow finally found acceptable, notably those on the freedom of religion and of travel. Now the split was spreading, reflecting the deepening division in Eastern Europe between reform-minded and reform-hostile regimes, both of which were increasingly out of step with Moscow. As the Vienna meeting neared its climax, reports of police brutality against dissidents in Czechoslovakia contrasted with those of an incipient dialogue between the government and the opposition in Poland.

While outside the CSCE the Soviet Union was still reluctant to take sides in squabbles among its East European allies, in Vienna it finally took them, and the change was dramatic. As late as September 19, 1988, a Soviet delegate at the conference vowed that his government would never end the jamming of foreign broadcasts that it considered hostile. Eight days later, Moscow announced the end of all jamming, except that of the allegedly subversive programs by the US-supported Radio Free Europe/Radio Liberty, based in Munich.

And in another three months, all jamming of Western broadcasts ended—not only by the Soviet Union, but also, under its strong pressure, by all its allies.[27] This was the largest opening of their closed societies so far.

By then, Moscow had been pressing hard to get approval for its controversial human rights conference, hinting at first that its consent to the Vienna final document might depend on this. Later on, Moscow added the telling argument that the conference was needed to strengthen the hand of the advocates of democratization inside the Soviet Union. Rejection of the project would presumably amount to their betrayal by the West. In the end, however, Soviet diplomats in the Austrian capital made it clear that the rejection would not jeopardize consensus on the final document. The way to a successful finale of the Vienna meeting had been cleared.

AN UNEXPECTED ACHIEVEMENT

On January 4, 1989, the United States government announced its approval of the Moscow conference despite opposition from both conservatives and human rights groups.[28] Critics charged that giving the Soviet Union the honor of hosting the conference amounted to acknowledgment that its human rights record was now adequate. However, the decision was based on the sound recognition of partial improvements and promises of more to come. The prospect of the conference actually encouraged the fulfillment of those promises by giving the Western nations the option of otherwise cancelling participation.

Soviet assurances that improvements would continue included not only the termination of jamming but also a wholesale release of political prisoners and even an inspection of a forced labor camp by Western journalists. Then, at the United Nations on December 7, 1988, Gorbachev made the sensational announcement that Soviet conventional forces in Europe would be drastically cut.[29] In addition, as a down payment for the projected talks on mutual reductions that he urgently wanted to be finalized, a unilateral withdrawal of Soviet forces began even before the Vienna conference ended.

The US consent to the conference in Moscow was a tribute to the key role that this project had played in inducing Soviet acceptance of a concluding document with many more explicit commitments on human rights than the West (and, by all indications, Moscow as well) had anticipated.[30] The document included elaborate provisions on the freedom of travel, including the right to leave one's own country and return to it at will, as well as paragraphs that made the flow of information across national boundaries considerably easier. Shevardnadze's remark that Vienna had "shaken the iron curtain" was no overstatement.[31]

The last obstacle to success at Vienna was not the Soviet Union but the Romanian regime of Nicolae Ceauşescu. His diplomats raised as many as 17 objections to the already agreed-upon text of the final document. After all the objections were predictably rejected, the Romanian delegation scandalized the conference by signing the document with the reservation that its government did not consider itself bound by the provisions it deemed objectionable, particularly the provisions concerning religious freedom and movement of people.[32]

Rather than suggesting the ineffectiveness of the Helsinki process, the desperate maneuvers to which the prospective violator had to resort testified to the CSCE's growing influence. This was also the reason that the United States, having reversed its former position, acceded to the Soviet desire, shared by many Europeans, to schedule after Vienna a large number of subsidiary meetings of experts. These would provide an opportunity for the CSCE to affirm its relevance in an increasing variety of areas pertaining to security in a broadly defined sense. There was to be one meeting on the flow of information, two on environmental issues, and as many as three on human rights. Moreover, as human rights were advancing while the military substance of European security was diminishing, Washington had less reason to be concerned that the Helsinki process might be distorted by scheduling, within the CSCE, two conferences on military matters.

The two conferences were to follow closely after Vienna. One was a continuation of the Stockholm talks on Confidence- and Security-Building Measures and involved all 35 participants in the Helsinki process. The other was a new negotiation on the reduction of Conventional Forces in Europe (CFE), which, though declared part of the process, included only the 23 members of NATO and the Warsaw Pact. It was at this conference that the removal of the military barriers to Europe's unification was to be decided, after the psychological barriers had already been shaken. Those who judged the former more formidable than the latter braced themselves for "most complicated negotiations."[33]

CONFIDENCE BUILDING
AND CONVENTIONAL DISARMAMENT

The reason the CSBM and CFE negotiations eventually turned out to be less difficult than the West had anticipated could be detected in the initial Soviet optimism about their outcome. It became evident later, though it was not at the time, that the Soviet Union, unlike NATO, went into the conferences knowing which concessions needed to be made to ensure its success, and determined to make them. Although this did not preclude Moscow's attempts at hard bargaining, already its opening positions differed diametrically from those that had previously paralyzed the MBFR talks. Not only did Shevardnadze amplify on Gorbachev's UN speech by announcing in January 1989 further, albeit unspecified, unilateral cuts of Soviet conventional forces, but he also made a proposal at the CFE talks that could form the basis of an agreement, assuming that his government was indeed reconciled to giving up the military advantages it had.[34]

Incorporating the two fundamental Western demands pioneered by the INF treaty—asymmetrical reductions and intrusive verification—the proposal called for proceeding in three stages over a period of up to six years. During the first stage, any imbalances and asymmetries would be ascertained and eliminated by setting up ceilings rather than by trying to reduce the existing levels—an exercise that had previously led to insuperable disagreements about just what the levels were. The equal ceilings would then be reduced by the same percentages. Finally, the opposing forces were to be restructured to serve demonstrably defensive purposes only.

As Shevardnadze candidly admitted, the viability of the plan depended on trust. It stood to reason that

> any ingenious stratagem or undisguised attempt to retain an advantage in a particular kind of arms could torpedo the negotiations. This is not a matter of arithmetic but more properly of morality. Honesty and fair play are indispensable components of the process of negotiations.[35]

This accent on trust added importance to the other set of talks—those concerning confidence-building measures. Yet precisely there the Western negotiators discovered enough remnants of "old thinking" in Soviet maneuvers for what seemed to them more like "advantage-building measures."[36] Moscow resumed its old demand for the compulsory notification of naval and air activities, although these were explicitly excluded from the mandate of the conference. It further blocked progress by trying to link conventional arms reductions to cuts in NATO's tactical nuclear weapons—another subject outside the mandate.

Yet regardless of these less than "ingenious stratagems," the announced unilateral reductions continued, thus materially reducing the Soviet Union's capability to wage war and consequently also altering the Western perceptions of the Soviet threat. With plans for the modernization of NATO's short-range nuclear missiles already untenable for domestic political reasons, the US was under growing pressure from its European allies to give the Soviets the benefit of the doubt and reciprocate with arms reductions of its own. An arms race in reverse was now on when President George Bush turned the tables on the Soviets; on May 29, 1989, he announced NATO's readiness to negotiate also about combat aircraft and to reduce troop ceilings even lower than Moscow had proposed.[37] He challenged the Soviet Union to conclude the CFE talks within six months.

The necessary trust for that to happen was still in short supply. However, there at least was a growing willingness to overcome mistrust by addressing its causes.[38] In September 1989, the CSBM negotiators agreed to convene a seminar that would discuss first the respective military doctrines, postures, structures, and deployments, then training and other military activities, and finally the budgets that supported all this. "Confidence is the key,"[39] the Vatican delegate to the seminar exhorted the assembled military brass when this extraordinary gathering took place in January 1990; indeed, enough confidence was bred there to give the Vienna talks a decisive push. By that time, however, it became imperative to move quickly in any case, merely to keep up with the developments in the streets of Eastern Europe that threatened to overtake whatever the negotiators might be able to accomplish in their conclaves.

THE LONDON INFORMATION FORUM

Not only was the CSCE changing because the world around it was changing, but, conversely, it also influenced in critical ways the form and pace of the wider change, especially in Eastern Europe. At the London Information Forum, which opened in April 1989, five weeks after the two Vienna conferences, the division between the region's reformist and anti-reformist states came more into the open. The debate provoked them to sharpen their differences on the one human right that epitomized the contrast between closed and open societies—the right to receive and impart information.[40] While Romania harped on the need for "responsibility" in spreading information,[41] the Hungarian delegation included for the first time members who dared to publicly criticize their own government.[42]

Suggesting its reluctance to interfere with the course that reform would take in Eastern Europe, the Soviet Union preferred to distance itself from both its reformist and its anti-reformist allies. At the London Forum, Moscow's representatives evidently relished the situation when Western delegates, trying to jostle the conservative East European regimes into action about their human rights misdeeds, sometimes held before them the Soviet example. But the Soviet Union pointedly distanced itself from the liberal Western notion of freedom of the media, referring to the media as an "instrument of glasnost," rather than its beneficiary.[43]

The London Forum helped to further aggravate a split between the conservative regimes themselves, setting those intent on gaining time by appeasing criticism against the aggressively unrepentant Romania. Thus the Czechoslovak delegate, dwelling on the alleged seriousness of his country's reform efforts, pleaded plaintively for their more sympathetic appreciation.[44] In contrast, the Romanian envoy proclaimed the Ceauşescu regime's undisguised contempt for the Helsinki principles by vetoing the conference's final document, because of a paragraph that pointedly reminded all CSCE members of their obligation to honor the principles, and another that indirectly mentioned the conference's discussions critical of Romania.[45] At London, Bucharest thus set a record for blocking final consensus at CSCE meetings for the third time—not counting its repudiation of the inconvenient parts of the Vienna document.

THE PARIS MEETING ON THE HUMAN DIMENSION

Far from slowing down the Helsinki process, Romania's self-imposed isolation helped to accelerate the CSCE's progress "from nag to nurture."[46] At the subsequent Paris meeting on the human dimension, held in May and June 1989, the focus was less on the rectification of the remaining human rights abuses than on the nurturing of political structures that would preclude them.[47] The Western proposals were, therefore, not intended to be incorporated into a final document that would receive consensus, but were aimed at encouraging Eastern Europe's reformist governments to go farther and make reforms irreversible. China's relapse into repression in the aftermath of the Tiananmen Square massacre, which occurred while the conference was in session, underscored the urgency of the task.

At issue were such practical matters as the presence of observers during political trials, the guarantee of the right to leave one's country and return, as well as the panoply of rights of the individual that had been the mainstay of Western liberalism. A common denominator of Western proposals in Paris was the need to safeguard those rights under the rule of law—something that Gorbachev also insisted must become the foundation of a reformed Soviet state. Unlike its conservative allies, Moscow therefore proved receptive to many of the proposals. Together with France, Germany, and Austria, it even cosponsored the call for the creation of a European "legal space," an expression of the belief that everywhere the rule of law should rest on the same basic values.[48]

Paris was the first CSCE meeting where Eastern Europe's mounting ethnic tensions produced open clashes. Although veiled polemics had taken place before, only now did Hungary accuse Romania forcefully (and by name) of denying the Magyars in Transylvania their minority rights, whereupon Bucharest's representative responded in kind.[49] The increasingly rigid Ceaușescu regime alone remained totally impervious to criticism; other East European violators of minority rights, trying in their own ways to preempt or divert criticism, tacitly if unwillingly acknowledged the criticism and exposed their growing weakness in the process.

The Czechoslovak government—remembered for instructing its police to beat up demonstrators on the very day it signed the Vienna document in January 1989—released from prison the country's leading dissident, Václav Havel, shortly before the Paris meeting opened in May 1989. It proceeded to answer, though not to satisfy, the numerous inquiries about its conduct that it had been receiving from other CSCE governments under the recently created human dimension mechanism.[50] It did gradually loosen press and travel restrictions, although, as a prominent Western critic promptly pointed out, not as much as the Soviet Union, its supposed model.[51]

Also on the eve of the conference, the head of state of Bulgaria, Todor Zhivkov, announced a sudden reversal of his regime's five-year-old policy of forcible assimilation of the country's large Turkish minority. He opened the border with Turkey to those "Bulgarian Muslims" who wished to emigrate. There followed a forcible expulsion of tens of thousands of members of a minority whose existence the regime pretended to deny.[52] The turnabout, which created outrage and consternation in Paris, was as puzzling as had been the initial launching of the assimilation campaign in the first place. Neither added stability or respect to the regime; indeed, the subsequent halt to the expulsions, under pressure from foreign public opinion, may have been the beginning of its end.

THE CSCE AND THE REVOLUTION IN EASTERN EUROPE

The CSCE assisted more directly in hastening the decline of the Zhivkov regime by holding in Sofia in mid-October 1989 an experts meeting on environmental matters—something that the regime had long desired for reasons of prestige. After the Budapest cultural forum in 1985, this was the second CSCE gathering held within the Soviet bloc, and the results were indicative of the extent of change there.

In 1985 in Hungary—then the most liberal country in the Eastern bloc—the Budapest dissidents had barely managed to hold a parallel forum in their apartments as a political gesture; in the repressive Bulgaria of 1989, the Ecoglasnost opposition group demonstrated in the streets and eventually gained official recognition. To be sure, pressure from the CSCE delegates present in town was needed in both cases to persuade the reluctant governments to yield.[53] In Hungary, further liberalization had then followed gradually; what followed in Bulgaria within days was the downfall of the Zhivkov regime, engineered by party reformists with Soviet backing.

By that time, the CSCE had already made its most important indirect contribution to Eastern Europe's revolutionary upheaval. On September 10, 1989, the Hungarian government invoked its Helsinki obligations and its recent adherence to the UN Convention on Refugees to justify the invalidation of its agreement with East Germany that provided for the return of potential defectors. This was the decision that triggered the mass exodus of East German citizens across the open Hungarian border into Austria, starting an avalanche that, in the end, swept away East Germany's communist regime and led to the reunification of Germany.

In Czechoslovakia, the downfall of the communist regime occurred with a minimum of violence and brought into power in No-

vember 1989 some of the leading human rights activists of the Charter 77 movement, whose endeavors had long been publicized and
supported at CSCE meetings. The CSCE, to be sure, could not claim
credit for the bloody overthrow of the Ceauşescu dictatorship in
Romania in the following month. Conversely, however, one of the
first foreign policy acts of the successor regime was to end the country's self-imposed isolation from the Helsinki process by revoking the
Romanian reservation to the Vienna Concluding Document.[54]

In a deeper sense, Eastern Europe's largely peaceful revolution,
which prevailed despite the presence in the region of hundreds of
thousands of armed personnel capable of preventing it, vindicated
beyond expectations the belief in the possibility of eventually eroding
Europe's divisions by adding weight to the nonmilitary dimensions of
its security. That belief had been central to the Helsinki process ever
since its beginning 15 years earlier. Certainly the outcome gave a
useful lesson on the limitations of *Realpolitik*—both to the self-right-
eous critics who viewed the CSCE as an allegedly sinister Soviet
scheme for the perpetuation of Europe's division, and to the haughty
skeptics who dismissed it as a hypocritical exercise in ineffectual
posturing about human rights.

Now, suddenly, the all-inclusive European conference began to
appear, even to its erstwhile opponents, as something of a panacea,
more pertinent to the problems of the changing continent than either
its obsolescent military alliances or its exclusive economic communities—if only the Helsinki process could be transformed into an institution. Not surprisingly, in trying to sort out the debris of their
empire, the Soviets were the first to publicly promote the idea, even
before the external empire's last rotten pillar fell in Romania.

EUROPE'S NEW ARCHITECTURE

On November 30, 1989, during his visit to Italy, Gorbachev proposed
to convene in the following year another Helsinki summit to address
the new European situation. The summit proposal was not entirely
new, but its meaning was different from what it had been on previous
occasions. Earlier, when the Vienna conference appeared to be stalled
in 1988, Gorbachev's call for a European summit, supposedly to
expedite disarmament, had been justifiably suspect because the United
States and Canada had not been included. Later on, the Soviet leader
had managed to avoid this elementary mistake, but his summit sug-

gestions still left much to be desired because of his overriding emphasis on military and economic issues at the expense of human rights.

Now Gorbachev's main concern was damage control. Still vowing that he would "see to it that no harm comes to the GDR," the Soviet Union's "strategic ally,"[55] he tried to at least slow down what appeared to be an irresistible movement toward Germany's unification. Musing that one cannot build the common European home if "the walls keep moving,"[56] he implied that the possible removal of the border between the two German states could be a violation of the Helsinki provisions about the inviolability of frontiers. However, since the provisions did not rule out peaceful changes mutually agreed upon, Moscow wisely chose not to pursue this spurious proposition. Instead, it proceeded in the course of the next year to abandon, one after another, all the obstacles it had been trying to erect on the road to German unification.

Gorbachev's call for a Helsinki summit received unexpected support from Senator Steny Hoyer, chairman of the US Congress' Commission on Security and Cooperation in Europe, a body otherwise suspicious of Soviet initiatives. At the meeting with Gorbachev off the coast of Malta in December 1989, Bush proposed economic aid to Moscow by adding substance to the CSCE's long-neglected Basket Two, but offered no encouragement about the summit project. Undeterred, Gorbachev secured backing for the project from French President François Mitterrand, another Helsinki enthusiast, who envisaged his country's growing role in an undivided Europe.

The United States was slower than Europe in adapting to the sudden disappearance of the familiar East-West cleavage that had been the hallmark of the Helsinki process for so long. But once adapted to the change, it proceeded with more practical and specific proposals. In a keynote speech on the "Architecture for a New Era," delivered in Berlin on December 12, 1989, Secretary of State James A. Baker conceded that "the CSCE process could become the most important forum of East-West cooperation."[57] With an eye on the continued importance of military security, however, he saw the immediate priority in an early conclusion of the Vienna negotiations on confidence- and security-building measures and conventional arms reductions.

Mindful of the former Soviet bloc's worsening economic plight, Baker elaborated on Bush's proposal to give more substance to Helsinki's Basket Two. But he saw greater need in making the recent political changes in Eastern Europe irreversible. In his view, the CSCE's main task should be to institutionalize the system of free elections in the region. With a rhetorical flourish, he described such elections as "the ultimate human right, the right that secures all others"[58]—a fitting counterpoint to the one-time Soviet proposition, now discredited and discarded, that the ultimate right was that of mere survival.

Endorsed three days later by NATO's foreign ministers, Baker's blueprint conveyed expectations and priorities different from the Soviet design. Speaking in Brussels soon after the removal of the Ceauşescu tyranny in Romania, Shevardnadze suggested that Europe had already become politically the most integrated region of the world. In his opinion, the agreements concluded as part of the Helsinki process proved so successful that they were in effect legally binding within an emerging European "legal space."[59] He suggested that no more than a short step was now needed to create CSCE institutions that would serve as the new framework of European security. He added that the unification of Germany and of the entire continent could be best managed within that framework.

Between these different, though not necessarily incompatible, visions held by the two superpowers, there was abundant room for Europeans in East and West to exercise their imagination concerning the continent's new architecture. Mitterrand greeted the new year, 1990, by exalting the CSCE as the core of a future confederation of European states, although he remained notably vague about specifics.[60] This absence of details helped East Europeans build on the idea.

Endorsing the confederation idea, Polish Prime Minister Tadeusz Mazowiecki linked it with the creation of a European Security Council.[61] Czechoslovak President Václav Havel proposed an even more ambitious plan for a European Security Commission that would have two chambers and would become a precursor of a United States of Europe.[62] But even the most daring of these visions risked becoming quickly obsolete because of the continued rush of events, as had already happened to the pending disarmament talks in Vienna.

DEMILITARIZATION OF SECURITY

With the Warsaw Pact crumbling while NATO remained relatively intact, Moscow was not alone in its concern about the evolving imbalance. Even its erstwhile allies initially saw merit in the preservation of the two alliances, which, through the CFE negotiations, seemed to provide the best guarantee for getting Soviet forces out of their countries. To further expedite the departure, NATO proposed at its meeting in Ottawa to lower even more the ceilings on armaments that were being considered at the Vienna talks.

However, growing local pressure for the departure of the Soviet troops stationed in Eastern Europe threatened to render obsolete the concept of balance of forces, on which the whole arms control process had so far been built. On the one hand, fears arose that propping up the concept in a CFE treaty could artificially preserve Soviet military presence in the region,[63] which would otherwise be untenable for local political reasons. On the other hand, there was a concern that the ongoing disintegration of the Warsaw Pact, together with the growing momentum of German unification, would actually make the conclusion of the treaty impossible.

Because the United States made the conclusion of the CFE treaty a precondition for its consent to the Helsinki summit, the future of the CSCE thus became thoroughly intertwined with that of the two military alliances—itself a controversial subject. In the West, where it lacked immediate urgency, the debate proceeded more slowly. On the Soviet and East European side, it evolved dramatically.

Previously, the Soviet Union had been verbally committed to the dissolution of both alliances. It had created its own only in 1955, six years after NATO had come into existence, and the Warsaw Pact's original mission had been political rather than military. At that time, Moscow's immediate need had been to offset the attractiveness for its East European clients of the neutral status it had allowed nearby Austria. In the hypothetical case that the two alliances were indeed to be negotiated away later on, presumably at a time of irresistible Western weakness, the Soviet Union would still have been left with its intact network of bilateral military pacts in Eastern Europe while the West would have dismantled the only security structure it had. Thus the professed Soviet desire to dispense with both alliances had not necessarily been a sham.

Now, however, those bilateral pacts, too, were in shambles, thus threatening to leave the Soviet Union, but not the West, without an international security structure of its own. Moscow therefore reversed itself by urging the preservation of both alliances and their simultaneous transformation into mainly political entities. There were people in the West who saw this as a good way of keeping the Soviet Union attached to Europe while facilitating at the same time its peaceful military exit from the region. But for most East Europeans eager to "return to Europe," there was never any appeal in remaining politically bound to the former hegemonic power that had kept them out of it. Nor did the West Europeans and North Americans need a special structure to facilitate their already vast cooperation outside the military sphere.

Amid the progressive demilitarization of European security, it therefore appeared more promising to try to assign more security functions to the CSCE while not tampering with the uneven transformation of the two military alliances. Italian Foreign Minister Gianni De Michelis, for example, saw a stronger CSCE necessary because of the collapse of the Warsaw Pact and the possible withdrawal of the Soviet Union, beset by internal crises, from European affairs.[64] But there was no inherent contradiction between that stronger CSCE and the continued existence of NATO. Hence, even staunch opponents of the institutionalization of the Helsinki process, notably the United States, the United Kingdom, Canada, and the Netherlands, gradually came around to the conclusion that some institutions had become both inevitable and desirable.[65]

The interaction between the CSCE's nonmilitary and military components favored its institutionalization. The three-stage human dimension mechanism, adopted at the Vienna follow-up meeting to help rectify human rights violations, served as the model to the conference on confidence- and security-building measures for designing a procedure to handle suspicious military movements. Conversely, the emerging consensus at this conference—that annual meetings of officials should review compliance and that a permanent communications network should be established to assist them—provided an example to be followed by the CSCE as a whole.

By the summer of 1990, the question was no longer whether institutions should be created but how extensively they should be developed. Austria and several other countries favored a secretariat and regular meetings of foreign ministers. The UK wanted the new CSCE to have a mechanism for dealing with Europe's mounting ethnic conflicts and likely territorial disputes. FRG Foreign Minister Genscher, who regarded the Helsinki process as an outstanding vindication of his long-controversial belief in a progressive demilitarization of the East-West rivalry, proposed a panoply of agencies, with responsibilities ranging from human rights and conflict resolution to transportation and environmental protection.[66]

After Gorbachev, at the Washington summit in June 1990, accepted the US condition that the CFE treaty must be completed before the Helsinki summit could take place, NATO took a decisive step forward. On July 6, 1990, it issued a communiqué that was

conspicuously vague about its own future role but all the more definite in recommending an extensive buildup of the CSCE.[67] Declaring
solemnly its original mission accomplished and its adversarial relationship with the Warsaw Pact turned into partnership, the document
proceeded to expatiate on the different components of a new CSCE.
These included, in addition to most of Genscher's ideas, a center for
the monitoring of elections and even a parliamentary assembly of all
Helsinki states.

The vision came closer to reality as encouraging developments,
including the successful CSCE conferences in Bonn and Copenhagen, brought the convergence of values between East and West
farther than could possibly have been expected before. The conviction took root that the democratization of the former communist
states had become irreversible, thus making it possible to proceed
with erecting a roof over the common European house. Rare were
those who wondered why the roof was needed at all if everyone
believed that the sun was shining.

THE TRIUMPH AT BONN

The first of the two successful conferences, the Bonn meeting on
economic cooperation in March–April 1990, concerned the fundamental policy principles that differentiated Western-style capitalism
from Soviet-style socialism. Because adoption of these principles materially affected the very survival of the Soviet system, the attitude
toward them by those responsible for the system's functioning could
be regarded as the acid test of the ultimate demise of communism.
Hence also the United States, originally lukewarm to the conference
project decided upon in Vienna two years earlier mainly to give some
shine to the lackluster Basket Two—economic cooperation—subsequently reversed itself and prepared its strategy carefully.[68]

Now the promise of Western economic aid became a much
stronger leverage in dealing with Moscow than it had ever been. It
was now also true that the Soviet leaders themselves—not to mention
the new East European democracies—had come to regard a shift
from a command to a market economy as indispensable for the
future of their countries. In this sense, nothing less than an uncondi-
tional surrender of communism to capitalism at the end of that final
battle that Marx had prophesied was being staged in the West German capital.

It was indicative of the historic victory that representatives of the United States and the European Community—those bulwarks of organized capitalism—drafted the elaborate concluding document that was then approved by consensus after hardly any discussion. Although the Soviet delegates grumbled about too many enthusiastic references to "private enterprise" and "free market," they seemed to lack the inner conviction and will to fight over the text as they used to do. The result came closer to a Magna Carta of free enterprise than any comparable document in history.[69]

Far from being limited to a ringing affirmation of principles, the document went into minute detail about the ways and means by which the Soviet-style socialist system needed to be subverted, dismantled, destroyed, and buried beyond resurrection. The operational provisions ranged from open access to accurate economic data to the convertibility of currencies, from the creation of capital markets to the creation of institutions that would protect entrepreneurs from state interference.

None of these accomplishments necessarily made the Bonn gathering "the most important economic conference the world had ever seen," as West German Economics Minister Helmut Haussmann eulogized it.[70] After all, the importance of the agreement depended, as always, upon its implementation. Still, the willingness of the participants to shed old stereotypes and affirm common values was greater than at any previous—or later—CSCE meeting. Bonn was the veritable climax of the Helsinki process, after which new disagreements began to appear. Indeed, the overwhelming emphasis in Bonn upon opportunities for individuals and the relative neglect of the protection of social groups heralded future trouble. This became evident already at the Copenhagen conference three months later.

THE LIGHTS AND SHADOWS OF COPENHAGEN

Resuming under more propitious circumstances the unfinished business of the Paris meeting the year before, the second conference on the human dimension met in Copenhagen in June 1990. It set itself the ambitious task of moving beyond Helsinki and Madrid, from the protection of individual human rights to the creation of safeguards that would protect minorities from the tyranny of majorities—the safeguards that constitute the essence of democracy.[71]

It was symptomatic of an extraordinary international harmony

that seemed to be spreading through Europe that the human dimension mechanism, hailed as such an accomplishment in Vienna, had
rarely been invoked since the communist regimes in the eastern part
of the continent had disappeared. That Romania still—or again—
struck a discordant note because of its treatment of minorities did
not initially disturb the unprecedented consensus about what was
needed in order to advance the progress of democracy. Even Albania, the last bastion of Stalinism, which had been boycotting the
CSCE since its inception, now sought to belong, pledging a readiness
to abide by the Helsinki principles. Appropriately, Albania was put
on probation as an observer after its representative, quizzed about
the country's opposition parties, tried to explain that under Albania's
special brand of "democracy" there was no need for any opposition.[72]

The creation of safeguards for political pluralism under the rule
of law was the leitmotif of Copenhagen. In effect, this meant breaking the political backbone of communism after its economic backbone
had already been broken in Bonn. Again the Soviet Union, along
with the East European states more advanced on the road from one-
party rule to democracy, was ready to collaborate on dismantling the
system that had so far held it together. Principles aside, there were
pragmatic reasons for doing so. Not only had the system plainly
failed, but its abandonment also was the price to be paid for ending
the Cold War and obtaining the Western assistance desperately needed
to overcome the country's economic catastrophe.

The result was the unanimous adoption of a final document
exuberantly affirming the fundamental principles of Western democracy.[73] The Copenhagen declaration echoed themes from the US
Declaration of Independence, the *Federalist Papers,* the Bill of Rights,
and other classics of Western political thought. At US insistence,
safeguards of the right to free elections—the right that supposedly
secures all the others—figured prominently in the text. As an added
insurance, however, guarantees for the exercise of those other rights
—political and civil as well as human—were also spelled out in detail.

Yet the triumph of democracy at Copenhagen was more apparent than real. This was not necessarily because some of the participants' professed commitment to democracy was questionable, although subsequent developments in such countries as the Soviet
Union, Yugoslavia, and Romania proved that indeed it was. More
pertinent were the emerging shortcomings of the Helsinki process
itself. The CSCE, so successful in helping to overcome Europe's
division, was now beginning to navigate in uncharted waters, for
which its instruments might be inadequate.

At Copenhagen, the Helsinki process reached the stage where the varieties of Western democracy, rather than differences between East and West, provoked disagreements because of the legal and constitutional problems involved. Thus Switzerland, despite its being closer to direct democracy than other nations, could not easily reconcile the principle of universal suffrage with its ancient voting habits. Similarly, the United States, regardless of its elaborate Bill of Rights for the protection of individual liberties, was constitutionally inhibited from assuming at the CSCE the commitment to abolish capital punishment. And many West European states, whose courts were otherwise models of responsibility, felt similarly inhibited from accepting the US principle of judicial review.

Ironically enough, the quintessentially American principle of the separation of powers elicited greater interest in the politically unstable postcommunist Eastern Europe than in the more solidly democratic parts of the continent. This was particularly true of the multiethnic Soviet Union and Yugoslavia, where the influence of the old communist elites remained strong. Right or wrong, the US model, with its well-functioning federalism, seemed most pertinent to the need to accommodate the rising aspirations of the region's many minorities. The status of these minorities emerged as the most contentious issue at Copenhagen.

MINORITIES AND EUROPEAN SECURITY

The disputes over ethnic minorities that erupted at the conference portended the most vexing of the new Europe's security problems, ones that the CSCE was ill-equipped to handle.[74] Their intractability could be gleaned from the now more civil, though no less sharp, exchanges between delegates from postcommunist Hungary and post-Ceauşescu Romania concerning the collective rights of the Hungarian minority in Transylvania.[75] Did the recognition of such rights, in addition to the civil and human rights of its individual members, entitle the minority to special protection by the government of the "mother country"—as Budapest claimed on behalf of compatriots not only in Romania but also in Czechoslovakia? And, if so, where was the line to be drawn between a minority's allegiance to its special protector and its state of residence?

Nor was the Hungarian-Romanian dispute the most intractable; that distinction always belonged to the Macedonian question. At Copenhagen, Yugoslavia accused Bulgaria of denying minority rights to Macedonians, whose existence as a separate ethnic group was denied by Bulgaria. Reminding the Yugoslavs of their own plethora of ethnic problems, the Bulgarian delegation asked rhetorically what had happened to their Bulgarians—whom the Yugoslavs considered Macedonians.[76] On behalf of these Macedonians, Yugoslavia then raised a voice in support of their alleged compatriots in Greece.

Tongue in cheek, the Greeks proposed convening a special conference to define what a minority really is—something that had always eluded experts.[77] In any case, as the delegate from Cyprus reminded the conferees, there was also an oppressed Greek minority in the Turkish-occupied part of that island. And, for good measure, his Turkish colleague could always refer to his compatriots in Bulgaria, leading a precarious existence either as subversive aliens or as Bulgarians in Muslim disguise.

As if the resurgence of these ancient disputes were not enough, new minorities asked for recognition. Turkey and Yugoslavia spoke up on behalf of Europe's growing population of migrant workers, asking the CSCE to confer on them the rights and protection due to minorities.[78] And outside of the conference hall, a spokesman for European Gypsies, himself a member of the Romanian parliament, called attention to their particular plight, demanding their recognition as a "non-territorial minority."[79]

Not surprisingly, the section on minorities in the Copenhagen document, though verbally extensive, failed in operational terms to advance significantly beyond Helsinki, Madrid, and Vienna. It was further weakened by Bulgaria's "interpretive statement," sadly reminiscent of the earlier Romanian antics, that each participating state was free to decide whether to apply in practice any "political provisions" affecting its own minorities.[80] Nothing came of the British idea of establishing a CSCE center for the mediation of ethnic conflicts—something that at least one country torn by such conflicts, namely Yugoslavia, tentatively indicated interest in. The most deplorable shortcoming of the document, however, was its utter neglect of what was rapidly becoming Europe's preeminent security problem—managing the likely separation or secession of different components of the existing multiethnic states.

Already the mounting crisis in the Soviet Union's Baltic republics, which for the first time raised the specter of Moscow's use of force while the Copenhagen conference was in session, highlighted the irrelevance to this new security threat of a process designed to preserve rather than alter Europe's territorial status quo. It was impossible to avoid the problem by ruling out CSCE intervention on behalf of Lithuanian independence on formal legal grounds, as Austrian Foreign Minister Alois Mock suggested, for the Helsinki process was, after all, a political one.[81]

Alert to the importance of international recognition for advancing their struggle for independence, the Baltic republics pressed for admission to the CSCE at least as observers, the status that even Albania received. They could not count on obtaining full admission because of the certainty of a Soviet veto; what they could count on were the CSCE's well-tested powers of persuasion—provided there was enough willingness to apply these. That willingness, however, was in short supply, at least for the time being.

Also, as far as further advances in human rights were concerned, critics argued that in the new international setting, the Helsinki process could be more of a hindrance than a help. A better mechanism was the European Court of Human Rights, which enabled individual citizens to sue any member government of the Council of Europe that had contracted to accept its decisions. Indeed, the Council itself, highly regarded especially by East Europeans as a vehicle facilitating their "return to Europe," seemed uniquely suited to take the lead in promoting the reintegration of the continent from now on.

Encouraged by the vigorous leadership of its activist secretary general, Catherine Lalumière, the Council of Europe's supporters campaigned for assigning it the function of the CSCE's representative assembly.[82] The Copenhagen document paid the Council of Europe a special tribute by referring in the section on minorities to its project on "Democracy through Law," which aimed at developing constitutional devices designed to mitigate ethnic conflicts. Into all these endeavors intruded suddenly the Gulf crisis, dramatically showing how much the progress of Europe's reintegration still depended on developments in far more turbulent parts of the world.

THE ELUSIVE PEACEFUL ORDER

The Iraqi invasion of Kuwait in August 1990 shattered the illusion of an incipient peaceful international order extending beyond Europe. The next month, at the CSCE meeting of experts at Palma de Mallorca, originally convened to address mainly environmental and other relatively unpolitical issues, Italy and Spain advocated the expansion of the Helsinki process to Arab countries of the Mediterranean, the

Middle East, and even the Persian Gulf.[83] They hoped to prevent Europe and the Islamic world from embarking on a collision course. Yet with a war looming in the troubled region, the proposed expansion risked making discord, rather than peace, contagious. At least the conference achieved, besides modest progress in environmental cooperation, an agreement to convene in the spring of the following year a conference on security in the Mediterranean—but outside the CSCE.

In Europe as well, the most profound transformation of its established state system—the unification of Germany as a result of the extinction of one of the CSCE's founding members, the German Democratic Republic—was rushing forward outside the Helsinki tracks. Although the pending Helsinki summit had originally been expected to give German unification the necessary imprimatur, this became redundant as the process was being effectively implemented by the Germans themselves with the reluctant blessing of the four occupation powers formally responsible for the settlement.

The conference of CSCE foreign ministers in New York on October 1–2, 1990—the first Helsinki meeting to be held in the United States—therefore merely registered its approval of West Germany's absorption of East Germany that was scheduled to come into effect the next day, October 3.[84] It was not so much the CSCE as the bilateral deal concluded between Bonn and Moscow the preceding July that had helped to make this difficult step so easy. The deal between Gorbachev and Chancellor Helmut Kohl at their meeting in Stavropol sanctioned the unification and approved the united Germany's membership in NATO—something that only months before Moscow had vowed never to permit. The Soviet Union acquiesced in the inevitable while exacting from Bonn a huge package of economic aid in return.

By that time, the disintegration of the Warsaw Pact had advanced so far as to leave NATO the only credible military structure of European security. The Soviet Union paid it a tribute by assigning an ambassador to its headquarters. As far as Moscow's nominal allies were concerned, Czechoslovak President Havel now publicly referred to the Western alliance as "a guarantee of freedom and democracy" while dismissing its Eastern counterpart as "an outdated remnant of the past."[85] Besides Czechoslovakia, Hungary also expressed interest in an association with NATO, while Poland made no secret about the fact that it hoped to establish a special relationship with the United States.

With the terminal agony of both the Warsaw Pact and its economic counterpart, the Council for Mutual Economic Assistance (CMEA) well under way, and the disintegration of Europe's two remaining communist multiethnic states—the Soviet Union and Yugoslavia—looming, the long-awaited CSCE summit was bound to be anticlimactic. Whatever substantive results it was expected to achieve, notably the conclusion of the CFE treaty, had already been achieved before it opened in Paris on November 19, 1990. Now it was the CSCE's inadequacies that were breaking ever more through the surface despite all the efforts to give it a smooth and shiny appearance.

Like the agreements on German unification, the Treaty on Conventional Armed Forces in Europe, while formidable in its 200-page bulk,[86] merely confirmed the spectacular collapse of Soviet power that had been an accomplished fact in the central and eastern parts of the continent. It described in meticulous detail the assorted arms control and disarmament measures that had to be taken to end the East-West military confrontation in Europe once and for all. Thousands of tanks were to be cut into pieces and thousands of controllers brought in to ensure that none would ever return.

No sooner did the ink dry on the treaty, however, than the Soviet Union was found to have removed beyond the Urals much of the heavy equipment it was supposed to destroy, proceeding also to reclassify army units as part of the navy to prevent them from being counted. While none of these evasive maneuvers could bring back the lost empire, they could make the loss much worse by adding to it a loss of credibility. Indeed, by January 1991, the follow-on talks designed to extend the armaments cuts to personnel had broken down over the evasion. Nor did the subsequent resumption of those talks dispel the disturbing thought that they might never be concluded, because the ascendancy in Moscow of reactionaries, in addition to the country's probable breakup, may have meanwhile prevented the Soviet government from ever again mustering the necessary will to finalize the treaty.

In contrast to the matter-of-fact CFE treaty, supplemented by an equally tight agreement strengthening the military confidence-building measures,[87] the grandiloquent Charter of Paris was abstract enough to be unexceptionable.[88] In its further reaffirmations of a desire for peace, friendship, democracy, and the flowering of human rights, the verbalization of the Helsinki process already may have exceeded its useful limits. More substantive, though as yet untested, was the annex to the document, which described the institutions the CSCE now decided to establish: the council of foreign ministers meeting annually, the committee of senior officials to assist it, the small permanent secretariat in Prague, the conflict prevention center in Vienna, and the office for free elections in Warsaw.[89]

THE NEW CSCE AND ITS INSTITUTIONS

The new institutions marked the beginning of a different CSCE in a different Europe. The provision for the meetings of high officials proclaimed a readiness to communicate and consult regularly, though not necessarily act in concert. It conveyed the recognition that the previous East-West conflict had been aggravated, even if not caused, by a failure of communication. The creation of the secretariat reflected the equally sound conviction that the Helsinki process, having made its contribution to bringing Europe together by its advocacy of principles and persuasive debate, should now move on to the formulation and execution of policies, albeit on a modest scale.

The two field offices in Vienna and Prague embodied this modesty of purpose. A far cry from a center for the prevention and management of political, especially ethnic, conflicts, the Vienna office was pertinent only to disputes arising from the implementation of the military confidence- and security-building measures. Thus it served as an extension of the CSBM negotiations, which also resumed to further improve on their accomplishment and proceeded without such snags as those marring the progress of the CFE talks. Alone among the new institutions, the Warsaw Center for Free Elections was concerned directly with the functioning of political systems and thus with the convergence of values on which Europe's future security hinged. Its mandate, however, was limited to gathering data and exchanging information without wielding any executive power.

No less important for the future of the process than the institutions created at the Paris summit were those that were not created there. Besides its failure to establish a mechanism for mitigating ethnic conflict, the summit also delayed decision about the formation of a representative body, a CSCE "parliament." It left open the question of whether the Council of Europe should assume that function, and if so, how. It called upon the Council of Europe to share its experience by taking part in the planned Helsinki seminar of experts on democratic institutions scheduled to meet in Oslo in November 1991. Even earlier, in July 1991, experts on national minorities were to gather in Geneva.

As 1990 turned into 1991 and the crisis in the Gulf turned into a war, the breakup of both the Soviet and the Yugoslav states gathered momentum, and the CSCE's moment of truth was at hand. Despite its impressive past record of enhancing security by helping to redefine it, the utility of the Helsinki process was less obvious than it had been when Europe was still divided. With the division gone and the more elusive goal of reintegration now foremost on the agenda, the CSCE's own mission became due for redefinition.

THE END OF THE EUPHORIA

After the Paris euphoria, with its deceptive simplicities, the Helsinki process grew more "complicated," a word that lately had often been used by Soviet and other communists as a euphemism whenever something had unexpectedly gone very wrong and they did not know what to do. This was a fitting description of the CSCE's new predicament as well.

The first thing to go wrong was the CFE treaty, that landmark agreement previously hailed as settled. It was not settled for those Soviet military and their high-ranking party supporters who rightly saw in it a humiliating reconfirmation of the loss of Moscow's strategic positions in Eastern Europe and who remained influential enough to sabotage it. That this was indeed the intention was freely acknowledged in their press organ, *Sovetskaia Rossiia*, on January 9, 1991.[90] The hurried transfer of equipment and matériel beyond the Urals— outside the area of the treaty's application—but especially the redesignation of several armored divisions as naval units, so that a few thousand tanks would escape the required destruction, flagrantly violated the spirit and letter of the agreement.

To help prevent this gathering storm from clouding the CSCE's sunnier sides, many West Europeans were inclined to let Moscow have its way. After all, much of its surreptitiously staved away weaponry was rusting under open sky anyway, while Eastern Europe's decisive political changes more effectively prevented a Soviet conventional threat from reemerging. But it was equally true, as the United States insisted, that the issue was one of principle, as well as a practical one. Knowing that the CFE treaty would be headed to defeat in the US Senate, President Bush delayed sending it there for ratification.

In the end, principles were thrown to the winds and a facesaving compromise was reached at the end of April 1991 between

Secretary of State Baker and his Soviet counterpart, Aleksandr Bes-smertnykh.[91] Moscow was allowed to keep its "naval" tanks in return for its promise that it would get rid of an equal number of tanks elsewhere. This superpower deal restarted the arms control process, eventually bearing fruit also in the conclusion of the crucial START agreement on the reduction of strategic nuclear forces. However, it did not add to the CSCE's prestige, nor did it discourage Gorbachev's reactionary enemies from further plotting against him.

SLOW MOVING AHEAD

While the disarmament talks were still stalled, CSCE experts on the peaceful settlement of disputes met at Valletta during January and February 1991. Unlike two meetings on this subject held in previous years, where no results had been achieved because of the Soviet Union's refusal to submit itself to any impartial arbitration, now the absence of the East-West split made serious discussion possible. Yet Switzerland was left alone in insisting on legally binding proce-dures,[92] while there was not enough political will to make them binding in any other way. Moreover, the exclusion of disputes concerning territory or national defense left a big loophole. The conference agreed on a "mechanism" for settling international disputes by arbitration, but not on any way to put it into effect. For that purpose, an unspecified institution was to be created, which would draw up a list of potential mediators.[93]

Further detracting from this meager accomplishment, the disputes to be mediated were only those between states, while the greater challenge was now disputes within states, which their feeble governments might be unable to manage regardless of any outside incentive or pressure. This was the problem in the Soviet Union and Yugoslavia, both increasingly torn apart by ethnic strife. After Soviet security forces cracked down on the independence-minded Baltic republics, Austria and other CSCE members invoked the human dimension mechanism on the assumption that the central Moscow government was still sufficiently in charge to be responsive.[94] It was, indeed, responsive enough to turn down what it described in familiar terms as unacceptable interference in its internal affairs.

In contrast, the mechanism was not invoked in support of the independence-minded republics of Slovenia and Croatia against the increasingly powerless government of Yugoslavia. The issue there was not so much a conflict between them and the central government as between the country's irreconcilably divided nationalities—something the CSCE was ill-equipped to handle. Rather than make itself a champion of their right to self-determination, it therefore called for the preservation of a unitary Yugoslavia, thus trying to hold together what was irretrievably falling apart.[95]

INSTITUTIONS TESTED AND FOUND WANTING

The call was issued on June 19, 1991 at the Berlin meeting of the CSCE's council of foreign ministers, its key new institution. At the meeting, the two superpowers were, for their own different reasons, most eager to further advance institutionalization. Bessmertnykh wanted to see the foreign ministers' grouping become a "European security council,"[96] thus filling the void left by the demise of the Warsaw Pact while not allowing it to be filled entirely by NATO. The concept also echoed Moscow's vain efforts after World War II to make the great powers' Council of Ministers the main instrument of its European diplomacy—not an encouraging precedent. On behalf of the United States, Baker singled out the CSCE as the most important instrument in the indispensable effort "to extend the trans-Atlantic community to . . . the Soviet Union"[97]—as if the fate of that crumbling superpower depended on how its embattled government would be treated by other governments rather than on the outcome of the internal struggle beyond their reach.

More to the point, the secretary of state made the crucial point that the CSCE was the only organization that linked North America to all of Europe. In his proposals for the further expansion of its institutions, the Helsinki process had gone full circle—from the time at its inception in 1975, when the West Europeans had placed their hopes in it while Washington had harbored skepticism, to the current reversed situation. While Baker hoped the CSCE could better safeguard his country's continued influence in Europe, most of his European listeners were skeptical about the utility of trying to strengthen the CSCE's already existing institutions.[98] All the same, they went along with the strengthening, although their skepticism was to prove well-founded.

The Berlin conference expanded the mandate of the Vienna crisis prevention center to deal not only with suspicious troop movements but with any kind of international crisis—but still only a crisis involving relations between states.[99] It also put more substance into the Valletta document by designating the Vienna center to be the institution that could set the proposed arbitration mechanism in motion. But the way of doing so would merely be to supply, if asked, a register of mediators that was yet to be drawn up.

More promising seemed the approval in Berlin of an emergency crisis mechanism, modeled after the human dimension mechanism.[100] The new procedures went further than anything before in authorizing CSCE interference in its member states' internal affairs for the sake of Europe's security. After much wrangling, the conferees bypassed the sacrosanct principle of unanimity by allowing the emergency procedures to start if at least 12 members could be found to request so. This was no mean accomplishment, even if the resulting meeting would be authorized only to discuss a crisis and, at most, recommend a way to its solution, but not to act on the recommendation. With an eye on the Yugoslav situation as an ominous precedent, the Soviet Union ensured that all states were able to veto the use of the mechanism in disputes involving themselves. Still, there was a hope that they would hesitate to risk the resulting opprobrium. All things considered, the CSCE at least acquired gums, though not yet real teeth.[101]

The test of the new equipment was not long in coming, as the Yugoslav conflict grew into a civil war, with the Serbian-controlled federal army trying to prevent Slovenia and Croatia from breaking away. On July 1, 1991, the Vienna center convened an emergency session, but no Yugoslavs came. It passed a resolution urging that the troops in Slovenia return to their barracks. But it adjourned before it could agree on a proposal to send observers there.[102]

The ramshackle Belgrade government was represented two days later at the subsequent meeting of CSCE senior officials in Prague.[103] The Yugoslav delegation supported the call for a cease-fire, which promised to give the government a chance to reassert its authority over its unruly armed forces. With Soviet help, it nevertheless refused to allow CSCE observers to monitor the cease-fire. Nor was it prepared to accept the offer of a mission that would provide the badly needed "good offices."

After the situation further deteriorated, another senior officials' meeting three weeks later—now attended not only by a Yugoslav government delegation but also by Serbian and Slovene representatives as observers—approved the dispatch to the battlefield of up to 500 cease-fire monitors.[104] But none ever left, thus underscoring the impotence of the Helsinki process in the Yugoslav situation. Rather than the CSCE, it was the European Community that at least managed to send into the troubled country a mediation team of three foreign ministers, though not for the moment succeeding any better.

Neither the CSCE nor the Community responded to the other major challenge emanating from the Balkans—the mass exodus during the summer of refugees from Albania to Italy. The Rome government was left alone to handle and mishandle the chaotic situation, although its urgent human rights problems were no less within the CSCE's purview than was the looming security threat of uncontrolled migrations from the impoverished and unstable parts of the continent.[105] This nightmare added to a growing feeling of insecurity in Europe that had not been there during the more predictable years of the Cold War.

THE GENEVA MEETING ON MINORITIES

The CSCE did address the burning issue of national minorities at its July 1991 Geneva meeting of experts, which had been placed on the schedule the previous November. At the meeting, problems were defined, narrowed down, and discussed seriously, though not without the predictable friction.[106] The discussion showed that, even after all governments had agreed on general propositions such as the idea that democracy was good and communism bad, there was still ample room for clarification of the particulars.

At Geneva, the main issue was not the division between proponents and opponents of minority rights; rather, the issue was reverse discrimination—the notion that a minority may sometimes have to be favored at the expense of the majority if the groups were to become genuinely equal.[107] The division created strange bedfellows, as both Romania and the United States found reasons to criticize the idea, while France joined with Hungary in sponsoring the proposal advocating elaborate "specific" solutions to take "particular circumstances" into account.[108]

Although the divergence of circumstances precluded an agreement at Geneva on universally applicable policies, the consensus reached there was nevertheless heartening.[109] Besides proclaiming common respect for minorities not only as individuals but also as groups, the conference's final report enumerated as examples for emulation solutions that included reverse discrimination. Although no specific cases were mentioned by name, the successful examples were all in Western democracies—the settlement of the South Tyrol question, the German-Danish treaties on the mutual protection of minorities, and Canadian multiculturalism, among others.

Adherence to the consensus did not prevent Romania from trying to cover up by tortuous argument the condition of its disaffected minorities.[110] Nor was there an end in sight to the predicament of the over 1.2 million Albanians who constituted 90% of the population of Serbian-controlled Kosovo—for Belgrade a minority not entitled to self-determination, yet for Tirana no minority at all but rather the other half of the divided Albanian nation.[111] While the clash prompted the CSCE's latest member to already distance itself from its consensus by proclaiming the final report inapplicable in Kosovo,[112] the document at least left no doubt that more democracy was needed if the minority problems in the East were to be dealt with as satisfactorily as those in the West. The crucial change of mind, to be sure, would have to be experienced by the people, not merely government officials.

THE NECESSARY TRANSFORMATION

That such a change was possible could be seen in the Soviet Union after its failed reactionary coup in August 1991. In an important sense, the country did not follow the example of Yugoslavia: the Russians, unlike the Serbs, proved immune to the temptation to use force for national aggrandizement, letting other ethnic groups assert their self-determination. This minimal certainty among the uncertainties brought about by the Soviet Union's disintegration allowed the CSCE conference on the human dimension to meet in September 1991 in Moscow, as scheduled 33 months earlier in Vienna, albeit with a very different agenda.

Now that the Helsinki principles had triumphed also in the Soviet Union, there was no longer a need to harangue its government about human rights; indeed, there was soon to be no Soviet government to harangue. The week that preceded the conference, the USSR Congress of People's Deputies issued a stirring proclamation of the rights and freedoms of the individual, before dissolving itself as the country did.[113] The collapse of the Soviet Union, as well as of Yugoslavia, then dominated the conference's agenda by drawing attention to the plight of human rights in those breakaway ethnic areas where freedom did not bring democracy, particularly not to the many minorities within other minorities.

In giving substance to the now accepted principle that in the new Europe such internal matters are a legitimate cause of concern for all of its states, the CSCE tried in Moscow to move forward where it had previously lagged behind. Not only did it quickly admit as its members the three recently independent Baltic states, whose right to self-determination it had been so incapable of advancing before, but it also drew conclusions from its impotence in dealing with the crisis in Yugoslavia.

The membership expansion, which brought the total number of members to 38 and set a precedent for more to come, constituted a radical break from the key Helsinki notion of preserving Europe's territorial status quo while altering its political content. With the political content altered beyond the CSCE's founders' wildest dreams or worst nightmares, their successors now at last reluctantly acquiesced in the realization that, for better or for worse, the emergence of new states on the continent was as inevitable as the drawing of new boundaries there.

The other Moscow breakthrough was the CSCE's departure from its principle of consensus, by now deprived of its original justification as a means of building a community of interests between the two estranged parts of Europe. In strengthening its human dimension mechanism, the conference provided for the dispatch of fact-finding missions into troubled areas at the request of no more than six of its member states, with or without the consent of the governments concerned.[114] It still failed to clarify how the fact-finders' recommendations were to be enforced against local opposition.

The division of opinion formed in Moscow on this issue showed a world very different from the one that had given birth to the Helsinki process. Now Germany and the Soviet Union—previously Europe's two chief troublemakers and champions of totalitarianism —joined in advocating more intrusive international intervention on behalf of human rights than such venerable democracies as the United States, Great Britain, and France found good for comfort.[115] With the eyes cast on US racial minorities, French Bretons, and Northern Ireland, these recent converts to the idea of CSCE's institutionalization had each its own reasons to wonder whether the process may have gone astray.

A growing, albeit informal, consensus that the CSCE ought to be radically changed emerged from the Moscow discussions; the feasibility of the change, however, remained uncertain. Even with its institutions strengthened and its rule of unanimity modified, the CSCE was not necessarily best suited to meet the new tasks of Europe's reintegration. Crises that might require at the last resort the use of outside military force could still best be handled by NATO, thus providing a major justification for the preservation of that alliance. The more mundane task of economic integration could also be better served by the well-established institutions of the European Community than by the CSCE's anemic Basket Two. And concerning the Basket Three agenda—in the past the CSCE's greatest pride—in the altered situation the Council of Europe was increasingly taking the lead.[116] Not only had its mechanisms proved effective in Western Europe, but its prestige was also high among the potentially refractory states in Eastern Europe.

None of these competitors has necessarily rendered the Helsinki process obsolete. Its forte has always been its ability to get results by generating political pressure for specific causes—in the past, mainly human rights causes. Even if the expectations of a diminishing need for campaigning on their behalf come true, there is unlikely to be a shortage of other worthy causes, from the preservation of the environment to the building of confidence in contentious situations, particularly topical in minority conflicts.

The CSCE's all-inclusive character has been its abiding asset. The presence of even ministates in the CSCE has been a model for integrating the conflicting legitimate needs of diverse ethnic and other groups into Europe's security framework. At a time when further states of uncertain viability have been emerging, that task alone is apt to keep the Helsinki process going for many years to come. At Moscow, Hungary's Zsuzsanna Hargitai grasped the challenge and the opportunity by urging the CSCE to become "a permanent forum to discuss the problems associated with the birth and rebirth of states."[117]

By inducing comprehensive, continuous, and open-ended debate on almost any subject broadly relevant to security, the CSCE proved uniquely successful in anticipating so well the long-term trends of development ultimately resulting in the end of Europe's post–World War II division. More recently, that accomplishment has been faltering as the Helsinki process resisted, rather than anticipated, the new fissures that inevitably opened up. With its balance restored, it can again become the "process to define the long-term direction of Europe"—an important enough function whether or not it also responds to "the short-term problems which arise along the way."[118]

The CSCE's predicament highlights the limitations of govern-

ments—its key constituents—in meeting the new challenges. The
expertise of diplomats, the CSCE's mainstays, is not necessarily most
germane to the growing involvement of the CSCE in matters internal
rather than external. Nor has the innovative addition of nongovernmental participants enhanced the effectiveness of the Helsinki process under the new circumstances. In adjusting to the changed situation, the CSCE may have to transform itself beyond recognition. This
would make it no longer the most successful experiment in multilateral diplomacy that it was during the first 15 years of its existence,
but something quite different, the precise description of which is yet
to be developed.

NOTES

1. "Das KSZE-Expertentreffen über Menschenrechte in Ottawa—eine
    Bewertung," *Europa-Archiv*, 1985, no. 19, pp. 573–80. Excerpted and
    translated in *Helsinki, Human Rights, and European Security*, ed. Vojtech
    Mastny (Durham, NC: Duke University Press, 1986), p. 306.
2. See Document 1 in this volume.
3. Document 6.
4. Document 2.
5. Report by Henry Hamann, London, April 10, 1986. RFE/RL B-Wire,
    FF085. (All RFE/RL wire reports as well as all other unpublished docu-
    ments excerpted or referred to in this book may be found at the CSCE
    Collection, Johns Hopkins University Bologna Center.)
6. Report by RFE/RL correspondent Roland Eggleston, Bern, May 12,
    1986. RFE/RL B-Wire, FF121.
7. Document 3.
8. Document 5.
9. Document 7.
10. Speech by Jerzy Nowak. CSCE Meeting of Experts on Human Contacts,
    Bern, May 26, 1986. RFE/RL B-Wire, CN004.
11. See document 8 for Genscher's speech.
12. Associated Press report, Stockholm, September 17, 1986. RFE/RL B-
    Wire, FF159.
13. Document 9.
14. Documents 10 and 11.
15. Document 13.
16. Editorial, *Die Presse*, November 8–9, 1986.
17. Philip Taubman, "Soviet Offers East-West Rights Talks in Moscow,"
    The New York Times, November 6, 1986.
18. Document 14.
19. Document 15.
20. Document 12.
21. Document 21.
22. Documents 19 and 20.

23. Document 18.
24. Document 24.
25. Document 25.
26. Document 22.
27. Documents 26, 27, and 28.
28. Document 30.
29. Document 29.
30. Document 31.
31. Speech by Eduard Shevardnadze. CSCE Review Meeting, Vienna, January 19, 1989. RFE/RL B-Wire, FF109.
32. Document 32.
33. Document 34.
34. Document 35.
35. Speech by Eduard Shevardnadze. CSCE Meeting of Foreign Ministers, Vienna, March 6, 1989. RFE/RL Special Report, CN46.
36. "US Says Soviets Seek to Gain Advantage at CSBM Talks" (article on Maresca news conference). CSCE Negotiations on Confidence- and Security-Building Measures, Vienna, March 8, 1989. USIS EUR44, Item 405.
37. Document 36.
38. Document 37.
39. "Intervention de la délégation du Saint-Siège au Séminaire sur les doctrines militaires dans le cadre des Négociations sur les mesures de confiance et de sécurité," January 19, 1990, *Seminar on Military Doctrine,* vol. 1 (Vienna: Institut für Militärische Sicherheitspolitik an der Landesverteidigungsakademie Wien, 1990).
40. Document 40.
41. Document 42.
42. Report by RFE/RL correspondent Roland Eggleston, London, May 5, 1989. RFE/RL B-Wire, FF122.
43. Document 41.
44. Document 43.
45. Report by RFE/RL correspondent Roland Eggleston, London, May 12, 1989. RFE/RL B-Wire, FF091.
46. "The Road from Helsinki," *The Economist,* May 20, 1989, p. 55.
47. Document 45.
48. Document 52.
49. Documents 47, 48, and 49.
50. Document 46.
51. Document 45.
52. Documents 50 and 51.
53. Document 55.
54. Document 56.
55. Document 58.
56. Gorbachev, as quoted by Italian Foreign Minister Gianni De Michelis, in Michael Dobbs, "No Return to Past, Soviet Says," *The Washington Post,* December 1, 1989.
57. Document 59.
58. Ibid.
59. "Europe: A Time of Change," Speech by Eduard Shevardnadze. Euro-

pean Parliament Political Commission, Brussels, December 20, 1989. *Foreign Broadcast Information Service,* SOV-89-243, December 20, 1989, p. 27.
60. Document 61.
61. Document 62.
62. Document 63.
63. Document 86.
64. David Usborne and Alan Murdoch, "EC Move Designed to Bolster Gorbachev," *Foreign Broadcast Information Service,* WEU-90-017, January 25, 1990, p. 1.
65. Documents 64 and 66.
66. Document 65.
67. Document 87.
68. Document 68.
69. Document 69.
70. Burkhard Rexin, "Bonn rüstet sich für erste KSZE-Wirtschaftskonferenz." Bonn, March 9, 1990. RFE/RL B-Wire, FF081.
71. Document 70.
72. Document 71.
73. Document 85.
74. Document 72.
75. Documents 73 and 76.
76. Document 78.
77. Document 77.
78. Document 79.
79. Document 80.
80. Document 82.
81. Georg Possanner, "Mock Not to Use 'CSCE Mechanism' for Lithuania," *Foreign Broadcast Information Service,* WEU-90-062, March 30, 1990, p. 7.
82. Document 96.
83. Document 88.
84. Document 89.
85. Document 101.
86. Document 91.
87. Document 92.
88. Document 98.
89. Document 99.
90. Document 103.
91. Mary Curtius, "US, Soviet Union Settle Two Disputes over Conventional Weapons Treaty," *Boston Globe,* April 26, 1991.
92. Valletta, January 15, 1991. CSCE/PSDV.1.
93. Document 104.
94. NCA/AP/Reuters report, Vienna, January 17, 1991.
95. Document 113.
96. Report by RFE/RL correspondent Roland Eggleston, Budapest, June 14, 1991. RFE/RL B-Wire, FF003.
97. Document 112.
98. Report by RFE/RL correspondent Roland Eggleston, Berlin, June 19, 1991. RFE/RL B-Wire, FF042.

99.   Document 115.
100. Document 114.
101. Report by Reuters correspondent Patrick Worsnip, Berlin, June 20, 1991. RFE/RL B-Wire, FF060.
102. Report by AP correspondent Drusilla Menaker, Prague, July 3, 1991. RFE/RL B-Wire, FF053.
103. Document 116.
104. Report by RFE/RL correspondent, Prague, August 8, 1991. RFE/RL A-Wire, CN0155. Associated Press Report, Prague, August 9, 1991. RFE/RL A-Wire, CN0001.
105. Document 94.
106. Document 106.
107. Documents 107 and 108.
108. Geneva, July 9, 1991. CSCE/REMN.11.
109. Document 111.
110. Document 110. See also Address by Ambassador Traian Chebeleu. CSCE Meeting of Experts on National Minorities, Geneva, July 1, 1991.
111. Statement by P. Pojani, head of the Albanian delegation. CSCE Meeting of Experts on National Minorities, Geneva, July 1, 1991. Statement by Ambassador Vladislav Jovanović. CSCE Meeting of Experts on National Minorities, Geneva, July 8, 1991.
112. Report by RFE/RL correspondent Roland Eggleston, Geneva, July 19, 1991. RFE/RL A-Wire, CNO126.
113. Document 117.
114. Documents 120 and 121.
115. Documents 118–121.
116. Document 107.
117. Document 122.
118. Commission on Security and Cooperation in Europe, "Conference on Security and Cooperation in Europe: An Overview," staff paper, Washington, DC, September 1991.

Part I

The
CSCE
in
Transition

Helsinki: For and Against

THE LONG HARD ROAD

1. *from* US Congress, Commission on Security and Cooperation in Europe, *The Long, Hard Road from Helsinki to Vienna* (Washington, DC: US GPO, 1986).

Positive Aspects of CSCE Principles
The "Declaration of Principles Guiding Relations Between Participating States" stands at the heart of the Helsinki Final Act. . . . As could be anticipated, the provisions of the Declaration . . . have not been fully implemented. . . .

The Declaration has, however, helped to focus public attention on three issues—human rights abuses, the Soviet invasion of Afghanistan and events in Poland during the past several years—which constitute instances of non-compliance. The principles have supplied the participating states with a justification and a useful diplomatic tool with which to call public attention to these and other violations of the Final Act. They have also constituted an international standard by which participating states can be held accountable. . . .

Among the political benefits of the CSCE process is that it "has provided a flexible, nearly continuous series of forums for dialogue on a wide range of issues among the participating states". . . .

. . . The commitments undertaken at Helsinki . . . have facilitated the United States' pursuit of a policy of differentiation in its relations with the countries of Eastern Europe. The Helsinki framework has enabled East European nations to engage in bilateral endeavors with the West, including the United States, that were not previously possible and has given the East European states marginally greater room for maneuver vis-à-vis the Soviet Union in conducting their foreign and domestic policy. . . .

Following the signing of the Final Act, Principle VII, respect for human rights and fundamental freedoms, unexpectedly sparked a new awareness of and demand for basic human rights throughout the Soviet Union and the rest of Eastern Europe.

From the US perspective, one of the most important contributions of the CSCE process has been the possibilities it has afforded for the strengthening of unity and cohesion among the NATO allies. . . .

. . . in Western Europe, as in the United States, the Helsinki Final Act . . . is considered to have brought several non-quantifiable yet important political benefits. Broadly speaking, these countries consider the central contribution of the CSCE process, embodied in the principles set forth in Basket I, to be the establishment of a lasting framework of East-West relations, within which both sides have been forced to confront and deal with a wide array of important political, military, social and cultural issues.

For the West Europeans, the CSCE process has added a new multilateral dimension to the relations in Europe, setting relations between them, despite occasional set-backs, on a new more forward-looking course, aimed at increasing dialogue and mutual understanding. More specifically, the Europeans see the principles of the Helsinki Final Act as having provided a series of political advantages to the West, including fostering high-level political contacts, the establishment of human rights questions as legitimate topics of international attention, and the establishment of a continuing monitoring process for human rights and other CSCE issues. Other benefits have included the encouragement of more independent activity by the nations of Eastern Europe and the increased significance of the role of the Neutral and Nonaligned (NNA) countries in solving the problems confronting contemporary Europe.

High on the list of significant contributions of the CSCE process in the view of many West European states is the notion that the Helsinki Final Act and its principles have enhanced the normal fabric of East-West bilateral relations by building upon established principles of mutual cooperation and supplementing them in fields not covered by existing bilateral treaties and arrangements. This has been particularly true in the case of the FRG-GDR relationship.

As Austrian Foreign Ministry officials have pointed out, the CSCE process has helped to maintain, in the troubled 1980s, a modicum of bilateral cooperation between East and West built up during the détente era of the 1970s. Corresponding to this view, French officials emphasized that the Helsinki process has provided the only forum within which all European countries (with the exception of Albania) can meet consistently together and currently contributes the only effective forum wherein East and West are talking on a regular basis. The French consider that the CSCE framework is the only concrete proof of the unity of Europe. Others consider CSCE as one of the few surviving elements of détente.

Some West European countries take this notion even further. Finnish Foreign Minister Paavo Vayrynen has expressed concern that, without CSCE, East and West currently would hardly be talking to one another and that there would be no instrument to discuss serious East-West issues. An official of the Dutch Foreign Ministry has emphasized the importance of the CSCE process as a natural channel of communication—a channel significantly kept open by the East when it had closed others in the wake of the NATO decision to deploy intermediate-range nuclear weapons in Europe. In fact, the CSCE process has provided the forum for all of the high-level political contacts held between the USSR and the US in 1983 to 1985, a time when bilateral relations were at a low point. . . .

The proven durability and timelessness of the Final Act's Declaration of Principles are viewed by some West European states as enabling the nations of Europe to deal with crisis management situations in times of East-West tensions. In the view of Austria, the Helsinki process has contributed to a more relaxed atmosphere in Europe and, in many respects, has contributed to the development of less complicated procedures in the shaping of European political relations.

However, most West European states stop short of directly crediting CSCE for specific improvements in bilateral relations with nations of the East. Many of these improvements had been set in motion before the signing of the Helsinki Final Act and thereby could not be attributable solely to the influence of the CSCE process. . . . A notable exception to this case was the Federal Republic of Germany which stresses that the FRG-Polish agreements of 1975, which eventually enabled 270,000 ethnic Germans living in Poland to resettle in the FRG, bore a direct relationship to the signing of the Helsinki Final Act.

Most Western European sources observe that high-level political contacts and visits with countries of the East had increased since the CSCE process began, but notably do not attribute this increase either solely or directly to Helsinki-related factors. However, many do emphasize that CSCE had created the framework, despite increased East-West tension in recent years, for bilateral and multilateral contacts to continue and even, in some cases, to expand. For instance, Greek officials note that they make reference to the Final Act in all agreements signed with the countries of Eastern Europe, but admitted that it was difficult to determine whether it was existing government policy or the Final Act which was responsible for the agreements themselves. Officials of the Federal Republic of Germany directly credit the CSCE process with having facilitated governmental contacts with the GDR, particularly the increasing high-level contacts of recent years.

In the view of the Western Europeans, the original Soviet goal of using the CSCE, particularly the Declaration of Principles, as a surrogate peace treaty ratifying the post-war political situation in Europe, has failed. CSCE has not led, as some had predicted, to a consolidation of Soviet domination over Eastern Europe. Nor has it generated measures towards change in Western Europe. On the contrary, according to officials of the United Kingdom, the Final Act established a standard of behavior and values which already existed in Western Europe. While the Final Act did not require any fundamental changes in the societies of the West, it has in the East.

In addition, as pointed out by UK officials, the Final Act's Declaration of Principles, particularly Principle I on the sovereign equality of states, by recognizing the right to change frontiers by peaceful means, has provided the opportunity for the West, and particularly the FRG, to address the question of German reunification, as well as the general problem of the division of Europe, in a peaceful way.

Several countries noted that the principles of the Final Act have helped increase the maneuvering space of the smaller East European states vis-à-vis the Soviet Union. In this view, which is shared by the US Government, the CSCE process has enabled the Soviet Union's Warsaw Pact allies to operate, at least marginally, more independently and more freely in multilateral endeavors in Europe. In addition, as noted by Foreign Ministry officials in the Netherlands, the people of the countries of Eastern Europe have attached great importance to the Helsinki principles as safeguards of national sovereignty.

A point stressed by many West European countries is that an important aspect of the CSCE process is the active participation of all European states, each having equal rights and, thereby, an equal voice in the future of the process. This political fact was deemed to be particularly important to the NNA countries who have endeavored to use their participation in the CSCE process to expand their political influence in Europe and their impact on issues heretofore considered solely in the domain of East-West relations. Noteworthy in this regard has been the key mediating role the NNA states have played at many fora held as part of the CSCE process, particularly at the Madrid Meeting and the Bern Human Contacts Experts Meeting. Similarly, the Stockholm CDE Conference[1] has given the NNA countries an unprecedented opportunity to participate directly in important security negotiations affecting Europe.

The West European CSCE states are in basic agreement that the CSCE review mechanism, embodied in periodic review conferences such as Belgrade, Madrid and Vienna have added a new and valuable dimension to the CSCE process. As one Western CSCE signatory emphasized, the Helsinki process has brought the issues of human rights and human contacts into the focus of international attention. These sentiments have been echoed by officials of the United Kingdom who emphasize that CSCE has helped raise certain issues in a direct way with the countries of Eastern Europe which, prior to the Helsinki era, would have been difficult. Through the CSCE review mechanism, these Eastern countries have been forced to confront and discuss issues they would prefer to avoid, most notably, human rights. Similarly, Dutch officials emphasize that meetings like Belgrade and Madrid provided useful fora for calling attention to Soviet and East European human rights violations. The pressure of review conferences of this sort has, in their view, a positive effect on implementation.

This view was also endorsed by many non-NATO countries. According to Swedish Foreign Ministry officials, the Helsinki Final Act and specifically Principle VII, the human rights principle, has legitimized international action and a process of criticism in matters relating to the safeguarding of human rights. Officials of the Holy See stressed that the CSCE principles opened a "Pandora's Box" permitting people recourse to action in terms of human rights and creating possibilities for concerned people throughout Europe to raise human rights issues directly with East European governments, thereby making human rights a legitimate topic of international discourse. Through the CSCE process, many countries stressed, both East and West have had to acknowledge the mutual right to monitor implementation of all provisions of the Final Act.

French officials carry this argument further. The principles of the Helsinki Final Act, they emphasized, permitted the West to maintain permanent pressure on human rights issues, and to make a direct connection between human rights and issues of security in Europe. Without the Final Act, they note, the human rights movements in the USSR and Eastern Europe would not have been able to operate as long as they have. The linkage of their activities to the principles of the Final Act has provided them extra latitude with the authorities of Eastern Europe.

The Europeans, however, are acutely aware of the limitations of the CSCE process and caution against excessive public expectations in human rights and other Helsinki-related issues as well. Most could agree with the sentiments expressed by Swedish Prime Minister Olof Palme . . . that despite progress in some areas, respect for human rights in Europe had certainly not increased to the extent aimed at in Helsinki. While recognizing this fact, many cautioned that the CSCE process was geared to the long-term. . . .

. . . French officials stress that the spirit of Helsinki should not be viewed as something already achieved but as a dynamic, ongoing process with its own fluctuations. Similarly, officials in the United Kingdom stress that because one country might violate certain provisions of the Final Act, these actions by no means signified that the provisions were worthless. On the contrary, the French assert that, while the Final Act had created the unfortunate illusion to some that relations with the Soviet Union had normalized, the CSCE process had nevertheless helped the West to maintain a fabric of relations with the East, even during the worst of times. The mere existence of the CSCE process, in this view, has had a beneficial effect on life in all of Europe. . . .

The Consequences of Renunciation of the Final Act
There have been suggestions that the United States unilaterally renounce, or threaten to renounce, the Helsinki Final Act on the grounds that continuing and egregious violations of the human rights provisions by the Soviet Union and its East European allies have, in effect, rendered the agreement meaningless. This argument views the Final Act as a trade-off between the Soviet desire for Western ratification of the post–World War II borders in Europe and the Western desire for Mutual and Balanced Force Reductions (MBFR) talks. In addition, to gain additional support for CSCE, the Soviets agreed to set provisions concerning human rights. Since Helsinki the Soviets and most of [their] allies in Eastern Europe have shown continuing and contemptuous disregard for the human rights commitments under the Final Act, and therefore, the US need no longer be bound by its commitments under the Act. Indeed, according to this argument, continued US involvement in CSCE serves to hide these violations and perpetuates the illusion that the Soviets have respectable humanitarian concerns.

The argument concludes that this "charade" should stop. . . .

Contrary to a widespread and continuing public belief, fostered by the Soviets and the Western press at the time of the Helsinki signing, the expert legal view of the effect of the Final Act on Europe's World War II boundaries is that, basically, the document makes no difference since it goes no further and, in some cases, not as far as previous international arrangements on frontiers. Moreover, rather than constitute a consolidation of Soviet territorial claims, the Final Act language is substantially less than what the Soviets sought at the outset of the negotiations. Consequently, the claim that the Soviets achieved legal ratification of World War II borders at Helsinki and that, by renouncing the Final Act, the US could withdraw its ratification, is a specious argument. . . .

US renunciation of the Final Act would most likely produce a strong negative effect among other participants. Since most West European nations hope for some concrete long-term results from CSCE and see the US emphasis on human rights as a possible impediment to progress in other areas, it is doubtful whether even its closest NATO allies could be persuaded to go along with the US. A more probable result would be that allies and others would interpret withdrawal as a sign of decreased US interest and influence in Europe. For many, there is the belief that there is a better chance of altering Soviet behavior through CSCE than without it. They could well conclude that the United States does not care to be a part of the first all-European effort to reduce tension and that the United States prefers retreat from a tough problem rather than fight for what it believes.

Dissidents initially reacted negatively to the Helsinki Final Act. They felt it legitimized Soviet annexation of the Baltic states and other territories after World War II. Soon, however, dissidents had discovered that the Helsinki accords made human rights a legitimate item on the international diplomatic agenda. Acting on the discovery, citizen Helsinki monitoring groups were established in various parts of the USSR; the movement also spread into Czechoslovakia and later into Poland. . . .

. . . US withdrawal from CSCE would presumably have a devastating effect on these individuals and others who might be inclined to follow them. How could they not help but think, buttressed by Soviet propaganda, that the United States had abandoned them?

Since there is little chance that the other Western participants would allow the United States to renounce its CSCE commitments vis-à-vis the Soviet Union alone, the only way open is renunciation toward all participants. Either way the US would lose its right to

review and criticize Soviet and East European shortcomings in violation of the Helsinki Final Act. As Belgrade and Madrid have shown,
without a strong US voice in the lead, there is little inclination among
other CSCE signatories to hold the Soviets to account on such politically sensitive subjects as human rights. The net result of a US withdrawal could be silence. . . .

    . . . In East-West relations, the Helsinki process has become a
vehicle by which concerns in humanitarian, military, political, economic, social, cultural and other fields routinely are raised and discussed. Helsinki's European focus ensures that debate remains cen-
tered on an area where Western ideas fall on fertile soil. The future
of the process will remain dependent on persistent efforts to bring its
promises to fruition.

NOTE
1. On Confidence- and Security-Building Measures and Disarmament in
    Europe.

Bern: A Meeting of Lost Opportunities?

TOWARD AN OPEN SOVIET UNION

2. *from* Speech by Michael Novak, head of the US delegation. CSCE Meeting of Experts on Human Contacts, Bern, May 1, 1986. In Michael Novak, "Toward an Open Soviet Union," chap. 14 in *Taking Glasnost Seriously* (Washington, DC: American Enterprise Institute for Public Policy Research, 1988).

The Soviet Union is a great nation among the world's nations. Its 270 million citizens occupy nearly a sixth of the world's surface. Its navy operates on virtually all seas; it is a great military power. The talents of its people have long been praised. Yet—and here is the puzzle . . . —why does such a great nation whose activities are international in scope remain so outspokenly insecure, hesitant, and fearful about human contacts? . . .

The reason cannot be ideology: (1) Marxist thought does not require the total control exercised until now by the Soviet regime; (2) other Marxist nations do differently; and (3) many Marxist thinkers propose much more open methods.

If the reason for the closed society cannot be ideology alone, neither can it be attributed to the fact that the Soviet social system is "different" from all others. For to assert that is to beg the question. *Why* is it different? What is the *reason* for such systematic control over human contacts as the Soviet Union practices, and concerning which every delegation in this room has considerable experience?

A great world power, one of the greatest military powers the world has ever known, has the right to be secure, unafraid, relaxed, and open. According to the Helsinki Final Act, it even has the duty to be so. And in the world of fact and ordinary reason, it has the full capacity of being so.

The Soviet state could remain a Marxist state and still be far more open than it is—open in its postal service, open in its telephone and telegraphic service, open in television and radio and every form of reading material, open in permitting visitors to travel as freely as they do in Switzerland and other nations, and open in allowing its own citizens to travel, to visit, and to emigrate, as they like, when they like.

The Soviet Union is powerful enough to be an open society. Why, then, is it not so? The people of the Soviet Union are attractive. The nation has to its credit immense accomplishments. All the world would like to know its citizens better, and to have its citizens know better all the great, buzzing, and vital world around them. Why not? Why not an open, large-hearted, free, and amicable Soviet Union?

Nothing in the ideology of Marxism prevents this. Nothing in the vast power of the Soviet Union requires otherwise. Logic, reason, experience, sentiment, the ideas of civilized people everywhere, the basic founding ideas of European culture—and the Helsinki Final Act, Madrid, and this very good dialogue we have been having in Bern—all these invite the governing bodies of the USSR to try a new path. All the world would applaud new decisions taken in this new direction.

These are the reasons *for* greater openness to human contacts. But there are also arguments *against* the closed society: (1) the closed society deprives its people of the stimulation of diversity, opposition, and unconventional ways of looking at reality; (2) any one culture is only one culture, but human creativity is fertilized by inputs from many cultures (and especially by the most contrary and opposite), for the human mind works by the clash of opposites; (3) the closed society leads to a decline in standards, from want of true intellectual challenge; (4) in a closed society, the roots of genuine culture—a true sensitivity to differences and to nuances—are slowly covered over by bureaucratic sludge; and (5) even the mode of controversy declines, since true argument is not permitted and true differences are not freely faced.

In sum, the closed society deprives its thinking citizens of intellectual air. They miss, they truly miss, the necessary contact of the human spirit with contrary ideas and opposing images and unaccustomed controversies. Surprise is the law of life. Surprise is the stimulus of the mind. The question for Soviet society, then, comes down to this: can it compete in a world open to surprise, to choice, to individual will? My own answer is, its people are worthy of the highest confidence, and they would benefit enormously therefrom.

Indeed, nothing would do more to build a new spirit of worldwide confidence, a humanitarian outlook, a new sense of a common humanity, than new policies of openness by the Soviet regime. Allow the peoples of the USSR to be seen and known and conversed with, as they are—an attractive and talented people. Allow them to know all the rest of us, as we are, in our strengths and in our weaknesses. All of us are only human beings: only that. But nothing less. This is the cry of Europe; this is the heritage of Europe: out of many, one. In diversity, a common humanity.

Europe has two branches, from one same set of roots. East and West are not antithetical; the two branches belong together. They should be open to each other. They should strengthen each other. They should enrich each other. Being closed, one to the other, violates our profoundest vocation, and wounds our duty to each other. The task of the younger generation of Europeans everywhere (including those who are children of Europe, in Canada and the United States) is to make Europe one—an open Europe, a Europe of respect and affection, one for the other, each for all, all for each.

NEUTRALS DRAFT A COMPROMISE DOCUMENT

3. *from* Roland Eggleston, "Neutral Compromise Effort in Bern." Report by Radio Free Europe/Radio Liberty correspondent, Bern, May 26, 1986. Radio Free Europe/Radio Liberty B-Wire, FF054.

The nine neutral and nonaligned countries made a last-minute effort to bring NATO and the Warsaw Pact together on a final document.

A few hours after the night session broke up, the neutral and nonaligned produced their take-it-or-leave-it paper and then an hour or two later still the Warsaw Pact produced its final document.

Neutral diplomats said that their hopes that their paper would be acceptable to the West were based on the inclusion of four major Western issues.

The neutral and nonaligned called on the 35 participating states to "guarantee the freedom of transit of postal communications, to ensure the rapid delivery of correspondence, including personal mail, and to ensure the conditions necessary for rapid telephone calls, including the use and development of direct-dialling systems wherever it is possible and to respect the privacy of all such communication." The Soviet Union and its allies had indicated earlier in the conference that they would accept such a paragraph.

Another paragraph aimed at satisfying the West required the 35 states to make accessible to their own people "all laws and administrative regulations relating to travel for family, personal or professional reasons on a permanent or temporary basis."

A third calls on the 35 states to "promote the possibility" for religious faiths and their representatives to maintain contact with those in other countries. This paragraph also says that religious institutions and their representatives should be allowed to "acquire, receive and carry with them, religious publications and religious objects for their own use."

A fourth paragraph calls on states to "review carefully" all travel applications which have not yet been decided or to which a formal answer has not yet been given. The head of the British delegation, Sir Anthony Williams, said the West appreciated the inclusion of these and a number of other measures sought by the West. But he said the West would have preferred far stronger language.

Sir Anthony said the West deeply regretted that there was no language in the neutral and nonaligned document specifically stating the right to an exit visa or other travel document. But there are several paragraphs calling on the authorities to deal favorably with applications for foreign travel for family visits.

The Canadian and Yugoslav delegates regretted the absence of any specific paragraph on the right of national and regional minorities to maintain contacts with similar cultures in another country. The neutral and nonaligned did include a paragraph calling on governments to favorably consider travel application "regardless of the cultural, ethnic or national origin" from people who want to have family meetings "with persons of the same, or any other, cultural, ethnic, or national origin" residing in another participating state.

Western diplomats were also disappointed in this reference to "another participating state." They said the West would have preferred wording such as "another country." The Soviet Union had rejected this wording throughout the conference to avoid any text that sounded like an encouragement of immigration to Israel. Israel, of course, is not a participating state.

Among other paragraphs in the neutral and nonaligned document which the West favors is one saying that governments should give special attention to reunification of families where minor children are involved. This reflects a proposal submitted by Nordic countries, partly in response to the pleas of the Randpere couple from Estonia who fled to Sweden leaving a baby child behind.

Other paragraphs call on the authorities to give priority attention to visa applications in the case of a death or serious illness in the family or when an individual needs to go abroad for urgent medical treatment.

Another Western proposal reflected in the document suggests the holding of bilateral meetings and roundtable discussions to deal with "questions concerning the development of contact among persons."

Western diplomats said they had wanted the text to say the meetings should be held on "humanitarian issues," so they could bring up specific cases of people refused permission to travel abroad. However some Western diplomats said even the language proposed by the neutral and nonaligned should give room for such opportunities.

Warsaw Pact proposals in the neutrals and nonaligned document include Polish suggestions on bilateral agreements on consular, medical and legal assistance. There are also paragraphs on the promotion of contacts between youth, student and educational organizations.

THE SOVIET CONCESSIONS

4. *from* Roland Eggleston, "Summing up the Bern Conference." Report by RFE/RL correspondent, Bern, May 30, 1986. RFE/RL B-Wire, FF095.

In the closing hours of the conference the Soviet Union and five of its partners tabled an eight-page document of their own. Unlike the neutral and nonaligned document, which was only circulated unofficially among delegations, the Warsaw Pact document was tabled formally as a conference document.

Western diplomats said that as such it has to be accepted as an official position and Western governments can legitimately use it as a standard for measuring Warsaw Pact performance.

The only non-signer of the Warsaw Pact paper was Romania. Western diplomats considered that unusual considering the strong pro-Soviet positions taken by Romania during the six-week conference. According to the West, it is probable that Romania disagreed with some of the positions in the Warsaw Pact paper, but this has not been confirmed.

Obviously the Warsaw Pact paper contains several standard Soviet positions which are unacceptable to the West and many of the paragraphs contain loopholes enabling East European governments to avoid implementing the initial promise. But, as the West says, the words are there.

One paragraph calls for measures to improve administrative regulations and practices concerning not only entry visas but also exit visas. Considering the Soviet and Romanian opposition to a discussion of exit visas during the conference, some Western delegates were surprised at its inclusion. They said the wording of the text could undermine its use, but the basic position is there.

Another paragraph says that applications from families who wish to travel abroad together for regular meetings on the basis of family ties should be dealt with favorably "when possible." The words "when possible" open a loophole enabling East European regimes to maintain their practice of holding some family members at home as hostage for the return of the others. But Western diplomats say the paragraph as a whole opens the way for critical examination of such cases.

The West and the neutrals also noted another paragraph in the Warsaw Pact document which calls for "immediate attention" to be paid to visa applications of "an urgent humanitarian character." It goes on to define these as (a) travel to visit a seriously ill or dying family member, (b) travel of the aged and those with urgent medical needs recognized by local medical authorities, and (c) travel to attend the funeral of a family member.

Apart from the qualification in regard to travel for medical needs this paragraph seems to contain no hidden escape clauses. Western diplomats say this paragraph in particular is one where Soviet and East European deeds will be measured against their words.

Another paragraph says regulations relating to travel out of participating states should be published "within a reasonable time" when this has not already been done. Some Western diplomats consider that this would be a step forward if truly all regulations are made public. The paragraph is similar to one proposed by Britain with the major exception that the British wanted publication of the laws within a year. There is some suspicion of what a "reasonable time" means in Soviet terms.

In another interesting paragraph, the Warsaw Pact recommended that governments "guarantee" the freedom of transit of postal communications and "ensure the conditions" necessary for the rapid establishment of telephone communications and respect their privacy. Diplomats said it was hard to imagine the Soviet Union and some of its partners honoring their own words considering their present record, but they would now find it harder to justify violations.

Western diplomats are understandably cautious about reading

too much into the Warsaw Pact paper, but they say a close watch will be kept in the next few months to see if any attempt is made to implement it. If not, the West will question the Warsaw Pact's good faith towards its own document at the conference reviewing the Helsinki Accords which begins in Vienna in November.

Some diplomats argue that the appearance of such a Warsaw Pact paper is a plus for the Bern conference, even if it cannot be listed as a success. More wary diplomats say that like everything else which happened in Bern, only the future can judge its value.

5. *from* Michael Novak, "The Endgame," chap. 32 in *Taking Glasnost Seriously.*

I had gone to bed about 5 a.m. Monday, May 26 [1986], supposedly the day of final formalities, after the Soviets had walked out of our negotiations at 4 a.m. It seemed then that the issue of a final document was dead. I felt relief. No more decisions would be necessary. . . .

. . . Afterwards, at 9:30 a.m., I was suddenly surprised by a last-ditch, take-it-or-leave-it compromise document worked out by the Neutrals and the Nonaligned. . . .

My heart sank as I looked over the compromise document. At the meeting of the western caucus, I said I would need to consult with Washington before accepting it and was extremely pessimistic. But Germany was most eager to accept and had so persuaded the caucus of the European Community (the EC12) in their earlier meeting. . . .

By noon, however, I had reached both the assistant secretary of state for European affairs, Rozanne Ridgway, and the assistant secretary for human rights, Richard Schifter. Once they heard the final wording of the proposed compromise document, the two assistant secretaries of state most responsible judged immediately that we should say no. Both agreed that the document was unacceptable. That relieved me greatly, even though I dreaded having to carry that word to others. . . .

At about 2 p.m., I was summoned to receive an urgent cable from our embassy in Moscow. It recounted how our consular officers there had been summoned to the Foreign Ministry at 9 a.m. and then told to come back two hours later. When they did so, they were made to wait. Then they were handed a list of thirty-six families that had been given permission to leave, with a pledge that thirty-six others would be given similar permission very soon. Some families well known to the embassy were on the list. Here at last, perhaps, were the "concrete cases," the "concrete results," we had waited for in vain since our trip to Moscow ten weeks earlier.

Sadly, though, these lists came too late to change our decision in Bern. We had twice earlier been given long lists by Ambassador Kashlev in Bern, and on both occasions the permissions given had been routine and did not reflect new movement. To agree to a document because of a movement on concrete cases would have set a bad precedent for future negotiations. It would be like trading agreements for hostages. . . .

. . . Some in our delegation thought that the "concrete results"— seventy-two cases, an unprecedented number—justified a different decision. I did not. But Washington had other issues to consider, and that decision would be theirs. Assistant Secretaries Ridgway and Schifter agreed with me.

By now Washington had the Bern document in hand by cable, as well as the Moscow cable. Secretary of State Shultz was reached in Washington by Foreign Minister Genscher from Ankara, Turkey, where he was on a state visit. After asking for a review, the secretary held firm and so informed the German foreign minister. . . .

It was my painful task to announce at the much-delayed plenary session . . . that the United States must withhold its consent. . . .

. . . I had, in one sense, given Moscow an easy propaganda victory.

THE US VETO

6. *from* Speech by Michael Novak, head of the US delegation. CSCE Meeting of Experts on Human Contacts, Bern, May 27, 1986. In Michael Novak, "Words versus Compliance: Concluding Plenary Address," chap. 31 in *Taking Glasnost Seriously.*

Many delegations among us repeated that free and open contacts among persons have deteriorated in recent years in certain vivid ways: divided spouses, disunited families. Compliance has declined. In such circumstances precious words lose meaning.

The strength of the founding documents in this process depends on the credibility of words. That is why, to even the scales of the demonstrated decline in compliance in recent years, my government knew that a Bern document would have to set a high standard.

Otherwise the public would lose confidence. And confidence building is the essence of the Helsinki process.

Every delegation here knows the brilliant and careful work of the coordinators from the neutral and nonaligned delegations. They fairly reflected the long, slow course of our negotiations. They performed at the highest human level.

But our CSCE process works, rightly, through consensus. Each step in our negotiations, rightly, demanded compromise. In order to achieve compromise, as is normal, loopholes creep into the text. To the right to travel, for example, was added the loophole "when personal and professional circumstances permit." Honest authorities will understand this one way, but cynical authorities will use it to alter such circumstances at will. Loopholes are sometimes necessary. But, cumulatively, they eat like moths into our founding documents. Inevitably, too, robust proposals lost weight. Until the end it was impossible to add up the weight of all together. When at last my government could weigh them, it found the document too thin, containing loopholes damaging to compliance.

My government takes words seriously. In our country, there is growing uneasiness about the growing gap in the Helsinki process between words and compliance. A document reduced in weight by many compromises, it judged, would injure the process all of us cherish and must protect.

THE THINKING OF YESTERDAY

7. *from* Speech by Iurii Kashlev, head of the Soviet delegation. CSCE Meeting of Experts on Human Contacts, Bern, May 27, 1986. RFE/RL B-Wire, CN104. Translated from German by Roger Malone and Jeannet Frössinger.

In the course of our work, the delegates in this hall mentioned several times the name of M. Gorbachev, quoting passages from his speeches. We thank our colleagues for that and look at it as an indication that they sensed the meaning of the new philosophy, the new way of thinking that the Soviet leadership has developed at the end of the twentieth century.

The new way of thinking, the mentality corresponding to today's and tomorrow's new realities, requires from all of us mainly to ensure security, cooperation and mutual understanding among people, and to reach a new stage of international relations.

We have supported sensible and realistic proposals by other delegations on questions of family reunion, family travel, and other questions that are important to many people. Through this, we have succeeded—for the first time in the history of the CSCE process and perhaps for the first time in history in general—in working out a unique document on a collective basis that is a declaration on human contacts that, without doubt, will satisfy millions of people.

But another mentality, another way of thinking comes into play here that has erased the results of our common work. This is thinking of yesterday, the thinking of a world policeman who is supposedly allowed to exercise a veto against the will of other people. Those from far away across the ocean have been threatening us with the fist, suggesting that Europeans be not allowed to continue and develop the Helsinki process and to broaden humanitarian cooperation. After numerous lectures about common people, now we are not even allowed to make a small step in the interests of those people.

A relic of the Cold War, a philosophy of the world policeman, a philosophy of the veto, contempt for the interests of other people—including the European people—this is how we interpret the actions of those who have defeated the constructive results of our work at Bern.

No matter how hard those who have brought our work to defeat try to maintain the relics of the past, the times are changing, especially in Europe. What we have tried to do here in Bern—to work out and agree to an important, major, fundamental document about human contacts—is a sign of the new era, of the new approach, and that cannot help but make us optimistic that the Helsinki process will continue and further develop.

The Breakthrough at Stockholm

TOWARD COOPERATIVE SECURITY

8. *from* Speech by Hans-Dietrich Genscher, FRG minister of foreign affairs. CSCE Conference on Confidence- and Security-Building Measures and Disarmament in Europe, Stockholm, January 28, 1986. RFE/ RL B-Wire, CN063.

The confidence- and security-building measures which are the subject of our negotiations here in Stockholm should not merely be the preliminary stage of disarmament measures in the conventional sphere. They should also lay the foundations for cooperative security arrangements which remove the incentive for the use of force as well as the fear of such force. That is why our readiness to carry out such measures is a test of our will to ban war from Europe forever as a means of achieving political aims.

The new proposals put forward by General Secretary Gorbachev on 15 January, 1986, can give the negotiations major impulses and open up possibilities for movement.

Mr. Gorbachev's statement with regard to verification deserves special attention. The fact that the Soviet Union is now prepared to accept strict controls, including international on-site inspections within the framework of a universal convention banning the use of chemical weapons is also of fundamental importance for the multilateral arms control negotiations, where a breakthrough can be achieved if effective verification arrangements now prove possible.

The aim is to strengthen confidence and security by means of a set of politically binding, militarily significant and verifiable measures which will have to be applied throughout Europe. All involved have become increasingly aware that confidence-building is an indispensable element of a policy aimed at détente and cooperation. Only on the basis of growing confidence founded on concrete measures will it be possible to make progress in mutual cooperation and toward an accommodation in the field of security among the participating states.

Our aim is to effectively and visibly reduce the danger of the use of military power by means of cooperative confidence-building measures. We share Mr. Gorbachev's view that the road leading to the use of force and to covert preparations for war must be blocked. The actual or supposed military conduct of the participating states must be subject to specific rules, thus making it calculable. Reliable verification is a crucial element of such measures.

Confidence should not be "blind." The one showing confidence must himself be able to see that the military efforts of the other side exclusively serve to maintain its own defensive capability. Affording proof of one's good intentions in a militarily relevant manner means convincing others of one's own peaceful aims.

THE VERIFICATION PROBLEM DOES NOT EXIST

9. *from* Speech by Marshal Sergei Akhromeev, Soviet chief of general staff. CSCE Conference on Confidence- and Security-Building Measures and Disarmament in Europe, Stockholm, August 29, 1986. RFE/RL B-Wire, FW 147.

The Soviet Union is prepared to agree with any reasonable verification measures promoting the limitation of the arms race and confidence-building among countries. Obviously, verification is not an end in itself. Its scope and methods depend on the character and volume of concrete agreements regarding measures of disarmament and confidence-building.

Any attempt to portray things as if the USSR is against inspections and hence it is impossible to agree on any real disarmament steps constitutes a deliberate lie. We accept the widest possible inspection to terminate nuclear testing.

We are ready to accept inspection to solve the problem of banning and completely eliminating chemical weapons.

In brief, the verification problem does not exist. The USSR is agreeable to various forms of verification, including international ones.

Of course, we regret that our most active interlocutor on the inspection issue among the participants of the conference while speaking in favor of "openness of all military activities in Europe" puts its own territory outside of verification. It seems likely that in this case there is a desire to open ("make transparent") Europe to the Urals and close its own military activities. Despite this, the Soviet government deemed it possible to agree to inspections in order to verify confidence-building measures.

Specifically, the USSR considers that each state participating in the Stockholm conference could allow the conduct of on-site inspections on its territory within the European continent based on the quota of one or two inspections per year on requests from other participating states, if suspicions arise regarding compliance with confidence-building measures which will be negotiated.

The inspection area specified in the request of an inspecting state forms an important element of this scheme. It should be an area where a notifiable military activity takes place—operational and tactical exercises, troop movements, transfers of forces and exercise- and movement-related concentrations of forces outside areas of permanent location above a notifiable level.

In order not to diminish the security of the inspected state, inspections should not be sought in closed areas or in military and defense installations with restricted access.

At the same time, we act on the assumption that such closed areas will be defined as applied to an agreement on verification of compliance with CSBMs.

Naturally, the number and extent of these closed areas should be kept within reasonable limits, i.e., they should be so as to assure compliance with agreements reached at the conference. They should not include areas where notifiable military activities take place.

There are still divergences at the conference regarding methods of inspection: NATO countries, in particular, insist on air inspection.

I shall be frank: to us, military men, inspection from the air has been a traditionally difficult question since the "open skies" doctrine proclaimed by President Eisenhower.[1] At that time, as is known, no agreement was reached to this effect.

However, time moves us to new frontiers, requires new political and military approaches to questions of ensuring peace and cooperation, confidence and security in the entire world and especially in Europe.

With this understanding and taking into account the situation at the Stockholm conference, we could think of adapting an air-ground version of on-site inspection on the clear understanding that inspections would be carried out from transportation vehicles and aircraft provided by the inspected state.

Such are constructive proposals of the USSR and other socialist countries aimed at achieving agreements on the major issues of the conference.

NOTE
1.   At the Geneva meeting of heads of state, July 1955.

A SENSE OF TRIUMPH

10. *from* Richard Wallis, "Triumphant Mood in Western Camp at Stockholm Talks." Report by Reuters correspondent, Stockholm, September 11, 1986. RFE/RL B-Wire, FF020.

A sense of triumph is spreading through Western delegations as a key European arms control conference draws to a close, set for an accord that resembles NATO's original proposals far more than the Warsaw Pact's.

NATO's taste of victory is, however, tinged by the knowledge that an agreement in Stockholm—even on the West's terms—will take the Soviet bloc one step closer to one of the Kremlin's long-standing foreign policy goals. This would be the start of talks on real disarmament in Europe, including huge cuts in conventional forces and combat planes, plus the withdrawal of short-range nuclear missiles.

The aim is to make military activities more predictable through new rules on notification, inspection and observation of military exercises and thus reduce the risk of war breaking out in Europe by accident or miscalculation.

This is a far cry from the Soviet goals spelt out when the conference began in January, 1984, at the height of a freeze in East-West relations when the Soviet Union had walked out of all major arms control negotiations.

Then-Soviet Foreign Minister Andrei Gromyko called on the Stockholm talks to produce a treaty renouncing the use of force, a ban on chemical weapons in Europe, a pledge to renounce first-use of nuclear weapons, a freeze on military budgets and the creation of nuclear-free zones in Europe.

All these have been discarded except for non-use of force. There is to be no treaty, however—just a reaffirmation that states renounce the use of force. It will at Western insistence be linked to a condemnation of terrorism and a statement linking human rights to security.

"The measures adopted [if the conference is successful] will be very much like the measures the West proposed at the beginning of the conference. The East initially tried to gain support for declaratory measures, but failed. The main result was to delay the conference for nearly one and a half years," the chief US delegate, Ambassador Robert Barry, told Reuters.

Warsaw Pact diplomats did not deny that the shape of the final accord will be a Western one. They are, in fact, keen to show the East made major concessions.

NATO diplomats say it is wrong to speak of Soviet bloc concessions when the East's original proposals were so extreme as not to be serious.

"But the fact that we will open military activities for inspection in societies that were always considered so secretive in the West will deal a mortal blow to the myth created in the West about a Soviet threat to Europe," a Soviet diplomat said.

Last June, the Warsaw Pact launched its Budapest Appeal calling for negotiations on cuts of 500,000 troops each by both military blocs in Europe. It suggested that negotiations could take place at a second stage of the Stockholm conference.

Moscow presented the appeal as being aimed at reassuring Western public opinion that the scrapping of nuclear weapons in Europe would not leave NATO at the mercy of Warsaw Pact superiority in conventional forces.

Although the Budapest Appeal also mentioned the possibility of an enlarged version of the Vienna talks on conventional troop cuts as another possible forum, Soviet diplomats said they have little faith in this alternative.

Stockholm also has wider implications for arms control. Its central theme is verification, the issue on which so many other East-West negotiations have got stuck.

If an agreement in Stockholm giving such rights as on-site inspection of military activities works, this could help solve the problem of inspection in other arms control areas, such as a nuclear test ban, Soviet diplomats said.

In the eyes of many Western delegates, the greatly added publicity a Stockholm agreement would give the military activities will make it almost impossible for the Warsaw Pact to repeat such actions as the 1968 Soviet-led invasion of Czechoslovakia.

Asked about this, Barry said he did not want to comment on specific cases in the past, but added:

"[An agreement] will require participants to announce significant

military exercises at least a year ahead. Any change in that announced schedule—any break in the routine—for example, a military exercise mounted in response to an unexpected political development, would sound the alarm, drawing public attention and allowing
other states to take political or diplomatic steps if required.

"In short, although [an agreement in Stockholm] might not prevent intimidation, it would raise significantly the political stakes for
any state that might think about trying it."

THE FINAL DOCUMENT

11. *from* Document of the Stockholm Conference on Confidence- and
Security-Building Measures and Disarmament in Europe. Stockholm,
September 19, 1986. CSCE/SC.9. In *Implementation of the Helsinki
Accords,* Hearing before the Commission on Security and Cooperation
in Europe, 99th Cong., 2nd sess., October 1, 1986 (Washington, DC:
US GPO, 1986).

Refraining from the Threat or Use of Force
The participating States, recalling their obligation to refrain, in their
mutual relations as well as in their international relations in general,
from the threat or use of force against the territorial integrity or
political independence of any State, or in any other manner inconsistent with the purposes of the United Nations, accordingly reaffirm
their commitment to respect and put into practice the principle of
refraining from the threat or use of force, as laid down in the Final
Act. . . .

They will abide by their commitment to refrain from the threat
or use of force in their relations with any State, regardless of the
State's political, social, economic or cultural system and irrespective
of whether or not they maintain with that State relations of alliance. . . .

They emphasize their commitment to all the principles of the
Declaration on Principles Guiding Relations between Participating
States and declare their determination to respect and put them into
practice irrespective of their political, economic or social systems as
well as their size, geographical location or level of economic development.

All these ten principles are of primary significance and, accordingly, they will be equally and unreservedly applied, each of them
being interpreted taking into account the others. . . .

They reaffirm the universal significance of human rights and fundamental freedoms. Respect for and effective exercise of these rights and freedoms are essential factors for international peace, justice and security, as well as for the development of friendly relations and cooperation among themselves as among all States, as set forth in the Declaration of Principles Guiding Relations between Participating States. . . .

They emphasize the necessity to take resolute measures to prevent and to combat terrorism, including terrorism in international relations. They express their determination to take effective measures, both at the national level and through international cooperation, for the prevention and suppression of all acts of terrorism. They will take all appropriate measures in preventing their respective territories from being used for the preparation, organization and commission of terrorist activities. This also includes measures to prohibit on their territories illegal activities, including subversive activities, of persons, groups and organizations that instigate, organize or engage in the preparation of acts of terrorism, including those directed against other states and their citizens. . . .

Prior Notification of Certain Military Activities
The participating States will give notification in writing through diplomatic channels in an agreed form of content, to all participating States 42 days or more in advance of the start of notifiable military activities in the zone of application for confidence- and security-building measures (CSBMs). . . .[1]

Each of the following military activities . . . at or above the levels defined below will be notified:

The engagement of formations of land forces . . . conducted under a single operational command independently or in combination with any possible air or naval components.

This military activity will be subject to notification whenever it involves at any time during the activity:

- at least 13,000 troops, including support troops, or
- at least 300 battle tanks

if organized into a divisional structure or at least two brigades/regiments, not necessarily subordinate to the same division.

The participation of air forces of the participating States will be included in the notification if it is foreseen that in the course of the activity 200 or more sorties by aircraft, excluding helicopters, will be flown.

The engagement of military forces in an amphibious landing or in a parachute assault by airborne forces in the zone of application for CSBMs.

These military activities will be subject to notification whenever the amphibious landing involves at least 3,000 troops or whenever the parachute drop involves at least 3,000 troops. . . .

Observation of Certain Military Activities
The participating States will invite observers from all other participating States to the following notifiable military activities:

- The engagement of formations of land forces of the participating States in the same exercise activity conducted under a single operational command independently or in combination with any possible air or naval components.

- The engagement of military forces either in an amphibious landing or in a parachute assault by airborne forces in the zone of application for CSBMs.

- In the case of the engagement of formations of land forces of the participating States in a transfer from outside the zone of application for CSBMs to arrival points in the zone, or from inside the zone of application for CSBMs to points of concentration in the zone, to participate in a notifiable exercise activity or to be concentrated, the concentration of these forces. Forces which have been transferred into the zone will be subject to all provisions of the agreed confidence- and security-building measures when they depart their arrival points to participate in a notifiable exercise activity or to be concentrated within the zone of application for CSBMs.

The above-mentioned activities will be subject to observation whenever the number of troops engaged meets or exceeds 17,000 troops, except in the case of either an amphibious landing or a parachute assault by airborne forces, which will be subject to observation whenever the number of troops engaged meets or exceeds 5,000 troops. . . .

Constraining Provisions
Each participating State will communicate, in writing, to all other participating States, by 15 November each year, information concerning military activities subject to prior notification including more

than 40,000 troops, which it plans to carry out in the second subsequent calendar year. Such communication will include preliminary information on each activity, as to its general purpose, timeframe and duration, area, size and States involved.

Participating States will not carry out military activities subject to prior notification involving more than 75,000 troops, unless they have been the object of communication as defined above. . . .

Compliance and Verification
. . . In accordance with the provisions contained in this document each participating State has the right to conduct inspections on territory of any other participating State within the zone of application for CSBMs.

Any participating State will be allowed to address a request for inspection to another participating State on whose territory, within the zone of application for CSBMs, compliance with the agreed confidence- and security-building measures is in doubt.

No participating State will be obliged to accept on its territory within the zone of application for CSBMs, more than three inspections per calendar year.

No participating State will be obliged to accept more than one inspection per calendar year from the same participating State. . . .

The participating State which requests an inspection will be permitted to designate for inspection on the territory of another State within the zone of application for CSBMs, a specific area. Such an area will be referred to as the "specified area." The specified area will comprise terrain where notifiable military activities are conducted or where another participating State believes a notifiable military activity is taking place. The specified area will be defined and limited by the scope of the notifiable military activities but will not exceed that required for an army level military activity.

In the specified area the representatives of the inspecting State accompanied by representatives of the receiving State will be permitted access, entry and unobstructed survey, except for areas or sensitive points to which access is normally denied or restricted, military or other defense installations, as well as naval vessels, military vehicles and aircraft. The number and extent of the restricted areas should be as limited as possible. Areas where notifiable military activities can take place will not be declared restricted areas, except for certain permanent or temporary military installations which, in territorial terms, should be as small as possible, and consequently those areas will not be used to prevent inspection of notifiable military activities. Restricted areas will not be employed in a way inconsistent with the agreed provisions on inspection. . . .

Inspection will be permitted on the ground, from the air, or both.

The representatives of the receiving State will accompany the inspection team, including when it is in land vehicles and an aircraft from the time of their first employment until the time they are no longer in use for the purposes of inspection. . . .

The inspection team will have use of its own maps, own photo cameras, own binoculars and own dictaphones, as well as own aeronautical charts.

The inspection team will have access to the appropriate telecommunications equipment of the receiving State, including the opportunity for continuous communication between the members of an inspection team in an aircraft and those in a land vehicle employed for inspection.

The inspecting State will specify whether aerial inspection will be conducted using an airplane, helicopter, or both. Aircraft for inspection will be chosen by mutual agreement between the inspecting and receiving States. Aircraft will be chosen which provide the inspection team continuous view of the ground during inspection. . . .

The participating States stress that these confidence- and security-building measures are designed to reduce the dangers of armed conflict and of misunderstanding or miscalculation of military activities and emphasize that their implementation will contribute to these objectives.

Reaffirming the relevant objectives of the Final Act, the participating States are determined to continue building confidence, to lessen military confrontation and to enhance security for all. They are also determined to achieve progress in disarmament.

The measures adopted in this document are politically binding and will come into force on 1 January 1987.

NOTE
1. Under the terms of the Madrid mandate, the zone of application for CSBMs is defined as follows:

On the basis of equality of rights, balance and reciprocity, equal respect for the security interests of all CSCE participating States, and of their respective obligations concerning confidence- and security-building measures and disarmament in Europe, these confidence- and security-building measures will cover the whole of Europe as well as the adjoining sea areas and air space. They will be of military significance and politically binding and will be provided with adequate forms of verification which correspond to their content.

As far as adjoining sea area and air space is concerned, the measures will be applicable to the miliary activities of all the participating States taking place there whenever these activities affect security in Europe as well as constitute a part of activities taking place within the whole of Europe as referred to above, which they will agree to notify. Necessary specifications will be made through the negotiations on the confidence- and security-building measures at the Conference.

Part II

The
Vienna
Conference,
1986–1989

New Thinking and Old

THE US STRATEGY

12. *from* "Objectives for the Vienna CSCE Review Meeting," Memorandum by the Commission on Security and Cooperation in Europe to the Interagency Working Group on the CSCE. Washington, DC, April 28, 1986.

Observations

Vienna will be seen as a watershed for CSCE by the press and public. Even those who over the past decade have argued in support of the process now question whether CSCE is producing diminishing returns for human rights.

From the beginning, the US has struggled to preserve balance in the CSCE among all its aspects, but particularly between its security and humanitarian aspects. The United States has worked to counter Eastern efforts to turn the process into a one-dimensional security platform for Soviet peace propaganda. CSCE's utility, when considered at all by the US press and public, is measured in terms of effectiveness as a human rights tool. In contrast, the security aspects of CSCE tend to be given more emphasis in Europe. . . .

Progress in CSCE has been defined largely in terms of a balanced array of post-review secondary meetings and in new commitments. But, neither balance nor new commitments have produced improved implementation in the human rights area—in fact it can be argued that the reverse has occurred. Without a marked improvement in human rights implementation, the credibility of the entire CSCE process is in dire jeopardy, at least in the United States. . . .

Recommendations

At Vienna, if we are to maintain US public support for CSCE, a comprehensive implementation review should be our paramount objective. According to past practice, the US Delegation should cite

illustrative cases, naming names when appropriate. The US Delegation should make clear from the outset that it will speak forthrightly
about Eastern deficiencies in performance in the post-Madrid years.
Speaking factually about continuing Eastern violations is not at all
inconsistent with a non-polemical approach to Vienna. . . .

Producing a lengthy concluding document of Madrid proportions at Vienna will not be a sufficient result. We agree that it is not
more words but compliance that is required. The carefully balanced
words in negotiated documents have not led to balanced progress in
deeds. For alliance management, we should join with our partners in
a good faith effort to negotiate a document. We should not, however,
settle for a document that contains new agreements in the military
security area but merely offers a reiteration of Helsinki and Madrid
language on human rights issues, or even marginal new language
that in all probability will not be implemented. . . .

With respect to Follow-up, we should insist on the fourth major
review meeting within 2 to 2½ years after the conclusion of the
Vienna Meeting. . . .

The Commission agrees that subsidiary or experts meetings between major reviews are helpful in keeping the process alive and
public attention focused on issues of concern. However, we also have
seen some drawbacks to the experts meeting arrangement. Subsidiary meetings having one-dimensional subject matter provide little
leverage with which to pressure for implementation or for actual
negotiations.

Agreement to an array of post-Vienna meetings absent any explicit linkage among them risks fracturing CSCE into its component
parts and upsetting CSCE's delicate balance. Therefore, the United
States should insist that the mandates for proposed experts meetings
always refer to linkage, emphasizing the need for constant, tangible
and balanced progress in the Final Act fields.

The United States should insure that any CDE agreement reached
contains language linking security-related principles to other Helsinki Final Act principles concerning human rights and fundamental
freedoms.

The United States should defer a CDE agreement in Stockholm
for further consideration at the Vienna Meeting so that such an
agreement can be balanced against agreements in other fields of
CSCE, particularly its human rights dimension.

A form of linkage between CDE and human rights/human contacts implementation would be the truest measure of balance. At
Vienna, we should consider not giving consensus to continuation of

the CDE talks until we see concrete progress in the implementation of human rights and human contacts commitments.

Another way in which balance can be preserved and linkage established through follow-up mechanisms is to propose subsidiary meetings with combined subject matter. For example, a post-Vienna forum on the connection between peace and human rights or the linkage between scientific, cultural and educational exchange and the freer flow of people and information could be proposed. Another approach reinforcing the concept of linkage would be to task subsidiary meetings to focus on key Final Act principles that tend to be addressed in tandem in CSCE, say the connection between Principle VI (Non-intervention/Terrorism) and Principle VII (Human Rights and Fundamental Freedoms) or between Principle XI (Cooperation among States, including the role of governments, institutions, organizations and persons) and Principle X (Fulfillment of Obligations under International Law). . . .

Inclusion of cultural figures on delegations to Budapest[1] drew greater public attention to the Cultural Forum and to the Helsinki Process as a whole. The Commission would recommend mandating at Vienna an Information Forum. Delegations would include media figures. The participation of the media representatives would ensure that journalists become better informed about CSCE and could generate more understanding of and interest in the process in the future. The West can make important points about freedom of the press, "the right to know," the free flow of information and jamming. Yet, such a forum would not be without appeal to the East, which seeks to use the openness of the Western media and new satellite technology to bring its peace propaganda to Western audiences. . . .

Setting a date for the conclusion of the Vienna Meeting is wise so long as it is only a target date in the sense of such dates set for Belgrade and Madrid. It can be argued that protraction of the Madrid Meeting in response to external events, such as the crackdown in Poland, served Western, not Eastern, interests. We agree, however, that barring unforeseen international developments, a protracted meeting could convey the impression of impotence. . . .

Finally, with respect to planning for Vienna, there should be early and frequent coordination meetings within NATO in order to minimize the possibilities of being presented with *faits accomplis* by the EC-12.

NOTE

1. CSCE Cultural Forum, October-November 1985.

THE SOVIET OPENING

13. *from* Speech by Eduard A. Shevardnadze, Soviet minister of foreign affairs. CSCE Review Meeting, Vienna, November 5, 1986. CSCE/WT/VR.3. Translated from Russian.

The Vienna Meeting has opened in a new time frame. The time has come for vigorous and immediate action. Europe is capable of accelerating developments by channelling them along the lines of new political thinking. The recent lessons of Geneva, Budapest, Bern and Stockholm[1] show that this is possible. The lessons of Reykjavik[2] urge that it is essential. Reykjavik has shown that a maximum of positive results can be achieved in a minimum of time. However, despite the attempts to demolish the structure that we started there, we affirm that the foundation is solid, the framework is intact, and the construction can go on.

The Vienna Meeting cannot sidestep Reykjavik for it was there that the turning-point was reached in Europe's advance towards a nuclear-free world. It was there that a historic chance emerged for Europe, too, and finally it was there that a great moment for the whole of mankind might have occurred. And why did it not occur? None of us can be indifferent to the answer. A profound and accurate analysis of the developments of 11 and 12 October has been given by Mikhail Gorbachev. It remains for us to add a few words in connection with the mounting wave of political speculation and biased interpretation of the Soviet-American meeting. The truth must be asserted, not for the archive, but for the present and the future: It is extremely important for all of us to know what were the points of mutual understanding recorded in Reykjavik because they can now serve as a point of departure for subsequent steps forward.

There is no doubt that the highest point in the talks was the convergence of positions of the Soviet and the United States leaders concerning the elimination of all nuclear weapons. . . .

. . . From the lessons of Reykjavik we draw the following conclusions:

First—however difficult the campaign for a world without nuclear weapons might be, it is far from being a hopeless one. . . .

Second—the position of some European leaders on nuclear disarmament is illogical. Now that a real opportunity has finally emerged to rid the continent of missiles, they have begun to speak of the need to retain United States nuclear weapons in Europe and to protect their own alleged privileges as nuclear States. . . .

. . . It is a pity that some political leaders have shown that they are not prepared to think of a nuclear-free Europe.

The third lesson is . . . of a moral and ethical nature. Here in Vienna, where at one time Metternich and Talleyrand[3] used to set records of duplicity, it would be appropriate to say that orderly relations among States should be based on elementary personal decency. The house which we are building for all Europeans, in which all of us would be equal, would surely not be safe and solid if deception, half-truths and misinformation were mixed into the mortar that should hold it together. It is wrong to create a deficit of trust because of misconceived national prestige or pre-election considerations.

However, in the light of what has been happening since Reykjavik we have to note that the virus of misinformation has affected the top echelons of leadership in some Western countries. . . .

Today, one cannot do without parity in dignity and honesty, nor can one hope without it to remove confrontational barriers. When pronouncements about the primacy of military might are made daily, this does not enhance our trust in our partners. Times have changed and no serious person can hear without an ironic smile talk about the need to deal with the Russians from a position of superiority. . . . Our ideal is not a policy of strength but the strength of policy. This is what the new political thinking means and we advise that it be reckoned with.

It calls for action, lest the historic chance to end the deadlock be missed. All this greatly increases the significance of the CSCE process. The Vienna Meeting attests to its vitality. All past zigzags and turnabouts notwithstanding, today this process is steadily moving along the main thoroughfare of modern life, reaffirming the notion of peaceful coexistence as a supreme universal principle of relations among States.

The concept of security, too, is acquiring new dimensions. It is increasingly seen as a task of creating, through joint efforts, political, material, institutional and other safeguards for preserving peace that would rule out the very possibility of war breaking out. In fact, the fundamental aspects of the CSCE process and the system of comprehensive security formulated by Mikhail Gorbachev are similar in many respects. . . .

The three "baskets" of the Helsinki accords constitute the component parts of the proposed concept of security. It is futile to argue which of them should be given preference. What is needed here is not to argue but to act and make real progress in each of these areas, with each one complementing and enhancing the others. Therefore, the all-European process, if developed in all aspects, could become a kind of model for establishing a system of comprehensive security.

The Soviet Union's initiatives proposed earlier are of course still in effect—the initiatives on the disbanding of opposing politico-military alliances, on non-aggression, on the non-use of force, and on strengthening security in the Mediterranean. All of them are clearly consistent with the proposal on comprehensive security. . . .

In the political area, lines of communication between governments have been restored, contacts among the States have become livelier and an increasingly broad range of problems are brought up for discussion at bilateral and multilateral negotiations and consultations.

Slowly but steadily contacts are being established between the Council for Mutual Economic Assistance and the European Economic Community.

A very significant step has proved possible in the area of military détente and confidence-building measures. I am referring to Stockholm.[4] We would like to think that this success will signal a new trend in the CSCE process.

Stockholm I leads on to Stockholm II, to measures of real disarmament in Europe. All European countries and governments favor this objective. After all, disarmament is the most sound and effective basis for tackling the numerous outstanding problems in every sphere of our life. Of course, States may have different ideas on how to proceed to disarmament in practice. This should become the subject of a broad-based, honest and frank discussion among the participants in the CSCE process. But what is important is to maintain the momentum, not to get the matter bogged down in protracted debate. We should like these discussions to become dynamic and flexible. Why not work on parallel courses and at several levels? It might be possible, for example, without waiting for the mandate for a conference on reducing armed forces and conventional arms in Europe to be finalized, to arrange contacts between working groups representing NATO and the Warsaw Treaty countries, as Mikhail Gorbachev has proposed.

We regard this as a practical step towards an all-European Conference. The future of Europe is above any bloc approaches and should be determined by all European nations. Our continent does not need concerts of "chosen" powers; what it does need is a harmonious polyphony in which the voices of neutral and nonaligned countries are heard as clearly as those of others. But work by groups of experts from two politico-military alliances can produce very interesting practical results.

At their meeting in Budapest[5] the Warsaw Treaty countries drew up a balanced program for European disarmament in a broad geographical zone, from the Atlantic to the Urals. It involved more than just reduction in arms and armed forces. The socialist countries have proposed a reduction procedure that would lower the risk of surprise attack, improve military and strategic stability and enhance confidence. Reliable verification of these reductions can be assured through national technical means and international forms of verification, including on-site inspections. Incidentally, inspections to be carried out as early as the beginning of next year in the context of the agreement on confidence-building measures will permit tests of possible methods of verifying disarmament in Europe.

We are steadily moving towards completely ridding the territory of Europe of chemical weapons. The Soviet Union will shortly put forward new, potentially helpful proposals in this regard, which significantly develop the ideas now being discussed and take into account the proposals made by Great Britain and other countries. Stability and confidence will undoubtedly be enhanced by establishing zones free of chemical and nuclear weapons in the Balkans, in the center of the continent, in Northern Europe and elsewhere. . . .

The political climate in Europe depends to a large extent on the development of the entire range of economic relations between the East and the West. This is a kind of economic guarantee of peace. Let us together think how to make international economic relations serve the needs of all peoples on this continent, how we can help bring nations closer to each other economically.

We support the idea, proposed by a number of countries, of convening an all-European economic forum. The Soviet Union will bring to that forum a broad program based on the measures being adopted in our country to restructure our domestic economy and streamline external economic activities. They open up favorable prospects for new promising forms of cooperation, including industrial link-ups, joint ventures and direct ties between firms and production associations. . . .

Having entered the second decade after Helsinki, one cannot avoid answering the question of what is the supreme meaning behind Helsinki. We see the goals of the CSCE process as promoting more democratic relations between States and greater democracy in the public life within each country. One is inseparable from the other. These are words not just for propaganda export. The 27th Congress of our Party has identified as a central task that of perfecting democracy in all its aspects, and we are moving ahead in this respect.

The strength of any society lies in its ability to perfect itself, to improve itself. The strength of the socialist system reveals this ability in a far-reaching way. The notions of democracy and freedom are not static. What is more, there can be no monopoly on their interpretation and practical implementation.

The Soviet Union attaches paramount significance to the seventh principle of the Helsinki Final Act, concerning the respect for human rights and fundamental freedoms, including the freedom of thought, conscience, religion or belief.

Major legislative or administrative measures are at present being adopted in our country for the further development of international contacts and to resolve in a humanitarian spirit problems relating to family reunification and mixed marriages. We have stated our readiness to be guided in practice in these questions by the draft document of the Bern Meeting of Experts,[6] although it was not formally adopted and everyone knows why. Incidentally, the Bern document itself has been published in its entirety in the Soviet Union. We expect that other countries too will take steps to bring their legislation and rules regarding contacts in line with international documents and obligations.

In our view, a fundamental document of the United Nations, the International Bill of Human Rights, has been unjustly forgotten. This unique and universal code establishes the rules of conduct for States in safeguarding individual rights, the right to work, housing, rest, free education, medical care and social welfare, access to cultural life, and involvement in the progress of science and in the use of its benefits and fruits.

We are deeply disturbed that this instrument has been ignored in some countries, above all in the United States, where violations of fundamental human rights are of a systematic and massive nature.

Since quite a few problems have accumulated in the field of humanitarian cooperation and all of them require close attention and should be approached with a new historic yardstick, the Soviet Union is proposing that a *representative conference of the CSCE participating States* should be convened in order to consider the whole range of such problems, including human contacts, information, culture and education. We are inviting this forum to Moscow. In extending this invitation we expect a comprehensive discussion oriented towards a practical result, a mutual understanding that would make it possible to improve the situation in the humanitarian area in all the countries participating in the CSCE process. I trust that this idea will meet with support.

NOTES
1. Meeting of Ronald Reagan and Mikhail S. Gorbachev, Geneva, November 1985; CSCE Cultural Forum, Budapest, October-November 1985; CSCE experts meeting on human contacts, Bern, April-May 1986; CSCE Conference on Confidence- and Security-Building Measures and Disarmament in Europe, Stockholm, concluded September 1986.
2. Reagan-Gorbachev summit meeting, October 1986.
3. Respectively the chief Austrian and French representatives at the 1815 Congress of Vienna.
4. See Documents 8–11.
5. In June 1986.
6. See Document 3.

"GROSS VIOLATIONS"

14. *from* Speech by Vladimir Morozov, senior member of the Soviet delegation. CSCE Review Meeting, Vienna, November 14, 1986. RFE/RL LL-Wire, F500–505.

We have heard with interest the statement made by the chairman of the US delegation, Ambassador Zimmermann, to the effect that peace is a human right.

Regrettably, the recognition in these words of the right to peace as a basic human right finds no reflection either in the US legislation or in its practical actions no matter where we look, be it the Mediterranean or Nicaragua or the nuclear test ranges of Nevada where nuclear explosions still go on or in outer space which the United States wishes to turn into a Star Wars testing ground.

Everywhere we see a demonstrative contempt for man's right to peace and, consequently, for the right to life.

The USSR delegation, like the Soviet public in general, are much worried by US attempts to dodge a serious discussion of human rights and to reduce this important problem merely to the issue of citizens leaving other participating States.

We are also very worried about the fact that a substantial portion of the US population is deprived of the right to work, education and access to cultural achievements.

How can it be possible to reconcile second-rate products of the motion picture industry which incite hatred of the peoples of the Soviet Union and which have filled the screens of American movie theaters with those key provisions adopted at Helsinki?

How can the delegation of the country in which 30 million people live below the official level of poverty, in which 15 million people are unemployed and two million are homeless and in which various special services keep 15 files for each and every American—how can the delegation of such a country play the part of mentor on human rights?

The Soviet Union has taken several specific measures aimed at facilitating contacts among citizens of participating States.

What is involved here is a reduction in time limits for considering and reviewing applications, a two-fold cut in state fees, a simplified procedure for handling entries into and exits from the USSR, and so on.

On January 1, 1987, we will enact new regulations on entering and leaving the Soviet Union, which take into account the international obligations of the USSR and the Bern document.[1]

All these steps taken by the Soviet Union substantially facilitate contacts on the basis of family ties and travel for personal or professional reasons. I may add that efforts to improve relevant legislation in our country are continuing and pertinent documents will be made public.

In the course of the debate, we have gained the impression that as soon as it comes to human contacts some people in this hall hasten to don a judge's mantle. They begin searching for faults in the implementation of the Helsinki and Madrid Accords everywhere but in their own countries. This applies above all to the US delegation.

There exist in the US lists of many thousands of names of those who are banned from entering the country for political reasons. The US hinders development of contacts among trade unions, refuses entry visas to many world-famous artists and performers, scientists and anti-war activists.

In violations of international agreements, the US arbitrarily reduced the personnel of missions accredited to the United Nations. In the US, Soviet diplomats are subjected to threats and blackmail. They are being shot at. They are becoming the targets of terrorist attacks. Their property is set on fire. There has been a case of an actual siege being mounted around the consular mission of the USSR in the United States. It was surrounded by a mob of thugs who burned the national flag of the Soviet Union.

Serious violations of the Helsinki Accords and the Madrid document are also committed by the closest allies of the US, whose delegations pay lip service to human rights.

I would like to ask the distinguished representative of Great Britain, who claims to be an expert on the situation in other countries: How many thousands of people have been killed in Ulster and for how long will these killings go on?

Permit me also to say a few words about the US record in issues of humanitarian cooperation. In that country, Soviet ballet stars have to dance on floors covered with broken glass. Singers have to perform amid explosions of tear gas grenades.

It is in that country that US Congress Resolution 457 was adopted. It says it is the policy of the US to stop trips of scientists and students from the USSR for a period of one year unless it is required by urgent national needs. It is in that country that Darwin's books are banned in some states and often burned. It is there that decisions are taken to foil exhibitions planned in advance. It is there that every year entry visas are denied to dozens of Soviet citizens.

This is by far an incomplete list of gross violations by the US of its obligations in the field of humanitarian cooperation. We shall have to raise these issues more than once. It is time to put an end to such violations.

NOTE
1.   See Document 3.

THE PICTURE REMAINS MIXED

15. *from* Statement by Ambassador Warren Zimmermann, chairman of the US delegation. CSCE Review Meeting, Vienna, January 27, 1987. In *The Vienna Review Meeting of the Conference on Security and Cooperation in Europe: Compilation of Speeches (January 27, 1987– April 10, 1987)*, 100th Cong., 1st sess. (Washington, DC: US GPO, 1987), pp. 3–7.

I begin with a candid assertion: It is idle to assume that significant developments are not unfolding within the Soviet Union.

First, we see a country which seems to be trying to come to grips with its past. . . . It is reported that Boris Pasternak's *Dr. Zhivago* will soon be published in one of the few countries in which it is banned: his own.

Second, the Soviet press describes what has heretofore seemed a contradiction in terms: the arrest of a KGB official for abuse of his official duties.

Third, Soviet cultural authorities are coming to realize that the greatness of the Soviet culture does not stop at the border.

It is reported that the Kirov ballet star Mikhail Baryshnikov, currently in New York, and the former director of the innovative Taganka Theater Yuri Lyubimov, currently in Washington, have been or will be invited to perform again in the Soviet Union.

These examples make an important point—that the Soviet Union is a different place than it was two years ago. But how different? Is what we are seeing superficial or profound? Is it the reality, or just the appearance, of change? The answer is not obvious. The picture remains mixed. Based on events of the past five weeks, let me describe that picture as I see it today:

In my statement at the end of the first round of the Vienna Meeting, I expressed concern that Mustafa Dzhemilev, who had been convicted six times for his work on behalf of his fellow Crimean Tatars, would be re-sentenced. I am glad to note that Dzhemilev has since been released. But the fate of most other political prisoners in the Soviet Union remains the same. . . . All here have noted Andrei Sakharov's appeal for the release of all political prisoners in the Soviet Union, and we have also noted Ambassador Kashlev's hints in the *New York Times* that there might be a response. May it be soon, may it be all-inclusive, and may it be untrammelled by limits and restrictions which could vitiate its effect. . . .

In early January 50 emigrants were permitted by the Soviet authorities to return from the United States to the Soviet Union, many after several years of trying. It is understandable that the move from Soviet to American culture, cultures based on such different principles, could cause serious problems of adjustment. If, as the Soviet Foreign Ministry spokesman has said, there are a thousand more in the United States who desire to return, then we can only hope that the Soviet Union will abandon its former practice of treating them as pariahs and will permit them to exercise their right, guaranteed by the Final Act, to leave their country and return to it. . . .

On a related issue, I referred earlier in my remarks to efforts apparently underway to bring back to the Soviet Union cultural figures who have left it. Why not go further and respect their right to leave in the first place, and the right of others to leave as well? . . .

In the area of family reunification, there has been some prog-ress. Of the American cases announced by Ambassador Kashlev in Bern, three-quarters have been resolved, although it remains a mystery why one-quarter of them are still unresolved after nine months.[1] During the Vienna recess favorable decisions were made in several cases and hints were made about several more. So far the hints outnumber the decisions. . . .

The end of the year 1986 set a record of sorts in the field of Jewish emigration from the Soviet Union. Those allowed to emigrate numbered fewer than 1,000, under 100 a month—the lowest figure since accurate statistics have been kept. The new Soviet legislation, which took effect January 1, shows no sign of alleviating this crisis in emigration, and may even exacerbate it. The law is inherently restrictive, limiting the right to leave to those with close family abroad, and so far it seems to be being applied restrictively. Applications for exit visas, which were previously at least accepted, are now being refused.

Finally in the area of information, the BBC Russian service has for the last few days reached the Soviet Union unjammed. We hope that this is a harbinger of a trend and that the Soviet Union will finally recognize the illegality of jamming by keeping the jammers off the BBC permanently, and taking them and keeping them off the Voice of America, Radio Liberty and Radio Free Europe, Deutsche Welle and the other stations prevented from reaching the Soviet people.

In closing, let me return to the questions with which I began. We have heard predictions and promises from Soviet officials—on a cultural Renaissance, on the release of political prisoners, on genuine openness. They seem to be telling us that Soviet society is at a turning point. But will it turn? The evidence is not conclusive.

NOTE
1. See Document 5.

HELP RUSSIA OUT OF EUROPE

16. *from* William Pfaff, "Eclipse of Reason: How to Help Russia Out of Europe?" *The Baltimore Sun,* November 3, 1986.

Compare the Soviet situation with that of earlier imperial powers. The Roman Empire's languages and institutions irrevocably changed

Western civilization. Spain in Latin America, and Britain, France and Portugal in Asia, ruled sophisticated societies, yet gave them institutions of modern administration and law and a modern political consciousness, without which contemporary history would not be what it is.

The contrary has been true in East European states. The USSR brought no advance of civilization. It brought unworkable ideas of command economy and collectivized agriculture, and the practices of the police state. . . .

The Soviets brought no inspiring ideas, no advanced and civilizing institutions to Eastern Europe. They came by military power and remained by that. . . .

Even in the Soviet Union of Mikhail Gorbachev, what passes for liberalism and reform today is actually a promise—as yet, only a promise—to rectify the terrible and destructive practices of the past. . . .

. . . Nothing has been settled in Czechoslovakia or Poland. The Hungarians, Czechs, Slovaks and Poles live as they do because the Soviet Union has demonstrated its inability positively to reform its system, or theirs, and at the same time, its mortal fear of change.

How long can this go on? How enduring is the Soviet ability to rule by power alone? In every empire what goes first is power. The basis of power and the willingness to use it begin to fail, as they did for Rome after the Fourth Century A.D., for Spain in the Eighteenth Century, and Britain and France after the First World War. . . .

In the West, virtually nothing has been done since 1956 to prepare a Europe from which Soviet power could safely be withdrawn. The problem is scarcely recognized to exist. Statesmanship is supposed to consist in an intelligent collaboration with the inevitable. Nothing is more inevitable than that the present situation in Eastern Europe will eventually end. Nothing could be more imprudent than to assume, as Washington usually does, that Soviet power is permanently and safely installed in these countries.

It is considered exotic or eccentric to question the future of Eastern Europe. Policy-makers' attention is concentrated on summit meetings and the control of nuclear weapons, when no one has the slightest thing to gain from nuclear war and no reason to risk it. Eastern Europe is ignored—where national aspiration has been suppressed for forty years, and Soviet authority is without a civilizing legitimacy; where people, living life as it is, may, as the saying goes, dream of revenge.

BRING RUSSIA INTO EUROPE

17. *from* Jan Reifenberg, "Was Europa sein könnte," *Frankfurter Allgemeine Zeitung,* November 15, 1986. Translated from German by Roger Malone and Jeannet Frössinger.

The doors of the hall of the Vienna Hofburg, where the plenary of the third CSCE follow-up conference meets, are closed. The real work of the 35 delegates now begins: to determine how the provisions of the Helsinki Final Act had been followed during the previous three years. The trick of this is, on the one hand, not to thrust aside the fundamental difference between Eastern and Western Europe, and, on the other hand, not to play up any progress, even the slightest, as a triumph against the Soviet Union. It must be made clear to Moscow that its own security is best served if it opens up to the interchange of people, ideas and the spirit of innovation. In the end, the military security of Europe must be strengthened through confidence-building measures, and the imbalance of conventional weapons between NATO and the Warsaw Pact must be reduced to create a balance based on the lowest level of armaments. This cannot be made dependent only on the "climate" between the two superpowers, or else the CSCE process would be paralyzed.

In Vienna, despite the dividing line between East and West, despite the unchanged ideological contrasts, despite the persistence of military confrontation, the attempt to reestablish common European features has continued—ultimately to give Central Europe once again a place in the world. That will not succeed if, as the Soviet Union clearly wants it, the security question is given such a high priority that other questions are pushed into the background. Every opening speaker at the Vienna follow-up conference emphasized the interrelationships between the three "baskets." For what would be the meaning of "security" if the desire for free intercourse remained stifled? What would "confidence building" mean if compulsory methods for the observation of maneuvers or troops movements were developed, but at the same time people were labelled as state enemies because of their desire to express their religious beliefs or to see their families again?

The Soviet Union tries to oblige in Vienna. Its representatives behave more openly. They do not evade embarrassing questions about observance of human rights. They play up the tune of the

"Common European Home" and, with that tune, want to separate their neighbors in the West from the military madness of the American superpower. Until now, there is only a "new style."

If the conference is to do justice to its mandate, the common European spirit must be reawakened. Certainly, Central Europe can no longer present itself, as it once did, as a vital element of order. The notion is alien to the Americans: In their conception of a Europe divided between the West (friend) and the East (foe), there is no place for this. From Poland, Czechoslovakia, Hungary or Romania, one gets another answer: In their ideal world, Central Europe remains a bridge to the West and the means of preserving their national European qualities. Above all else, it remains the formula for dealing with the German question without getting out of hand. That is the basis of the CSCE and also its trouble spot. The CSCE "process" is like a lecture—a gradual comprehension of the fact that Europe is more than a continent divided into two camps and that the search for overcoming its division has to be accomplished by coming to grips with its historical development. Ideally, the CSCE might lead the Soviet Union to one day understand the true content of the European dimension.

The Emerging Linkages

THE HUMAN DIMENSION

18. *from* "Proposal on the Human Dimension of the Helsinki Final Act," by the Delegation of Belgium and those of Canada, Denmark, France, the Federal Republic of Germany, Greece, Iceland, Ireland, Italy, Luxembourg, the Netherlands, Norway, Portugal, Spain, Turkey, the United Kingdom, and the United States of America. CSCE Review Meeting, Vienna, February 4, 1987. CSCE/WT.19.

The participating States, having recognized the universal significance of human rights and fundamental freedoms [and] the fact that respect for human rights and fundamental freedoms is an essential factor for ensuring the peace, justice, security and well-being necessary for the development of the friendly relations and cooperation among them, . . . decide forthwith to make new, tangible, concrete, precise and intensive efforts to improve implementation of the undertakings they have already entered into:

1. By acceding to such requests for information and representations as may be made to them by governments of other participating States and by private persons or groups on questions relating to human rights and fundamental freedoms that arise in their territory.

Such requests or representations may be addressed to ministries of foreign affairs or to any other agency that the participating States may designate;

2. By holding bilateral meetings with any other participating State that so requests, in order to examine with a view to resolving them, cases or situations of non-respect for human rights, and humanitarian cases or situations relating to human contacts.

3. By instituting a notification procedure allowing participating States that so desired to refer particularly difficult cases or situations to the other participating States at any time.

4. By giving every participating State the possibility of requesting

and securing at the shortest possible notice a special meeting of 35 to discuss and resolve specific situations or cases.

The participating States undertake to take part in meetings at which questions concerning them are to be discussed [and] decide to set in motion a continuing action with a view to holding a conference on the human dimension of the CSCE (date and place to be determined at the appropriate time), starting with the convening of a meeting to be held at. . . . . on. . . . . ., and having as its task:

- To evaluate the working of the system of requests for information, the outcome of bilateral consultations, the working of and conclusions emerging from notifications and from special meetings of the 35;

- 10 proceed to a general review of developments in the situation with regard to human rights and to human contacts;

- To elaborate and recommend the adoption, at the conference on the human dimension, of new measures with the view to improving the implementation of the undertakings entered into by the participating States and facilitating human contacts (a list of items to be discussed will be included in the mandate).

The meeting will be declared closed only when it has been able, in the light of its assessment, to reach a consensus on the date and place of a conference.

That conference will have as its mandate to record the progress it has proved possible to make at the above-mentioned meeting, to discuss such items as are submitted to it, to adopt such measures as are recommended to it and to elaborate new efforts to improve the implementation of the human dimension of the Final Act and of documents adopted in the course of the CSCE process.

THE SECURITY DIMENSION

19. "Proposal Submitted by the Union of Soviet Socialist Republics Concerning the Need for New Thinking on Security Questions." CSCE Review Meeting, Vienna, February 20, 1987. CSCE/WT.84.

The states participating in the Conference on Security and Cooperation in Europe, declaring their invariable aspiration to reduce military confrontation and promote disarmament in Europe, realizing that the continuing production and accumulation of nuclear and conventional armaments threatens human life, as the supreme value, and the very existence of mankind, convinced that the realities of the nuclear and space age demand a new approach to the solution of international problems, based on the renunciation of the use or threat of military force and on the settlement of problems that arise by political means alone, express their readiness:

- To break decisively with ways of thinking and acting that were based on the acceptability and admissibility of wars and armed conflicts,

- To be guided in their mutual relations by the realities of the nuclear and space age, which have confronted humanity with a choice between survival and annihilation,

- To promote the creation of a comprehensive system of international security, providing for the renunciation of the building of one's own security at the expense of the security of others,

- To promote the cessation of the arms race on earth and the prevention of its transfer to outer space,

- To take, in accordance with the Final Act, effective measures for the creation of an atmosphere of confidence and respect among peoples in the spirit of the new political thinking.

A FLOOD OF PROPOSALS

20. *from* Roland Eggleston, "Vienna Conference Flooded with Proposals." Report by RFE/RL correspondent, Vienna, March 12, 1987. RFE/RL B-Wire, FF092–93.

As of today, 115 proposals are on the table. The number will probably rise to about 120 in the next few days but that is expected to be all. Then the diplomats must begin the laborious task of fashioning a final document out of the mass of words.

The proposals can be divided into six general sections. The biggest is human rights and humanitarian issues, in which there are 32 papers. Another three deal with religion and religious freedom.

There are 13 proposals on various aspects of military security and détente, 17 on economic and scientific cooperation, 13 on environmental protection, another 13 on culture and education and seven on information. Other proposals do not fit into any general category.

Western diplomats say the figures are deceptive. They argue that at least half the proposals could be discarded immediately as having no chance of inclusion in the final document for various reasons.

For example, many of the 13 proposals in the military field are Warsaw Pact declarations on issues which have nothing to do with the Vienna Conference. There is a statement about the desirability of withdrawing medium-range nuclear missiles from Europe, another on the desirability of the United States and the Soviet Union continuing negotiations on nuclear weapons, and a third which declares that it would be a good thing if countries broke decisively with ways of thinking based on the acceptability of war.

Many diplomats are puzzled by the introduction of these documents. The Warsaw Pact insists that all proposals introduced in Vienna should be restricted and not released to the press or the public. The West sees little propaganda value in presenting them for Western and neutral diplomats who will discard them.

Some of these military proposals are simply out of place. The Vienna Conference deals only with conventional weapons—it is not intended to concern itself with nuclear arms.

There is similar deadwood in some of the other areas. But the West assumes that the Warsaw Pact will insist on taking conference time to talk about them for a period before dropping them.

The biggest problems in drawing up texts for the final document are expected to be in the areas of military security and human rights and humanitarian issues.

Military security has unique problems. There is a general agreement on the need for a new meeting to discuss confidence-building measures such as an exchange of military information. But NATO, the Warsaw Pact and the Neutrals all disagree on the areas in which new confidence-building measures should be sought.

NATO and the Warsaw Pact also want a conference to negotiate cuts in conventional weapons across Europe from the Atlantic to the Urals.

The Warsaw Pact and France say this should be "linked" in some manner to the Helsinki process. But they are vague about what the "link" should be. The preliminary contacts about drawing up a mandate have nothing to do with the Vienna Conference and are taking place in other parts of Vienna.

There is also no decision about whether the Neutral and Non-aligned countries should be included. Several of the Neutrals and Yugoslavia are already angry at their exclusion from the preliminary contacts.

The 32 proposals on human rights and humanitarian issues cover a broad range of problems. Many are a response to human tragedies.

Western diplomats believe it will take months to reach agreements although the basic ideas have already been extensively debated at expert meetings in Canada and Switzerland. Diplomats say the Warsaw Pact appears to have retreated from many of the humanitarian measures to which they tentatively agreed a year ago at the meeting in Switzerland.

The West's goal is to win benefits for the ordinary man. Its proposals emphasize humanitarian issues such as the right to travel abroad and meet family members or to emigrate to join them. The West (and the Neutrals) argue that the Soviet Union and its allies should give written explanations when travel rights are refused and allow appeals against the decision.

The West has also urged the Soviet Union and other Warsaw Pact countries to relax the burdensome bureaucratic procedures necessary to obtain exit visas. In particular it wants speedier action in urgent situations, such as death or illness in the family or in other situations.

A critical Soviet diplomat provoked sharp comments when he saw nothing urgent about visiting a family grave. Western diplomats point out that the Soviet bureaucracy moves so slowly that often a sick family member is dead before the exit visa is granted. They argued that at least a visa could be granted to visit the grave.

The West also wants to establish the right of the family to travel abroad together instead of leaving some members behind as hostages for their return. Other proposals call for an end to interference with the mails and telephone calls. The West has also called for the publication of all the secret regulations controlling the life of citizens of the USSR and other countries.

Soviet delegates in Vienna say many of these things are coming as a result of the "new thinking" in the administration led by Mikhail Gorbachev. But the West would like to see them enshrined in the final document of the Vienna Conference. Some argue that the Soviet delegation should have no problem in supporting them if there is a genuine change in Soviet thinking.

Other Western concerns involve human rights. Among them is

the protection of the culture and heritage of minorities, such as the Hungarians in Romania and the Jews, ethnic Germans and others in the Soviet Union. Other proposals define the meaning of religious freedom. Another reaffirms the rights of a citizen to check on whether his government is really honoring the pledges it made when it signed the Helsinki Accords and to publicize his findings.

Most Western diplomats believe that negotiating these problems will take most of the year unless there is an unexpected change of approach by the Soviet Union, Czechoslovakia, Bulgaria and Romania. Diplomats say their overall impression is that these countries have little interest in real improvements in the humanitarian sphere.

Diplomats say that long negotiations are also expected on the proposals about economic and technological cooperation. Western and Neutral negotiators say some Warsaw Pact proposals are unrealistic considering East-West rivalries.

In culture, there has been some favorable interest in Poland's idea for a forum on the common cultural heritage in the Polish city of Cracow.

In sum, the Vienna conference has a full palette of proposals.

MAKE THE SOVIETS PAY

21. *from* Roland Eggleston, "USSR Showing New Hard Line at Vienna Talks." Report by RFE/RL correspondent, Vienna, April 1, 1987. RFE/RL B-Wire, FF065–66.

Diplomats at the Helsinki review conference say the Soviet delegation has apparently received orders from Moscow to be more aggressive.

The reports circulated after Soviet diplomats unexpectedly reverted to the hardline anti-Western approach common at the end of last year. The Soviet delegation has generally taken a softer line since the talks resumed on January 27.

Diplomats say the Soviet delegation has also become very hardline in corridor discussions on the human rights and humanitarian issues which are at the heart of East-West differences at the conference.

Eastern delegates have told Western colleagues the orders were given when Soviet delegation leader Yuri Kashlev went to Moscow ten days ago for a "consultation."

Some analysts believe that by taking a hard line Moscow hopes to dampen Western hopes that major concessions can be won from the USSR in humanitarian areas.

Some Western diplomats have said openly that the Soviet Union is anxious to have a new conference on military security and should be made to pay for it with concessions in the humanitarian fields.

The West has been joined in its demands by Neutrals such as Austria, Sweden and Switzerland. One of the boldest proposals on the table is an Austrian-Swiss initiative which says the Soviet Union and its allies should give travel permits to all present applicants by September 30. Later applicants would be promised speedy handling of their papers.

The Soviet delegation has reacted with anger and sarcasm to the various Western and Neutral proposals. Its major tactic, however, has been to suggest that the natural right of a citizen to leave his own country should be matched by the right to enter a foreign country. This has been rejected out of hand by the West, which says that entry visas have to be controlled for a variety of economic, social and political reasons.

The Soviet demands on entry visas refer only to peace groups and other official or semi-official organizations—individuals are not mentioned.

Diplomats say there is no doubt that the Soviet Union sees a new conference on military security as the major goal of the Vienna Conference. There are 13 Warsaw Pact proposals on various aspects of military security or the Soviet view of détente. There is not one Soviet proposal on individual human rights.

Last week, senior Soviet diplomats separately told a number of Western delegates that there should be no agreements on any humanitarian issues until the military issue is settled.

The Soviets said they were not opposed to negotiating on humanitarian issues now or even to reaching agreement in principle on various issues. But the agreement should hang in the air while the military negotiations continued.

Diplomats say there is a strong suggestion in all these conversations that the USSR is prepared to be "generous" on humanitarian issues if the West will make concessions on the terms of the military conference. It is hinting very broadly that humanitarian issues could be settled in two or three weeks.

Most Western diplomats have reacted skeptically. They doubt whether it is possible to obtain worthwhile texts on such major issues as religious freedom, travel for family reunification and minority rights in two or three weeks. The West insists that it will not be satisfied with platitudes and worthless promises.

LINKAGE AND LEVERAGE

22. William Korey, "The Helsinki Accord: A Growth Industry," *Ethics and International Affairs* 4 (1990), pp. 63–67.

As early as June 1986, several months before the review conference began, the State Department's principle policy maker on Helsinki, Rozanne Ridgway, suggested that a strategy of leverage and linkage was essential to the promotion of the human rights aims of the United States. Testifying before the US Helsinki Commission she commented that "it may prove easier to achieve real progress on humanitarian issues" since "all the 'baskets' . . . will be under consideration."

The observation was an outgrowth of concern registered by many regarding the Helsinki-sponsored experts' conference on "human contacts" held at Bern in April through May of 1986, which had then just been completed. The two-month-long experts meeting had produced, from the US vantage point, such an inadequate concluding document—even considered in various quarters as counterproductive—that the US, after some hesitancy and confusion, felt compelled to veto it. An earlier Helsinki-sponsored human rights experts' meeting held in Ottawa, Canada, in July 1985, had also ended in a frustrating deadlock without a concluding document.

Ridgway's comment to the Helsinki Commission implied that the problem of Bern as well as Ottawa lay in the fact that only one basket —Basket 3 with its focal point on human rights—was under discussion and this provided little leverage. At Bern, a British diplomat, highly experienced in Helsinki matters, privately noted that single-issue meetings are certain to prove unproductive, as the West has nothing to offer the USSR that will be enticing to her. He expressed the opinion that such single-issue meetings ought to be rejected by the West in the future as they extend no leverage in dealing with the East.

The Ridgway perspective, bolstered by informed experience, gave emphasis to the strategy of linkage. If a link was established between a Soviet aspiration in a particular area and what the West was seeking in another area, a complicated bargaining process could ensue. Once completed, trade-offs could be made between one basket and another in the Helsinki accord. Secretary of State George Shultz later, in December 1986, pressed the linkage theme with his NATO colleagues and prevailed upon them to accept it.

Linkage, indeed, was built into the Helsinki Final Act itself, particularly in the Decalogue—the Ten Principles—which is at its core. The text specifies that each of the principles are of "primary significance and, accordingly, they will be equally and unreservedly applied, each of them . . . taking into account the others. . . ." Most of the principles deal with security issues, of which Principle 3— "inviolability of borders"—is the cornerstone. However, "human rights and fundamental freedoms," the language of Principle 7, is given equal status and is to be taken "into account" when dealing with security issues.

Reflecting the linkage was the notion of "balance" between the three baskets, especially Basket 1 on security and Basket 3 on "human contacts." (Basket 2 on trade did not become a part of the linkage or the balancing process during the 14 years of the Helsinki experience, although in the future its inclusion is far more likely.) In practical terms, balance was perceived as being realized when progress in Basket 1 was accompanied by or was immediately followed by progress in Basket 3.

At Vienna, the Soviet Union had two major military-security objectives. The first was to move quickly toward a Stockholm II conference on confidence-building measures for reducing surprise attacks, which would ultimately concern itself with disarmament. Another type of security meeting focusing on arms reduction assumed, with time, an even higher priority with Soviet decision makers. In June 1986, even before the Stockholm I conference ended, Gorbachev publicly recommended that new initiatives were essential to reduce conventional arms and armed forces at their flash point in Central Europe. The proposed new initiative of Gorbachev took the form of a "Budapest Appeal" issued by the Warsaw Pact in the same month—June 1986. It called for an end to the deadlock by bringing the former MBFR discussions under the Helsinki umbrella.

That the maneuver might be attractive to France was clearly in the minds of Moscow. At the very beginning of the MBFR talks in the early seventies, France, in keeping with prevailing Gaullist security notions, had absented itself lest it be overshadowed on the NATO side by American strategic objectives. But if a serious renewal of arms-reduction talks was in the offing, which would inevitably attract

France's keen interest, a new format would be necessary that would legitimize Paris' special NATO status. It was precisely on the eve of Mitterrand's visit to Moscow in July that the "Budapest Appeal" was extended.

The proposed conventional stability talks under the Helsinki umbrella stirred enormous concern among the human rights advocates. Especially feared was the possibility that the new emphasis given military and security issues would seriously affect the delicate balance of the Helsinki accord arrangements between Basket 1 and Basket 3. Diplomats with long memories would recall that the initial threat of Soviet policy of the fifties and sixties was a European security conference bereft of its human rights dimension. The ghost of Kremlin past hovered incessantly over the Vienna deliberations. Frequent reiteration by Western ambassadors of the need for "balance" never quite exorcised the ghost. Not surprisingly, in the spring of 1988, when considerable progress had already been reached on security issues—including a mandate for the conventional arms stability talks—and at the same time that human rights progress was totally stymied by Soviet stonewalling, a Western diplomat expressed fear that Moscow was seeking to break the linkage between security and human rights. "It would mean an end of the whole Helsinki process," he added.

But if some stressed the possibility of security issues overwhelming human rights issues, others saw the additional Helsinki responsibilities as opportunities for greater leverage upon the Soviet Union in advancing human rights. That was the import of Ridgway's comments to the Helsinki Commission in June 1986. It stood also at the core of Secretary of State George Shultz's thinking. In Shultz's strongly held view, there existed "a very great limitation on the kind of progress that we can make in establishing a more stable and workable situation between our countries as long as the human rights situation remains what it is. . . ."

What intimately tied human rights to security issues at Vienna was a very crucial time factor that involved the peculiar and complex relationship between CSCE and the conventional arms mandate talks. The 35 Helsinki signatories comprising CSCE met regularly in one part of Vienna. A different team, mainly specialists on military affairs, comprising only the NATO and Warsaw Pact powers—23 instead of 35—met elsewhere in Vienna. Its function was to formulate the mandate for the Conventional Forces in Europe (CFE) talks, which would then be adopted by the CSCE. Since conventional arms stability talks had come under the CSCE umbrella, whatever decisions were made by the mandate negotiators could not be finalized unless and until approved by the CSCE. In the same way, further discussions on confidence-building measures would depend also on the completion of the CSCE meeting in Vienna.

Since the US and the West had placed a high priority on reaching a significant agreement on human rights issues, it was self-evident that those from the Soviet bloc especially interested in getting the mandate completed and the conventional arms stability talks started had to be generally and favorably responsive to Western human rights demands. Otherwise, the US, for example, might determine to sit endlessly at Vienna CSCE awaiting such responsiveness. Because the mandate was wrapped into the CSCE package, its operational effectiveness, if any, was totally dependent upon further progress in the human rights field.

How the strategy would operate was explained in a candid letter of Ambassador Zimmermann addressed to the chairman of the US Helsinki Commission, Congressman Steny Hoyer, as early as April 9, 1987. He told Hoyer:

> The Soviets are in a hurry to finish the Vienna meeting because it must end before they can move from the mandate negotiations to the actual negotiations on conventional arms reductions. *This right gives us considerable leverage on human rights* [emphasis added].

Zimmermann went on to note that "we will not end the Vienna meeting without an adequate human rights result" and that this "condition also applies to the concurrent mandate discussions." "Performance" and "deeds" were stressed, although "a substantive and balanced final document" was also desired.

Among the "deeds" urged upon the Soviets were "the full release of political prisoners, resolution of family reunification cases, a steep increase in emigration and an end to jamming." Equally important for Zimmermann were requests dealing with the institutionalization of the process:

> We are asking the Soviets to provide credible assurances that compliance will continue to improve beyond the Vienna meeting. Examples would be: abolition of Articles 70 and 190 of the Criminal Code, abolition of the psychiatric hospitals run by the Interior Ministry, a mechanism to ensure higher levels of emigration, and unambiguous commitments in the Vienna final document.

In the spring of the following year, 1988, Ambassador Zimmermann addressed the issue again in a private letter to the chairman of an important nongovernmental organization. He specifically discussed the strategy of Vienna with reference to the concluding document. "Unless," he wrote, the concluding document of Vienna advances "significantly further the documents we agreed to at Helsinki and Madrid," the United States "will not end the Vienna meeting." Repeatedly, at press conferences, in speeches and in private meetings with various delegates, including the Soviet delegates, this theme was stressed. The US would be prepared to sit and negotiate for a very long time until it was satisfied with the progress made in the human rights aspects of the concluding document.

The consensus feature of the Helsinki process, of course, made possible the application of a tough leverage strategy even as the trade-offs between Basket 1 and Basket 3 had always been a built-in component of the Final Act of the Helsinki phenomenon. In an interview, Zimmermann capsulated his thinking about the leverage strategy: "Tensions between the military and human rights aspects of the Helsinki process have provided the dynamic by which that process has developed and has established itself as a major phenomenon in East-West relations."

Elaborations of the strategy came from Ambassador Robert Frowick, who served as Zimmermann's deputy, principally specializing in security issues. He explained in an interview that Zimmermann's strategy was to keep the security discussions, which ran on a separate track, a step ahead of human rights. Progress on the security track could be used as a trade-off for accompanying movement in human rights.

Clearly, the incorporation of conventional arms stability into the Helsinki process proved not to be a feared albatross but rather a powerful lever for change.

Trading Apples and Oranges

THE COMMON EUROPEAN HOME

23. *from* Mikhail Amirdzhanov and Mikhail Cherkasov, "Our Common European Home," *International Affairs* [Moscow] 1988, no. 12, pp. 29–36.

It would not be an exaggeration . . . to consider the Helsinki Final Act, which laid the groundwork for the European process, unique. . . . This process . . . is today at the threshold of a quantitatively new stage—the transition from recommendations to decisions, to real disarmament and the strengthening of military-political stability and the creation of a mechanism of humanitarian cooperation. . . .

. . . The CSCE is a highly effective instrument capable of exerting an impact on the situation on the continent in the broadest sense of the word. It is legitimate to assume that the Helsinki process is also the optimal basis for erecting the European home. . . .

When the point at issue is the common European home today, what we imagine the clearest of all is precisely military-political measures. . . . The issue of a transition from a military to political means of ensuring security is being raised for the first time. In short, if we are asked how to build the military-political wall of the home in question, we can offer a wide selection of well-considered and carefully elaborated initiatives. This is only understandable, as the desire to survive can be characterized as an imperative intrinsic to the national interests of all countries.

All the same, merely a "desire to stay alive" is insufficient for building a common European home; its foundation must rest on much broader interests. In this connection, the conclusion suggests itself of the need for a *definite reshifting of accents in relations* between the residents of the home, specifically the transition from a negative orientation (the threat of mutual destruction) to a positive one, to a lessening of the role of the military component and to greater weight for humanitarian, ecological and other elements.

. . . Take the *human dimension of European politics.* The revolutionary process of *perestroika* and the development of democratization and *glasnost* apace in the USSR have in effect torn down the fence behind which we used to hide from attacks by the West in the human rights sphere. The situation has changed—in a move that was unexpected for our partners we have stated our readiness to hold all-round discussions aimed at practical results in order to arrive at a mutual understanding that would improve the state of affairs in the humanitarian sphere in all the CSCE countries. It is in this light that the Soviet initiative on holding a conference in Moscow on a wide range of humanitarian issues should be viewed. . . .

It is difficult to even imagine the scope of the possibilities that are opening up: people's diplomacy, communal (local) ties, ties between parties and between trade unions, meetings between young people, athletes, etc. This will be the shortest road to putting an end to the cultivating of the notorious image of the enemy and to the removal of the blinkers that artificially narrow people's view of the complicated and contradiction-filled world around them. But the shortest path does not mean the simplest. This choice will be difficult not only for those who are used to regarding each critical remark as slander and ideological sabotage but also for those who like to shout in a proprietary manner if something does not accord with the old traditions and notions.

The following three factors can be an earnest of the maintenance of normal, benevolent relations in the humanitarian sphere: (a) the obligation of states to ensure conditions as favorable as possible enabling citizens to exercise their human rights; (b) cooperation among states in implementing human rights, cooperation that is based on the appropriate international agreements; (c) exchange of experience accumulated in this sphere.

The creation of a mechanism of humanitarian cooperation in the framework of which the above three components could be implemented and the activity of the requisite consultative apparatus set in motion would definitely play a useful role. The draft of such a mechanism is already being elaborated by the members of the CSCE Vienna meeting.

This is, of course, only the first step in a qualitatively new stage of interstate humanitarian cooperation. However, in combination with the rights of citizens to contribute, independently or as members of unofficial associations, to the development and protection of human rights and the main freedoms of their country, such a step would definitely speed up the erection of the home. . . .

A detailed analysis of humanitarian issues is all the more necessary in that in a number of Western countries it is today advancing to the forefront of their state policies. However, whereas in the USA these matters are a traditional priority for its foreign-policy propaganda, in the FRG they are quite often presented as a component of the *"German question."* Specifically, West German Defense Minister Rupert Scholz has stated that "the unity of the people of Germany is one of the most important elements and treasures of Europe and an element of its unity" and that he pictures very well a united Germany in the European home.

This motif is being heard rather frequently in the context of the creation of the common European home. It appears as though some in Bonn believe that in this context it would be much easier to tackle such a task step by step. With this in mind some West Germans are oriented to the goal of fitting this home with the "amenities" that should lead to greater openness between the two German states, to a further broadening of their multifaceted ties and to the establishment of more "permeable" borders and their gradual removal. And in the light of the increased flexibility of Soviet foreign policy certain West German politicians are apparently nurturing the dream of some "turn" in the Soviet stand. . . .

. . . the USSR proceeds from the belief that the preservation of the territorial status quo in Europe, the existence of the two sovereign German states, the strengthening of socialism in the GDR and the quadripartite responsibility in the issue of West Berlin are an inalienable part of the foundation of the common European home. Advance of the slogan of "reunification of Germany" as a prerequisite for a convergence of all Europeans will hardly garner support in the other Western countries, for that matter. However, it is our view that it would be incorrect to make the long-term forecast that this problem will not be raised altogether or will dissolve in the broader context of general European cooperation. . . .

. . . The human dimension of the development of cooperation in Europe is one of the priority areas of the policies of our northern neighbors as well. "The individual and his rights and living conditions—this is the main bench mark of the European process," Finnish Foreign Minister Kalevi Sorsa pointed out at the CSCE Vienna meeting last May. Finns are vigorously implementing the Helsinki ideas; they are reacting sensitively to our new European course. They constantly show a readiness to be mediators between the West and us and they are exploring common ground in the interests of a multi-faceted Europe.

An understanding of the ecological catastrophe threatening man is only now beginning to penetrate deeply the consciousness of our countrymen. In the West, however, the significance of the *ecological factor* came to the fore much earlier. It is not fortuitous that Finland, like all the Nordic countries, is setting the pace in the discussion of environment protection issues at different European forums and meetings. It is largely thanks to the activity of the Nordic and socialist countries that ecological questions were broadly covered in the draft of the Vienna meeting document. . . .

The right of each to live in the "common home" will largely be determined by the *intensification of integrational processes* in both parts of the continent. Even though the existence of regional economic systems cannot itself be a prerequisite for the creation of the economic foundation of the common European home, the development of integrational cooperation in both East and West will unquestionably create additional conditions for their participation in inter-regional economic cooperation. The overriding problem here is the EEC's[1] degree of integration, which is much more advanced than the CMEA, and the Community's course for unifying domestic and foreign economic policies and creating an integral common market.

By all indications, the consequences of these changes will be ambivalent for the CMEA countries. This, of course, will largely depend on the accords reached on bilateral relations between the EEC and East European partners. However, the determinant will be capacity of socialist countries to overhaul their economic relations.

There is no time to waste in getting the ball rolling. If our countries fail to revamp our integrational mechanisms by creating a common socialist market in the immediate future, we will be unable to place on the basis of equality and parity of possibilities the institutional foundations being laid today for relations between the European Community, on the one hand, and CMEA and individual socialist countries, on the other. At the present juncture the level of coordination of the foreign economic policies of the socialist community countries vis-à-vis the European Community is not adequate to the tasks of building the European home.

By virtue of a number of objective factors the East European region has always been integrated into the general European system of relations to a much greater extent than the Soviet Union has. With progress toward the formation of an integral domestic market by 1992 the attractiveness of the European Community for the East

European countries will continue to grow. Also deserving attention are the proposals that appeared in the spring in the press of the EEC countries regarding a higher level of EEC-CMEA ties, which is manifest in the plans for major capital investments in East European countries which are to be financed by the Community, i.e., the so-called new Marshall Plan for Eastern Europe. Even though many Westerners are somewhat skeptical of this project, calling it the brainchild of West Germany which is out to tether the German Democratic Republic more tightly to itself, a thorough analysis of the possible consequences of the initiatives of this kind is imperative.

Will this, as well as the overall economic influence of the EEC, lead to the emergence of centrifugal tendencies among the socialist countries? Obviously, this can be avoided above all by an overhaul of economic cooperation among CMEA countries. It is the Soviet Union that has the most difficult changes to make. . . .

Nor should the unifying importance of *bilateral relations* of European countries be underestimated. The right of each state to "special" relations with any other partner within the new European structure being created has been called into question during the discussion of the issue. All the same, it is incorrect to assume that with the passage of time some of the residents of the European home will reject centuries-old traditions and rules of communication, forget history or prefer a new language of intercourse. Privileged, "special" relations will organically enter the future of Europe and become a connecting link. Why not, for that matter, use the "favorites" of the home for mediatory, peacemaking functions? The development of bilateral ties in the political, economic, scientific and humanitarian spheres will become a prerequisite for building the common European home.

The role of *subregional structures,* among them the countries of Northern Europe and the Balkan Peninsula, is enhancing as well. Despite the growth of their political authority of late we have a rather foggy notion of the significance of such associations for the future of the European continent. The development of subregional relations will also proceed along the lines of extra-bloc and inter-bloc structures which are to be based on the historical and cultural commonality of nations and the orientation of state policy on universal values. The idea of Central Europe as an unofficial historical public association incorporating Hungary, the GDR, Czechoslovakia, Poland, the FRG and Austria is widespread in a number of socialist countries today. Evidently the point at issue is shaping the first islands of the future Eurostructure. . . .

The idea of a common European home is new political thinking developing on European soil. Even though cooperation in Europe will still long be cooperation between its two parts, existence in it is no longer possible without recognition of all its elements, without a transition of this interdependence into a practical positive dimension, without a search for and determination of interests common to all Europeans.

NOTE
1.   European Economic Community.

THE DAWN OF FREEDOM

24. *from* "Glasnost: The Dawn of Freedom?" Speech by Richard Schifter, US assistant secretary of state for human rights and humanitarian affairs. Annual meeting of American Academy of Political and Social Science, Philadelphia, April 28, 1989 (Washington, DC: US State Dept. Public Information Series, June 1989).

A Change in the Human Rights Climate
Toward the end of year 2 and the beginning of year 3 of the Gorbachev era [1987] we, at last, began to see change in the air as far as the Soviet Union's human rights climate was concerned. The change was most clearly evident in the arts and literature. The controls on the theater and on films have been significantly relaxed. Long-suppressed books, we were told, were now to be published. Neither painters nor musicians were any longer required to let the party apparatchiks define the limits of their creativity.

A West European diplomat told me of his experience in Moscow in those days. The Foreign Ministry had provided him with a ticket to a new play, a play highly critical of the Stalinist past. A Soviet diplomat well known to us for his rigid espousal of what has since become known in the Soviet Union as "old thinking" came along as an escort. My West European friend, a man fluent in Russian, told me of the enthusiasm with which the Soviet audience responded to the play, the thunderous applause as the play came to a close. Through it all my friend's escort sat on his hands. As they walked out, he kept shaking his head and said only: "It's so difficult to understand. It's so difficult to understand."

Early in 1987 we heard the first announcement of the large-scale release of political prisoners. I recall a staff meeting at the State

Department at which Secretary Shultz turned to me to ask for my comment on the announcement. I replied that I thought it was significant. He laughed and said that if even I thought so, there must be something to it.

Finally around this time we also got the first inkling of possible genuine change in Soviet emigration policy. In January 1987, quite a number of long-term refuseniks began to receive exit permits. By February the number of departures was up 50 percent; by March the figures were up 370 percent.

We were not aware at the time of another change which had occurred in the Soviet Government's human rights policy. Without giving the matter any publicity, the Soviet authorities stopped, either late in 1986 or early in 1987, prosecuting dissidents and religious activists under the articles of the criminal codes which described as felonies such acts as "anti-Soviet agitation or propaganda," "defamation of the Soviet system," or participation in or organization of unauthorized religious groups.

To illustrate how these laws were applied, let me cite the case of Irina Ratushinskaya. In 1983, at the age of 29, this young woman, who had done nothing other than write poetry, was convicted of having written poems which were alleged to constitute anti-Soviet agitation and was sentenced to 7 years at hard labor plus 5 years of internal exile. She was amnestied and released after 3 years, in year 3 of the Gorbachev era.

At any rate, only after some time had passed without any prosecutions under the infamous Articles 70, 190–1, 142 and 227 of the Russian criminal code did we recognize that the Soviets had adopted a policy no longer enforcing those repressive provisions of law.

Though we were not yet aware of the implications of this unannounced change of Soviet policy, we did, of course, notice a good many changes that were, by 1987, clearly in evidence. I recall making an assessment in the early months of that year of developments in the Soviet Union relating to human rights. The conclusion which I reached then was that the Soviet Union was for the second time since 1953 engaged in an effort to purge Stalinism from its system. The goal, it seemed, was to return to what was viewed as a purer form of Leninism, the state of affairs that prevailed in the Soviet Union in the early 1920s.

I thought that that would, indeed, offer an improvement, but that we needed to keep in mind that Lenin conceived the idea of the one-party dictatorship; that he had reestablished the secret police, then known as the Cheka, which had been abolished by Russia's

short-lived democratic government; and that the evidence was clear
that a Leninist system provided a fertile breeding ground for Stalinism.

The Development of Glasnost and Perestroika

Nevertheless, as we entered year 3, we were, indeed, able to observe
a new openness in Soviet society, an openness comparable to
Khrushchev's thaw and approaching the conditions of the early 1920s.
There was even a label for this new development. It was called
glasnost.

Glasnost, we thought at the time, was a way of enlisting the help
of the Soviet public in what the leadership considered its most important undertaking: perestroika. Perestroika, the restructuring of the
Soviet economy, was clearly necessary to get the country out of its
disastrous slump. Glasnost, it seemed, would help advance the goals
of perestroika in that if the citizens were allowed to criticize low-
ranking officials for inefficiency, corruption or drunkenness, this
would help the leadership spot these people, who were thought to
bear principal responsibility for the country's failures. Once they and
their policies were identified, corrective measures could be taken by
the leadership. Similarly, if the general public could offer constructive ideas on how to improve the governmental and economic operations which they personally observed, this, too, could help the leadership improve the quality of work done by governmental agencies
and economic enterprises. Glasnost, as it was then practiced, required
the person willing to speak up to operate within the system, to accept
collectivism and the one-party dictatorship as a given, and to offer
ideas on what improvements can be effected subject to the understanding that the system as such must be maintained.

But as year 3 progressed we saw some changes in Soviet reality
beyond the narrow limits which we assumed had initially been set.
The most spectacular of these changes related to the new assertive-
ness of the Soviet Union's ethnic minorities. In the summer of 1987,
Crimean Tatars—members of an ethnic group which had been forc-
ibly relocated in 1944 from its ancestral home in the Crimea to
Central Asia—demonstrated for weeks in Moscow to press their case
for a return to their homeland. They did not reach their objective
and were ultimately detained and returned to their places of residence in Central Asia. That showed the limits of change. But what
was, nevertheless, remarkable was that the demonstrations had been
allowed to go on for quite some time and none of the demonstrators
had been charged with a felony and sent to Siberia.

Shortly after the Tatar demonstrations had been in the news, we heard of large-scale demonstrations in the Baltic republics. Here too, the police moved in after a while, but once again not with the ferocity which would have characterized police action at another time. (That this change was not irreversible was demonstrated at Tbilisi a year and a half later.)[1]

As we looked at the newspapers and magazines in year 3, we found that many writers were no longer limiting themselves to denunciations of miscreants who strayed from the path of socialist righteousness. These writers were posing increasingly profound questions about the basic structure of the system and, in this context, also urged a review of past history. Not only was Stalinism denounced, but Brezhnev and the "period of stagnation," for which he was held responsible, were subjected to severe criticism. Glasnost was beginning to challenge some beliefs which had long been held as sacrosanct.

And Jewish emigration had now climbed to a level 700 percent above the January 1987 starting point. Armenian and ethnic German emigration had climbed even faster.

Party Conference Institutionalizes Reforms
By the fall of 1987, still in year 3, we first heard rumors and then saw evidence of the fact that the Soviet leadership was no longer fully united. There appeared to be agreement that the economy was in disastrous shape, and that perestroika was required, although there may have been differences as to what it should consist. Beyond that, there seemed to be profound disagreement on the subject of glasnost. Yegor Ligachev, presumed to hold the number two position under Gorbachev, and Viktor Chebrikov, head of the KGB, were heard as sharply disapproving the new trends toward greater openness. This was confirmed by Boris Yeltsin, one of the younger personalities elevated to high rank by Gorbachev, who bluntly denounced Ligachev. Gorbachev now repudiated Yeltsin. He was quickly demoted and was expected to disappear from the political scene.

As year 3 drew to an end, we had seen the forward spurt toward greater freedom in the early months, the development of opposition to this relaxation of controls, and the creation of an uneasy balance between the two contending forces, which made it difficult to predict the direction in which the country would now move.

Year 4 [1988] began on an ominous note. In our part of the world, it is difficult to appreciate that a mere letter to the editor could shake a country, but in the Soviet Union that is precisely what happened. A newspaper known for its conservative outlook, *Sovietskaya Rossiya*, printed a letter purported to have been written by a Leningrad teacher by the name of Nina Andreyeva. The letter forcefully criticized the new trends toward freedom, defended Stalin, and appealed for a return to the stability and the verities of the recent past. *Sovietskaya Rossiya* would clearly not print such a provocative letter from an unknown schoolteacher without a signal from on high. The letter was assumed to be an authoritative statement of position from personages in the leadership. Were they laying down the new line? Many Soviet citizens, particularly those who belonged to the intelligentsia, were now wondering whether this was the death knell of glasnost. Millions of Soviet citizens were figuratively holding their breath. Lest we forget, I am talking about developments in March and April 1988.

Then, after an agonizing wait of about 3 weeks, came the counterblast, an editorial in *Pravda,* the official newspaper of the Communist Party. It was a ringing endorsement of glasnost. The split in the leadership was now undeniable. The decision evidently made by the reformers was to push onward, to accelerate the pace of change. A party conference was to be called to obtain institutional blessing for the reforms. And both before, during and after the conference of June 1988, a careful examination of the latest articles authored by Soviet reformers suggested a new development regarding doctrine: the reformers were not merely denouncing Stalin's terror state and Brezhnev's stagnation—they were beginning to challenge Lenin's precepts on maintaining power. When I asked one of these reformers whether he wasn't deviating from Leninism, his truly heretical response was: "Lenin said different things at different times."

The deviation from precepts which had long been assumed to be Leninist orthodoxy was not limited to theoretical writings. It was soon reflected in the program adopted by the party conference and put into practice, thereafter, through constitutional reform and the initial stab at a relatively free electoral process. The principal new developments deviating from traditional Leninist precepts were:

- The tendency to concentrate governmental operational authority in the party, at the expense of the state, was reversed: state agencies were to be reinvigorated.

- The practice of ending debate on an issue on which the party had reached a decision, euphemistically called "democratic centralism," was abandoned. "Old thinkers" now bitterly complain that their country has turned into a debating society.

- Decision-making power, for long concentrated at the very top, was to be transferred to the general population through the process of real elections.

Another change, minor in doctrinal terms, but of symbolic significance, has been the disappearance of such uplifting slogans as "The Communist Party represents the people's will." Lenin, who authored the slogan "All power to the Soviets," believed in demagoguery; Gorbachev seems to abhor it. And all over Moscow the Communist Party slogans which once adorned the street scene appear to have been taken down. An effort is being made to appeal to the good sense of the individual citizen rather than to his herd instinct.

These changes in doctrine and theory notwithstanding, much of the Soviet Union's day-to-day reality appeared mired in its Stalinist and Brezhnevist past. But there were also changes that transcended the theoretical sphere; for example, the transfer of Ligachev and Chebrikov to positions of reduced authority. We also saw late in 1988 the release of all persons who had been convicted under the political and religious articles of the Soviet criminal codes, an opening toward greater freedom of religion, Jewish emigration at a level 30 times that at the outset, and the beginning of an electoral process of which we can say that with all its serious shortcomings, it was no longer a complete farce.

There is one other doctrinal change which came clearly into focus in 1988. It had previously appeared in Gorbachev's speech in November 1987 on the 70th anniversary of the Bolshevik revolution. It was the concept that the existence of nuclear weapons and the resultant ability of some nations to end the human race made the idea of class warfare on the international scene obsolete. That idea was restated more fully and given practical application in the Soviet Union's evident reconsideration of its, theretofore, expansionistic policies. The withdrawal in Afghanistan, the agreement on Angola, and the expected Vietnamese withdrawal from Cambodia appear to reflect a new approach to foreign policy.

As year 4 was drawing to an end, the Soviet reformers moved from tinkering with the system to what could conceivably mean profound change.

NOTE

1. At Tbilisi, army units used poison gas to disperse demonstrators, causing numerous casualties.

HUMAN RIGHTS CONFERENCE IN MOSCOW?

25. *from* Roland Eggleston, "NATO Allies Drawing up Conditions for Moscow Conference." Report by RFE/RL correspondent, Vienna, November 10, 1988. RFE/RL B-Wire, FF071–72.

The United States and its allies are drawing up a list of conditions under which they might consider attending a human rights conference in Moscow.

This week, diplomats are studying and refining a proposed list of conditions suggested by the United States. Few details are known outside the negotiating rooms, but those who have seen the list say it is in two parts.

One deals with improvements in the Soviet human rights record which must be achieved before the end of the Vienna Conference in a few weeks. It includes the release of political and religious prisoners and exit visas for long-term refuseniks.

The second part is made up of other human rights and humanitarian steps which the USSR must guarantee to take by the end of next year.

The question of a human rights meeting in Moscow is one of the most controversial issues still to be resolved by the Vienna Conference.

Several NATO countries, particularly the US and Britain, are reluctant to agree because it could be seen as a betrayal of all those held in prison, labor camps and psychiatric institutes for struggling for human rights. They argue there has been no change in the laws which were used against human rights activists despite many hints from Soviet officials over the past two years that this is about to happen. The Soviet Union continues to restrict freedom of travel and emigration and still jams some Western radio broadcasts.

Other Western states argue that these are the very reasons why a human rights conference should be held in Moscow. In their view, it would point up the failings in the Soviet record. Most of the Neutral countries support this approach. They also argue that a meeting in Moscow would win more international publicity for human rights than a meeting anywhere else.

Three special meetings on human rights are planned to follow the Vienna Conference. There is wide agreement that the first two should be in Paris and Copenhagen. It is only the location of the third which is in doubt. Geneva is considered to be the most likely site if Moscow is rejected.

The Soviet Union is conducting a vigorous international campaign on behalf of Moscow. Foreign Minister Eduard Shevardnadze has put pressure on France, Italy and West Germany to support it. Diplomats from these countries say one of Shevardnadze's arguments is that holding the meeting in Moscow would help the reform program of President and General Secretary Mikhail Gorbachev. Most diplomats consider this argument to be too transparent to be taken seriously.

According to diplomats, Shevardnadze is engaged in a constant campaign to persuade the United States to agree to a human rights meeting in Moscow. His latest message was sent to outgoing Secretary of State George Shultz only this week.

The Moscow conference is expected to be high on the Soviet agenda for next week's visit to Moscow by the assistant secretary of state for humanitarian affairs, Richard Schifter.

It will also be discussed by a team of US congressmen led by the chairman of the US Helsinki Commission, Steny Hoyer, who are going to Moscow next week. The congressmen will have a series of meetings with members of the Supreme Soviet and will discuss the present situation in the Soviet Union with refuseniks and dissidents.

The Soviet Union also has to convince Britain, whose prime minister, Margaret Thatcher, has strong reservations about a human rights conference in Moscow. Britain says it has never rejected the idea out of hand, but needs to see dynamic improvement in the Soviet record with guarantees that it will continue. Above all, Britain wants to see the abolition of the laws used to send human rights activists to prison, labor camps, psychiatric institutions or into internal exile.

Diplomats say Britain is waiting to see how the Soviet Union reacts to a list of conditions being drawn up in Vienna before it takes another look at its position.

US and British diplomats in Vienna are unimpressed by the much-publicized Soviet statements that it will soon release all those considered by the West to be political prisoners.

Senior Soviet officials such as government spokesman Gennadi Gerasimov say there are only 11 of these. US and British diplomats say this alone exposes the emptiness of the Soviet promises. The West is reluctant to discuss the numbers of those it considers to be political prisoners, but the number is closer to 250 than 11.

The West believes there may be many more political prisoners of whom they have not heard. That is why they do not want to commit themselves to calling for the release of a specific number.

Diplomats say there is no time frame for the internal discussions in Vienna on conditions for the Moscow conference. Eventually, the list will be sent to Moscow to see how the USSR reacts. Then the West will consider the situation again.

UNJAMMING SOVIET PRIORITIES

26. *from* Roland Eggleston, "USSR Rejects Ban on Jamming." Report by RFE/RL correspondent, Vienna, September 19, 1988. RFE/RL B-Wire, CN130.

The Soviet Union today told the Helsinki review conference it would never agree to a Western proposal to end the jamming of Western radio stations.

Soviet delegate Vladimir Morozov called on the West to abandon its efforts on behalf of what he called propaganda establishments trying to encourage unrest in other countries.

Our correspondent in Vienna says the Soviet delegate did not mention any station by name. But Western diplomats were told later the comments were directed particularly at Western efforts to ban the jamming of Radio Free Europe and Radio Liberty.

Morozov also said some Warsaw Pact countries could not accept Western proposals calling for an end to regulations requiring foreign visitors to exchange a minimum sum of currency. He said these countries regarded the regulations as a protection against attempts to undermine the currency by black market operations.

British delegate Phillip Hurr said both issues had been on the agenda since the Vienna Conference began two years ago and could not be dropped now simply to satisfy a few countries.

27. *from* Roland Eggleston, "Jamming of RFE/RL an Issue at Vienna Conference." Report by RFE/RL correspondent, Vienna, September 27, 1988. RFE/RL B-Wire, FF130.

Western diplomats told correspondents that Soviet refusal to consider texts which would oblige it to stop jamming RFE/RL is one of the issues delaying agreement on a final document.

Soviet delegates have said the USSR is prepared to agree to a text which would end the jamming of most Western radio stations. But they insist that RFE/RL must be excluded from the agreement. NATO and the European Community refuse to accept such a deal.

Soviet delegation leader Yuri Kashlev put the Soviet attitude at a recent meeting of the full conference when he said: "The time has come for the West to abandon attempts to protect the fossil remnants of the Cold War—that is, the propaganda establishments designed to foment political, nationalist and religious fervor in other states through their broadcasts." Other Soviet delegates have since repeated Kashlev's statement in working groups.

The agreement in Vienna centers on a text included in the draft final document presented by the Neutral and Nonaligned countries in May. It would require governments to "permit direct and normal reception of foreign radio broadcasts." It is virtually the same language as in the original proposal rejected by NATO and the European Community.

The Soviet response is that it will agree to unimpeded reception —but only from radio stations broadcasting from the territory of their owners. This would exclude RFE/RL, which is American-controlled but has its transmitters in Western Europe.

In the past few days, Soviet delegates have offered another possibility. This would allow unimpeded reception of those broadcasts "which are in accordance with the regulations of the international telecommunications union and other international instruments."

To an outsider, that may appear to be acceptable. But Western diplomats say the catch is in the reference to "other international instruments." Past experience has shown this to mean an international convention on the use of broadcasting in the cause of peace which was drafted by the League of Nations in 1936.

That convention urged states to prohibit broadcasts detrimental to international understanding, or of a character likely to incite populations to act against the security of their own states.

The convention is often cited by Soviet delegates as legalizing jamming. In fact, the Soviet Union came to it very late. Although it was agreed in 1936, it was not ratified by the Supreme Soviet until 1982, when the USSR needed an argument to justify jamming.

28. *from* Roland Eggleston, "Soviet Delegation Will Press for Moscow Conference." Report by RFE/RL correspondent, Vienna, December 2, 1988. RFE/RL B-Wire, FF192.

[On December 2] the chief Soviet negotiator at the conference, Yuri Kashlev, said the Soviet delegation would continue to press for a human rights meeting in Moscow in 1991.

Kashlev told reporters in Vienna: "The proposal is on the table here and we will continue to press for it. We have instructions to solve the problem here in Vienna. That is the position and we will continue to discuss it here in Vienna."

The Soviet negotiator had been asked about reports that Soviet President Mikhail Gorbachev had said the USSR would not insist on the Moscow meeting now if the West did not want it. "The USSR could wait because the time for the meeting would come."

Kashlev said: "My personal understanding of the statement by Gorbachev is that he once again sent a message to the West saying: Please think again."

Kashlev said he personally would add another sentence to the message to the West: "Do not make a historic mistake."

Kashlev said he believed the Soviet offer to host the meeting in Moscow in 1991 had the support of a majority of the countries at the Helsinki review conference.

Kashlev said the Moscow conference could be on the agenda for Gorbachev's upcoming talks in Washington and London.

"But for the time being, our proposal is still on the table and we will continue consultations with all of the delegations here at Vienna. Generally speaking, we favor solving all the problems of the CSCE conference in Vienna, not somewhere else."

Kashlev was also asked why the Soviet Union had stopped jamming the broadcasts of Radio Liberty and the Deutsche Welle at this particular time.

"Our democratization is developing according to our own priorities," he said. "If one of our priorities coincides with the situation at the CSCE meeting here, then it is good for the CSCE and good for us.

"I know that our government, in taking the decision to stop the jamming, took into account the text worked out here at the Vienna Conference on that problem. But I don't think that was the main reason for our decision on jamming.

"The level of glasnost is now so high in the Soviet Union that we can afford to hear three more voices or 20 more languages—because this radio station is transmitting in more than 20 languages. So stop-

ping jamming corresponds to the level of our development. This is
the main reason. Not because of pressure somewhere."

GORBACHEV OFFERS TROOP WITHDRAWAL

29. *from* Speech by Mikhail S. Gorbachev, president of the USSR.
United Nations, New York, December 7, 1988. *Vital Speeches of the
Day* 55, no. 8 (February 1, 1989), pp. 231, 235.

The Helsinki process is a great process. In my opinion, it is still valid.
It should be preserved and deepened in all aspects—philosoph-
ical, political, and practical, but with due account of new circumstances. . . .

Today I am able to inform you that the Soviet Union has decided
to reduce its armed forces.

Over the next two years their strength will be reduced by 500,000
men, and substantial cuts will be made in conventional armaments.
These cuts will be made unilaterally, regardless of the talks on the
mandate of the Vienna meeting.

By agreement with our Warsaw Treaty allies, we have decided to
withdraw six tank divisions from the German Democratic Republic,
Czechoslovakia and Hungary by 1991, and to disband them.

In addition, assault-landing formations and units and some others, including assault-crossing support units with their armaments
and combat equipment, will be withdrawn from Soviet forces stationed in these countries.

The Soviet forces stationed in these countries will be reduced by
50,000 men and 5,000 tanks.

The Soviet divisions which still remain on the territory of our
allies will be reorganized. Their structure will be changed: a large
number of tanks will be withdrawn, and they will become strictly
defensive.

At the same time we shall cut troops and armaments in the
European part of the USSR.

The total reductions of the Soviet armed forces in European
regions of the USSR and the territory of our European allies will
amount to 10,000 tanks, 8,500 artillery systems, and 800 combat
aircraft.

In taking these important decisions, the Soviet leadership is expressing the will of the Soviet people, who are engaged in the radical
overhaul of their entire socialist society.

The Vienna Achievement

US SANCTIONS MOSCOW CONFERENCE

30. Announcement by the White House Press Office in California, January 4, 1989. Secretary of State to CSCE Collective, Washington, January 5, 1989. Unclassified State Department Dispatch 001640.

President Reagan has authorized the US delegation in Vienna to support, in cooperation with like-minded allies, US participation in an agreed schedule of Conference on Security and Cooperation in Europe Follow-on conferences dealing with human rights. The first conference will be in Paris in 1989, the second in Copenhagen in 1990, and the third is scheduled for Moscow in 1991.

The president decided to agree to this schedule, including the Moscow conference, as a means of encouraging continuation of the significant progress in human rights that has taken place in the Soviet Union over the past three years. That progress has included the release of hundreds of political prisoners and exit permission for many people long refused the right to emigrate. Emigration rates for the Soviet Union are substantially higher, and jamming of the Voice of America, Radio Liberty and other Western broadcasters has ceased. New laws respecting individual liberties have been promised to the world by President Gorbachev in his recent speech to the United Nations.

Such new laws—the institutionalization of reform—are crucial, and the president recognizes that there is much yet to be done in the Soviet Union before that nation meets acceptable and universal human rights standards. We will make it clear to the Soviet Union that the lack of future and institutionalized progress or a reversal of progress made to date will cause us to reconsider our decision to attend a Moscow conference in 1991. At present, we believe that Western concurrence in principle in such a Moscow conference may be the best way to encourage and support future improvement in the

Soviet human rights performance. The Soviet Union now has a unique opportunity to take further action to demonstrate its continuing and irreversible commitment to achieve commonly accepted human rights standards.

A HISTORIC SET OF MARKERS

31. *from* Roland Eggleston, "Vienna Review." Report by RFE/RL correspondent, Vienna, January 13, 1989. RFE/RL B-Wire, FF092–98.

There is widespread agreement that the success of the Vienna conference is the strong chapters on human rights and associated humanitarian issues.

NATO and the European Community came to Vienna determined to plug the loopholes which had enabled the Soviet Union and some East European countries to ignore the commitments they had made at previous meetings in the Helsinki process. Most Western diplomats in Vienna feel this goal has been achieved.

The West's particular goal was to obtain an improvement in travel regulations, not just for emigration but also for the sick and for those who just want to travel to the West and return home.

Despite the promises of "glasnost" it was not easy. On more than one occasion, angry Western diplomats accused the Soviet delegation of deliberately slowing progress on humanitarian issues despite the positive reports coming from Moscow on Soviet plans. Bulgaria, Czechoslovakia and East Germany were also reluctant to accept the West's humanitarian proposals at first.

These are some of the highlights of the human rights and humanitarian chapters of the Vienna document.[1]

Monitoring Human Rights
Three special meetings will be held to monitor whether human rights and humanitarian agreements are being honored. The first is in Paris in June this year, the second in Copenhagen in June-July next year and the third in Moscow in October-November 1991.

This year's meeting in Paris will allow the West to examine the Soviet human rights record and see whether it is maintaining the progress which persuaded others countries to agree to the Moscow meeting.

The Vienna document also contains a permanent mechanism for

monitoring human rights violations. It gives any country the right to call a meeting with another to discuss human rights or humanitarian problems.

This "mechanism" for examining human rights abuses was the key Western proposal at the Vienna conference. It is intended to ensure that human rights do not come secondary to the two semi-permanent conferences on military security.

Freedom of Movement

Freedom of movement in all its variations is considered in different chapters of the final document.

The basic provision is expressed in the first chapter. It says governments "will respect fully the right of everyone to leave any country, including his own, and to return to his own country." This text prompted some of the most bitter East-West arguments at the Vienna Conference. It took Western negotiators months of argument to persuade the Soviet Union and some other Warsaw Pact countries to accept it.

The same paragraph also requires governments to respect the right of everyone to "freedom of movement and residence within the boundaries of the state."

Family Reunification

Governments "will take the necessary steps to find solutions" to all outstanding family reunification and marriage cases within six months of the end of the conference.

When this proposal was offered by Sweden and Austria in December 1986 it was considered a bold step forward but one which was expected to be rejected by the Soviet Union. The Austrians and Swiss wanted a two-month time limit, but six months was considered acceptable.

The final document says applications to emigrate for family reunification or to marry a citizen of another state should normally be decided within three months. (The 1983 Madrid document said six months.)

Application to meet other members of the family living abroad should normally be decided within one month.

Another chapter of the final document concerning contacts between peoples says specifically that religious believers should be allowed to maintain contacts with those in other countries through travel, pilgrimages and participation in assemblies and other religious events.

Emergency Travel

Application to visit a seriously ill or dying member of the family living in another country should be decided within three working days. A decision should also be made within three days for those who want to travel to the funeral of a family member.

There is a similar three-day time limit for those who have a "proven need" to seek urgent medical treatment abroad or "can be shown to be critically or terminally ill."

This is a priority for the West because of the many Soviet cancer patients denied permission to obtain medical treatment in the West.

Defectors' Families

The authorities should not ban someone from travelling abroad because of acts committed by other members of the family.

This provision was proposed separately by the West and by the neutrals Austria and Sweden. It is intended to stop discrimination against the relatives of defectors or people who stayed abroad illegally. The sponsors argue that it was wrong that relatives should be punished for the acts of others.

For a long time the Soviet delegation said this text would "never" be accepted by the USSR.

Possession of State Secrets

This NATO text seeks to help those refused permission to emigrate or travel abroad because they have had access to state secrets. It says the travel restriction should be as "short as possible." Refusals should be reviewed within six months and at regular intervals thereafter. People entering a job associated with national security will be warned in advance that it could affect their travel rights.

The US wanted the travel ban to expire one year after the individual stopped having access to state secrets. It proved impossible to persuade the Soviet Union and some other members of the Warsaw Pact to accept this. Some Western countries then suggested a limit of five or seven years because of reports that this will be contained in new Soviet legislation. However, there was no agreement on this either.

Another measure says those who are refused a travel visa for any reason should be given a written explanation. As a rule he should also be informed of the measures he can take to appeal against the refusal.

All the documents needed for obtaining a travel visa should be easily accessible to the applicant and should remain valid throughout the application procedure.

Religious Freedom
This is one of the chapters of which the West and the neutrals are most proud. It contains ideas presented by both groups. Its 16 paragraphs are a big step forward from the bare mention accorded religious freedom in the 1975 Helsinki Accords and the 1983 Madrid document. They spell out in detail the practical meaning of "religious freedom."

The text begins by requiring governments to "take effective measures to ensure the freedom of the individual to profess and practice a religion or belief."

A particularly important paragraph says governments should "respect the right of everyone to give and receive religious instruction in the language of his choice." Another text refers specifically to freedom of parents to ensure the religious and moral education of their children in conformity with their own convictions.

Other paragraphs require governments to respect the right of individuals and communities to acquire, possess and use sacred books and religious publications in the language of their choice. The document says religious faiths and institutions should be permitted to produce, import and disseminate religious publications and materials.

Another text says religious communities have the right to establish and maintain places of worship, to appoint and replace their personnel and to solicit and receive voluntary financial contributions.

Helsinki Monitors
An important text reaffirms the right of individuals to observe whether the Helsinki Accords and other agreements are being honored. It requires governments to "facilitate direct contacts and communication among these individuals, organizations and institutions" and remove legal and administrative impediments to their work.

The United States, Britain and Canada tried unsuccessfully to insert a specific reference to "Helsinki monitors." They were vigorously opposed by Czechoslovakia and Romania although the Soviet delegation said it could accept the reference.

Psychiatric Abuse
In a key provision directed against the mistreatment of political prisoners by incarcerating them in psychiatric institutions, the Vienna document requires governments to "protect individuals from any psychiatric or other medical practices which violate human rights and fundamental freedoms." It says governments should punish those responsible for such practices.

The same chapter deals with the treatment of prisoners. It begins by saying governments "will ensure that no-one will be subjected to arbitrary arrest, detention or exile." It prohibits torture and other cruel, inhumane or degrading punishment.

Another text deals with the right to a fair and public hearing within a reasonable time before an independent and impartial tribunal. It says the individual has the right to be represented by legal counsel of his own choice.

In addition, it says the individual has the right to be promptly and officially informed of the decision taken in an appeal case and given a written explanation of the legal grounds for the decision.

Minorities
The rights of national and regional minorities and cultures are considered in several chapters of the document.

The basic provision says the state "will take all the necessary legislative, administrative, judicial and other measures to ensure the protection of human rights and fundamental freedoms" of the minorities within their territory.

It requires governments to "refrain from any discrimination" against minorities. Governments are required to create conditions in which minorities can exercise their ethnic, cultural, linguistic and religious rights.

It requires governments to ensure that national minorities and regional cultures "can give and receive instruction in their own culture." One measure specifically refers to the right of parents to instruct their children about their language, religion and cultural identity.

The debate on minorities took place in the shadow of the conflict between Hungary and Romania. It never came into a public exchange. But in the working groups Romania frequently opposed texts which were supported by Hungary. The speeches of Hungarian delegation leader André Erdös often contained veiled references to Romania's repression of its minorities.

Interference with the Post
Governments are required to respect the privacy and integrity of postal and telephone communications. They will also ensure there is no interference with the delivery of correspondence, including personal mails and parcels.

This measure was prompted by complaints from Soviet civil rights activists that the authorities were opening or delaying mail in violation of international agreements.

Contacts Between People
There are many measures on the right of national minorities, religious believers and others to maintain contact with their fellows in other countries.

Another measure urges governments to encourage contacts between citizens and foreign tourists. It says foreigners should be permitted to meet citizens and stay in private houses if invited to do so.

It was vigorously opposed by Romania, whose domestic regulations restrict contacts with foreigners.

Jamming of Foreign Radio Broadcasts
In the Vienna document, the 35 governments have agreed to "ensure that radio services operating in accordance with the ITU[2] radio regulations can be directly and normally received in their states."

In effect, this is a pledge not to jam foreign radio stations which are operating in accordance with international regulations. Jamming was a priority issue for the United States, Britain, West Germany and the Netherlands during the negotiations. All jamming of Western radio stations by the Soviet Union and Eastern Europe had ended by December 1988. However, the West insisted on maintaining a paragraph on jamming in case it resumes in the future.

The information chapter also attempts to protect journalists carrying out their profession. The text says journalists should not be expelled or have their accreditation withdrawn because of what they write. Another text says they should be allowed to maintain contact with public and private sources of information.

Terrorism
The final document condemns all acts of terrorism no matter who commits them and says terrorism cannot be justified in any circumstances.

The concern at the growth of international terrorism is reflected in the fact that the final document contains 10 paragraphs on the problem. The final document of the Madrid Conference had only two paragraphs on terrorism.

The Vienna document requires governments to "prevent illegal activities of persons, groups or organizations which instigate, organize or engage" in acts of terrorism and subversion or other activities directed towards the violent overthrow of another government.

It also calls on governments to ensure the extradition or prosecution of those implicated in terrorist acts and to cooperate in bringing them to justice.

Trade, Environment, Science

The most important result of the negotiations on economic and trade problems was the decision to convene a special meeting in Bonn in March next year.

But in general, neither the West nor the Warsaw Pact is very satisfied with the two years of discussions on trade, scientific exchanges and problems of the environment. Both had hoped for clearcut agreements on subjects of special interest. But most of the chapter consists of expressions of good intentions.

NATO and the European Community wanted governments required to permit direct contacts between businessmen and potential buyers and end-users of the product. It said direct contacts should be allowed at all stages of the business transaction, including negotiation and implementation of contracts. The West also wanted businessmen to be able to visit the factory or business to see how the product could be adapted to individual situations.

The text in the final document is considered to be much weaker. It says governments "will facilitate direct contacts between business people, potential buyers and end-users, including on-site contacts relevant to the business."

Other measures require governments to continue efforts to reduce obstacles to trade.

Other texts call on governments to provide economic and commercial information necessary to businessmen, including data for the United Nations Trade Data Bank, COMTRADE. Until now the Soviet Union and East European countries have been reluctant to provide detailed information to the UN data bank.

A text on joint ventures tries to overcome some of the problems Western businessmen find in Eastern Europe. It says governments will "promote the exchange" of all necessary information, including information on management, labor conditions, accounting and taxation.

It says governments should also provide information on repatriation of profits and measures for the protection of investments.

The final document tries to overcome some of the problems in business deals involving compensation trade. This involves payment by goods instead of cash and is common in many Eastern European countries.

The Soviet Union and Eastern Europe were disappointed in their hope for concrete agreements on exchange of high technology and engineering know-how. The West bans the transfer of some technology to Eastern Europe. Another difficulty is that most technology is owned by private companies who cannot be ordered to sell it to Eastern Europe.

The final document recognizes the importance of scientific and technological cooperation. It calls for governments to improve conditions for exchange of information of scientific and technological achievements.

The document contains strong texts on the need to combat pollution in all its forms. It says states should take individual action to protect the ozone layer in the atmosphere and become parties to the international conventions of the ozone layer.

The text also stresses the need to cooperate in reducing the pollution of lakes, rivers and seas. It calls for measures to protect national resources and flora and fauna.

The West is particularly satisfied with what are often called the "human rights" sections of this chapter on science, technology and the environment.

The chapter on the environment refers specifically to the importance of individuals and organizations concerned with the environment and says they should be allowed to express their concerns without hindrance by the authorities.

The section on tourism calls for contacts between tourists and the local population. It says governments should develop cheap accommodation for travellers with not much money and for young people.

It said this should include small-scale private accommodation, in other words, bed-and-breakfast in private homes.

Despite East German opposition, the document calls for an end to the practice of compelling foreign tourists to exchange a fixed amount of foreign currency every day.

Another paragraph stresses that respect for improving fundamental freedoms provides a foundation for improving international scientific cooperation. Western diplomats say they were thinking particularly of contacts between scientists and the freedom to travel abroad for meetings and conferences.

Two Military Conferences
The Vienna Conference sets up two new arms conferences, both of which will be held in the Hofburg Palace in Vienna.

The first involves only NATO and the Warsaw Pact. It will reach agreements on reducing their conventional military forces from the Atlantic to the Urals.

Diplomats expect this to make a major contribution to easing tension in Europe and reduce the danger of surprise attack. However, it could take years to produce effective results.

NATO has already published proposals calling for severe cuts in the number of tanks in each alliance. More detailed proposals are being drawn up in Brussels and are expected to be put on the table soon after the conference begins in March. The Warsaw Pact is known to be drawing up its own proposals.

Both sides agree that the alliance with the superior forces in any category must make bigger reductions. But there are already arguments over how to measures these asymmetries.

The new conference will replace the MBFR talks which attempted to reduce conventional forces within a smaller area of central Europe. For a variety of reasons, they have never achieved a single agreement since they were established in 1973.

Turkey obtained permission to exclude certain areas from the zone in which reduction of forces will take place. All are close to the borders of Iran, Iraq and Syria. Turkey argued that the forces within these special areas were not assigned to NATO.

But the arrangement led to a bitter argument with NATO ally Greece. Turkey included in its special zone the seaport of Mersin, which is a major supply base for its occupation forces in Cyprus. The Soviet Union and the Warsaw Pact countries accepted this. But when all other issues had been settled, Greece suddenly objected.

Most diplomats believe Greece acted on behalf of neutral Cyprus, with which it has close ties.

The second conference agreed in Vienna, involving all 35 states of the Helsinki process, will continue the work of the highly successful Stockholm conference on military confidence-building measures.

The chief US delegate at the Vienna Conference, Warren Zimmermann, has praised the final document as historic.

He said the 26 months of negotiations had produced a "really historic set of markers in human rights—perhaps the most far-reaching markers on human rights issues that we have ever had in an East-West context."

NOTES
1. For full text, see *Concluding Document of the Vienna Meeting 1986 of Representatives of the Participating States of the Conference on Security and Co-operation in Europe, Held on the Basis of the Provisions of the Final Act Relating to the Follow-up of the Conference* (Vienna, 1989); also published as *CSCE: A Framework for Europe's Future* (Washington, DC: US Information Agency, 1989).
2. International Telecommunications Union.

ROMANIA'S EVASION MANEUVER

32. *from* Statement by the Romanian delegation. CSCE Review Meeting, Vienna, January 15, 1989. Journal No. 397, 162nd Plenary Meeting.

With regard to the Concluding Document of the Meeting, the delegation of the Socialist Republic of Romania is authorized to make the following statement . . . :

As far as human rights are concerned, the Concluding Document of the Meeting contains a number of important provisions with which Romania is in agreement.

It is, however, regrettable that this Document should not have incorporated, in an appropriate manner and as a firm commitment by States, certain proposals by Romania concerning a number of fundamental principles of human rights and humanitarian problems, such as: the commitment of the States to ensure employment for every citizen in their countries and the elimination of unemployment; vocational training, education and guaranteed employment and dignified living conditions for young people; the right to equal pay for equal work; the establishment of appropriate housing conditions for each family; wide access by the entire population to the achievements of modern science and technology; the guarantee of dignified and civilized living conditions for all citizens.

At the same time we note that—on the pretext of concern for human rights and religious freedom—provisions have been introduced and maintained in the Concluding Document that are not in conformity with the principles and spirit of the Helsinki Final Act or with the realities of the age in which we live, and that we are not in agreement with the international norms and regulations to which the States have acceded. Such provisions may open the way to interference in the internal affairs of other States and to the violation of national independence and sovereignty, and can stimulate and encourage activities and manifestations of obscurantism that are retrograde. Similarly, provisions have been retained in it that in fact are capable of stimulating emigration and encouraging the brain-drain, harming the economic and social development interests of the peoples, primarily those that are less developed.

Romania has, during the work of the meeting, submitted its observations and reservations, chapter by chapter, indicating in a concrete manner what were the problems for which an appropriate solution had not been found in the Document; they are observations and reservations that we still maintain.

In view of all the above, the Romanian delegation states that Romania assumes no commitment to implement those among the provisions of the Concluding Document regarding which it has presented observations and reservations that have not been accepted— provisions that it considers to be inadequate. . . .

The Romanian delegation requests the Executive Secretary to take the necessary action . . . to ensure that the present declaration is registered and circulated to the participating States as an interpretive statement of reservations concerning the acceptance as a whole of the Concluding Document of the Vienna Meeting.

UNREST WITHIN ALLIANCES

33. *from* "Vienna Agreement Stirs Unrest in the Two Military Alliances." Associated Press report, Vienna, January 22, 1989. RFE/RL B-Wire, FF031–33.

While the landmark human rights and security accord approved by 35 nations has narrowed the gap between East and West, it also has widened the fractures within Europe's two military alliances.

The Vienna agreement promising broader individual freedoms and mandating new arms-reduction talks has been praised by both superpowers as a bellwether for future disarmament successes. Yet the very success of the conference has stirred unrest within the military alliances led by the United States and the Soviet Union.

European members of the 16-nation North Atlantic Treaty Organization are showing increasing resistance to US views of how disarmament should proceed on their continent. And the Kremlin's allies in the Warsaw Pact have shown markedly different degrees of commitment to the human rights protections spelled out in the Vienna Accord. It remains to be seen whether the internal divisions will widen to cause disabling rifts within the alliances, and much will depend on the superpower leaders.

Soviet President Mikhail S. Gorbachev's reforms face widespread resistance at home, as well as in some East European nations, because of poor and unimproving living conditions and fears the East bloc might bargain away its military might.

US President George Bush is expected to continue the policies of his predecessor, Ronald Reagan, but mounting pressure from European allies could eventually shake Washington from its dominant role in NATO and result in a disarmament approach more receptive to Soviet overtures.

At the moment, Gorbachev desperately needs to cut arms spending to stabilize the Soviet economy and improve the living conditions of his people. The Western allies are aware of the pressure faced by the Soviet leader, as well as the consequences for arms control if Gorbachev succumbs to conservative opponents in the Kremlin. US diplomats concede the Vienna conference succeeded primarily because of the Soviet Union's political reforms.

Soviet Foreign Minister Eduard Shevardnadze, in Vienna for the closing session of the conference, said the Kremlin would fully disclose its count of troops and armaments in Europe before the start of the CAFE talks.[1] Arguments and secrecy over existing conventional force strength have stymied the current negotiations since they began 15 years ago.

Asked why he was so confident the CAFE Talks would be able to avoid the pitfalls of the older forum,[2] Shevardnadze said the East and West military alliances are under increasing internal pressure to improve international relations.

"I have confidence that progress will be achieved because it's something our peoples want, and their governments, if they are true governments, should express the will of the people," the Soviet official told reporters in Vienna.

In his speech Tuesday, the closing day of the Vienna meeting, Shevardnadze announced that the Kremlin would be unilaterally removing some of its short-range nuclear arms from Eastern Europe and called for NATO to negotiate for the removal of its remaining European-based missiles with ranges of 500 kilometers (300 miles) or less.

All missiles of intermediate range are being withdrawn and dismantled under an accord signed between the superpowers in Washington in December 1987. And the US and Soviet negotiators say they are making good progress on a pact to cut deeply into their stockpiles of strategic nuclear weapons.

The US government has repeatedly stated that it does not want to negotiate or remove short-range nuclear missiles until a Soviet advantage in conventional forces is reduced.

"There's not going to be anything left except the short-range," a senior US diplomat commented, referring to the progress made and envisioned in removing medium- and long-range missiles from Europe. "If we want to keep the flexible response doctrine credible, I don't see any way we can negotiate these in the foreseeable future."

NATO's "flexible response doctrine" holds that the Western Alliance must keep its nuclear weapons option until the Soviet advantage in troops, tanks, artillery and other conventional weapons is reduced. But West Germany and other NATO members have been chafing under that doctrine and other constraints on the pace of disarmament. Stephen Ledogar, the US ambassador to the CAFE talks, said Washington wants to see a reduction in conventional forces first.

Within the Warsaw Pact, the Soviet Union's planned pullouts are popular with the general public, but problematic for the communist leaderships that have traditionally relied on Kremlin military backing.

Even more divisive to the Warsaw Pact is the question of human rights and the varying degrees of willingness among the East bloc allies to emulate the Kremlin's policies of glasnost, or greater frankness on selected social and political issues, and perestroika, or revamping the economy.

Hungary played a maverick role at the Vienna meeting, siding with Western positions long before the rest of the bloc and promising to review and revise all laws relating to individual freedoms.

Czechoslovakia made no such commitment, and Romania claimed it had the right to exempt itself from the provisions for international review of an individual nation's compliance with the accord.

In the first days after the agreement, police broke up demonstrations in East Germany, Bulgaria and Czechoslovakia and arrested activists.

The accord earned the approval of the entire Warsaw Pact, but the Soviet Union, Poland and Hungary have shown themselves to be significantly more willing to put it into practice than the four other East-bloc allies.

NOTES
1. Conventional Armed Forces in Europe, later renamed Conventional Forces in Europe (CFE) talks.
2. The MBFR talks.

Part III

The Demilitarization of European Security, 1989

Confidence Building and Arms Cutting

MOST COMPLICATED NEGOTIATIONS

34. *from* Doyle McManus, "Vienna Talks Raise Hopes of Ending Cold War," *Los Angeles Times,* March 4, 1989.

A new round of East-West negotiations begins in Vienna next week, seeking an agreement to shrink the NATO and Warsaw Pact armies that face each other in Central Europe.

But behind the steely debates over tank divisions and troop levels, the superpowers and their European allies are grappling with a more fundamental question: After 40 years, can the Cold War be brought to an end?

An increasing number of Western experts say changes in Soviet foreign policy made by President Mikhail S. Gorbachev offer a new chance to reduce the East-West military confrontation in Europe— and, eventually, to end the Continent's political division.

"The imminent opening of [the Vienna] conventional arms control negotiations will ... generate the imperative of a European political settlement," former Secretary of State Henry A. Kissinger wrote last month. "Side by side with an unprecedented opportunity, there is an unprecedented challenge to Western statesmanship."

Egon Bahr, a foreign policy spokesman for West Germany's opposition Social Democratic Party, agreed, noting: "We are on the eve of a new phase. For the first time since World War II, we can envision that the military confrontation in Europe will be replaced by economic competition and peaceful coexistence."

The issue of ending Europe's division into two hostile camps is on the table largely because of two new Gorbachev policies: his decision to seek significant cuts in Soviet defense spending, including a unilateral withdrawal of 50,000 troops from Europe, and his apparent tolerance of more diversity among Soviet satellite nations in Eastern Europe. . . .

"We're a little bit optimistic, because some of the differences we had before are beginning to disappear," said a US official who has been involved in preparing the NATO position for the talks. He continued:

"There have been two significant changes in the Soviet position. First, they have accepted our argument that there are asymmetries" (unequal levels of armed forces, with Soviet advantages in most categories). "And second, they have accepted in principle the concept of on-site inspection, which you would need to verify any agreement on conventional forces."

At the same time, he said the talks will not be simple or quick. "You're looking at the most complicated negotiations we have," he said. . . .

. . . The CFE talks will include the 16 member countries of NATO and the seven members of the Warsaw Pact. They will cover the entire European continent, from the Atlantic Ocean to the Ural Mountains east of Moscow. And within that area, they will seek to reduce an array of armies that includes more than 7 million troops, more than 12,000 combat aircraft, more than 67,000 tanks, more than 106,000 other armored vehicles, and so many pieces of artillery that they literally are uncounted.

The two sides have already drawn up their initial proposals.

NATO, which contends that the Soviet bloc is ahead in virtually every category of weaponry, plans to ask for a cut to about 20,000 tanks for each side—a target that could require the Soviet Bloc to scrap more than 27,000 tanks (by NATO estimates) while the Western alliance would reduce by only about 2,000.

Overall, NATO says it plans to propose that each side cut its tanks, armored vehicles and large artillery to about 95% of current Western levels—a target that would require minimal changes in NATO's armies but large cuts in Soviet Bloc forces.

The Soviet Union has not responded directly to that proposal, but Soviet officials have indicated they will seek even deeper cuts— and, especially, cuts that will target categories such as troops and combat aircraft, where the two sides are closer. . . .

Senior US officials acknowledged that the initial NATO proposal may not go far enough and said NATO is considering deeper cuts.

The talks also will be bedeviled by the two sides' disagreement over how to count each other's weapons. For example, NATO says it has 16,424 tanks, but the Warsaw Pact insists that the West actually has 30,690 tanks. The discrepancy occurs because the NATO number includes only heavy, "main battle" tanks; the Warsaw Pact counts both light and heavy tanks. . . .

Both sides are considering proposals for a zone in central Europe—essentially, along West Germany's border with East Germany and Czechoslovakia—from which offensive forces such as tanks could be banned.

THREE-STAGE REDUCTIONS

35. *from* Speech by Eduard A. Shevardnadze, Soviet minister of foreign affairs. CSCE Meeting of Foreign Ministers, Vienna, March 6, 1989. *Foreign Broadcast Information Service,* FBIS-SOV-89-043, March 7, 1989, pp. 1–4.

The negotiations of 35 and of 23^{1}—the two new branches of Helsinki—are starting at a time when in Europe things that a few years ago seemed impossible have become routine.

The routine nature of these things reveals new standards of international existence.

Soviet and American nuclear missiles are being destroyed as a matter of routine.

Inspections of military facilities are being conducted on a workaday basis.

Notifications of planned military exercises, troop movements and strategic missile launches are being sent in an equally ordinary way.

These routine things have become the norm, the rule, the canon. It is our duty to extend that also to the reduction of conventional armed forces. . . .

Now, let me present to you our specific positions.

They call for a three-stage reduction of armed forces in Europe down to levels sufficient exclusively for defense.

Recently NATO, too, has put forward a proposal on stability at lower levels of armaments.

These two approaches can be bridged. Notwithstanding serious differences, they can be brought together. For both NATO and the Warsaw Treaty Organization call for eliminating the potential for carrying out a surprise attack and launching large-scale offensive operations. Furthermore, both sides believe that a lower level of overall military confrontation in Europe has to be attained. . . .

This is what we propose. In the first phase, with a duration of two or three years, imbalances and asymmetries would be eliminated, as regards both troop numbers and the main categories of arms.

To achieve this, it is proposed that reductions focus mainly on the most destabilizing kinds and categories of arms such as frontline attack combat airplanes of tactical aviation, tanks, combat helicopters, combat armored vehicles and armored personnel carriers and artillery, including multiple rocket launcher systems and mortars.

NATO and the Warsaw Treaty would reduce their armed forces and conventional arms down to equal collective "ceilings" which would be 10–15 percent lower than the lowest levels possessed by either of the political-military alliances. . . .

The next element: Strips (zones) with reduced levels of arms from which dangerous and destabilizing types of conventional arms and hardware would be withdrawn, reduced or restricted and within which there would be limitations on military activities, would be created along the line of contact of the military-political alliances.

Tactical nuclear arms would also be withdrawn from those zones. Nuclear weapons delivery vehicles would be pulled back from the line of contact to a distance that would make it impossible for them to reach the other side's territory. . . .

In the second phase, lasting 2–3 years, further cuts would be carried out on a equal percentage basis to reduce the identical ceilings attained during the first phase.

During that stage the armed forces on each side would be reduced by another 25 percent (i.e., approximately by 500,000 men) with their organic armaments. At the same time, other categories of arms would be reduced, and further steps taken to restructure the armed forces on the basis of the principles of sufficiency for defense.

Finally, during the third phase the armed forces would be given a strictly defensive character, and agreements would be reached on the ceilings limiting all other categories of arms and on the principles of armed forces development by which the participating countries would have to abide.

One of the most difficult problems, it would seem, is how to avoid the sterile data debate which Vienna has already heard as the requiem for talks on disarmament in central Europe.

It is clear even now that the published figures are causing a great deal of mutual arguments and objections. That is understandable. Differing approaches were applied, and hence the conclusions turned out to be different. We would think it is not productive now to argue who is right or who is wrong.

Would it not be better just to avoid sterile arguments about data while giving priority to strategy and large-scale politics?

We are not citing any absolute figures for future "ceilings." This is what experts should work on: it is for them to develop a common approach, a single method of account, which must be scientific, fair and objective. . . .

The issue of naval forces has been raised on the eve of these negotiations not as a condition but with only one aim in mind: We have to understand clearly even now that the scope of eventual agreements will to some extent be affected by, among others, the factor of naval arms.

This is equally true of the question of modernizing tactical nuclear arms, if such plans are translated into practical actions.

The reason is not even that modernization is a way to maintain and build up nuclear arsenals. What is more, it can destroy the fragile trust that has just begun to emerge in Europe as a result of decisions genuinely significant militarily, and important politically and psychologically.

If it happens, Europe will be pushed back to what it was before the conclusion of the Soviet-American treaty eliminating INF missiles.

The Soviet Union proposes that separate negotiations be started as soon as possible on reducing and completely eliminating tactical nuclear weapons in Europe. . . .

At the negotiations of 35 we would like not only to improve what was done in Stockholm but also to reach agreement on a new generation of large-scale confidence-building measures under which openness and general glasnost would go hand in hand with limitations on all kinds of military activities and with confidence-building measures extended to naval and air forces.

NOTE
1. 35 CSCE members and 23 NATO and WTO members.

ARMS RACE REVERSED

36. *from* Mark Thompson, "US Arms Control Experts React Cautiously to Proposal." Report from Knight-Ridder Tribune News, May 30, 1989. RFE/RL B-Wire, FF005.

President Bush tried to trump Soviet leader Mikhail Gorbachev's recent series of arms control initiatives with the broad proposal . . .

requiring Moscow to pull 10 soldiers from Central Europe for every American GI who returns home.

But because the proposal echoes a month-old Soviet offer for deep cuts in military hardware and adopts the Soviet stance that limits on manpower and aircraft should be part of the negotiations, US arms control experts sense that the superpowers are lumbering into negotiating positions where real progress is possible.

Such deep and balancing cuts in non-nuclear arms would set the stage for additional cuts in both sides' nuclear arsenals, they added.

"We're getting the Soviet bogeyman out of Central Europe," said Jack Mendelsohn, deputy director of the Arms Control Association, a nonprofit group based in Washington. "If the Soviets buy anything like what Bush is talking about, it's clearly going to diminish the chances of war."

The whole notion of an "arms race" has been reversed, he said. "We're in a bidding war—but the bidding is going down rather than up in terms of confrontation," Mendelsohn said. "Everybody should be pleased by that". . . .

"With our concessions on counting aircraft and troops, there's no difference in principle between the two sides," said Barry M. Blechman, a top arms control official during the Carter administration. . . . "There's a lot of underbrush to clear away, in terms of what's counted and what's not, and in terms of specific types of weapons, but with this change in our position there are no differences in principles."

Bush's proposed cuts in forces based between the Atlantic Ocean and the Ural Mountains echo those Gorbachev proposed last week in Vienna—which, in turn, are similar to NATO's March offer.

Bush called on the Soviets to cut their European forces from 600,000 men to 275,000—a week after Gorbachev said he would be willing to cut his forces there to 325,000 troops. The proposed cuts would remove about 325,000 Soviets, and a similar ceiling on US forces would require sending about 30,000 GIs home.

Both sides would cut their tank forces to 20,000, requiring a Warsaw Pact cut of about half while requiring little or no cuts in NATO tank forces, according to NATO calculations.

Under Bush's proposal, personnel carriers would be limited to 28,000 on each side, and artillery pieces would be trimmed back to between 16,500 and 24,000 per side, depending on how they are defined. The Warsaw Pact currently has roughly four times as many personnel carriers and artillery pieces as NATO, according to NATO's counts. Warsaw Pact figures generally acknowledge a smaller edge in Soviet firepower.

Bush's proposed aircraft cuts would require each side to trim its airplane and helicopter forces to 15 percent less than NATO's current aircraft tally—meaning the Soviets would be forced to cut their total aircraft in the region from about 12,000 to 5,500, while NATO forces would trim their planes and choppers from 6,400 to about 5,500, according to NATO figures. . . .

Some arms control experts greeted Bush's proposals coolly. George A. Carver, Jr., a former CIA official who served as a special advisor to US ambassadors in West Germany, warned that "the devil is in the details" in negotiating conventional arms accords. . . .

. . . Carver expressed concern over Bush's call for the conventional negotiations to be concluded within a year, with cuts taking effect as early as 1992, well before the 1997 target set by Gorbachev.

"The worst way to negotiate is under a self-advertised deadline," he said. . . .

. . . Bush's call for haste is designed to relieve West German concerns that NATO is adamant about modernizing its short-range nuclear missile force, a nagging political problem for West German politicians.

"We have made a major concession to the German concerns about the need to negotiate, by saying that we are willing to negotiate on short-range nuclear forces after an agreement is achieved on conventional forces," a top Bush administration official, speaking anonymously, told reporters travelling with the president.

"And what the president's initiative this morning says is, that it is not simply a way of putting off negotiations into the far distant future —we're determined to move quickly on conventional forces, and that means we would be able to move quickly, following up on them, on short-range nuclear forces."

The Bush proposal, unlike earlier NATO gambits, explicitly requires weapons to be destroyed and troops to be demobilized. "The president stressed this morning what has been implicit, but so far, not explicit in our NATO proposals, and that is the importance of destroying the equipment that's taken out, not creating a situation simply where the stuff can move back in, . . . in fact, making real reductions in the military threat," the Bush administration official said.

Helmut Schmidt, the former West German chancellor, said that

Gorbachev needs an arms control pact so he can convince Soviet citizens he is not jeopardizing their security by diverting military resources into the beleaguered Soviet civilian economy.

"No government in the world can easily . . . , with no regard to what the adversary does, decrease one's own military expenditure by a considerable chunk, let us say—20 percent, 25 or 30 or 50 percent," Schmidt told reporters in Washington. . . . Only a treaty, requiring cuts by both sides, makes such drastic cuts feasible, he said.

"The window of opportunity is, in my view, open as long as there is hope and effort on the side of the Soviet leadership to make perestroika a success," Schmidt said. "If it fails . . . then this window certainly will not any longer be open."

TOTALLY DIFFERENT ATMOSPHERE

37. *from* Interview with Ambassador Stephen Ledogar, US representative to the CFE Negotiations. Vienna, July 24, 1989 (Washington, DC: Worldnet, US Information Agency Television and Film Service).

[QUESTION]: In your opinion, sir, the CFE talks, how has their progress been and how does the progress compare to what you would have expected in March?

AMBASSADOR LEDOGAR: Well, it may seem a bit of a bizarre term to use, but as conventional arms negotiations go, they have almost been breathtaking in the rapidity of progress. Compared to March, I would say better than we expected, and even back in March we had already seen signs that the East was taking a whole new approach to this new negotiation. . . .

QUESTION: . . . I was wondering if you could give me your thoughts on the time frame for the negotiations. President Bush has said that he thinks an agreement is possible within six to twelve months.

Is that realistic . . . ?

AMBASSADOR LEDOGAR: If I may refine your question a little, sir, President Bush proposed that the allies challenge the East to try to move this negotiation forward so that the first agreement would occur within one year. All of his fifteen chiefs of state, heads of government, NATO allies, accepted this proposal, so it is now not just a Bush idea, it is a NATO idea.

We think that that is very doable. Of course, we cannot do it by

ourselves. One could say it takes two to tango, it takes two to waltz in
Vienna. We cannot do it all alone, but the challenge is there . . . and
thus far the rate of progress is such that I think we have a very good
chance of making that timetable.

Indeed, the NATO side is ahead of schedule in that we have
already proposed what I would say is more than fifty percent of the
promised fully elaborated position. . . .

QUESTION: . . . I would like to ask whether the measures and
announcements of the Soviet Union and the Warsaw Pact countries
to reduce their forces and their defense budget could have any
relevance for the Vienna talks?

AMBASSADOR LEDOGAR: Yes indeed, it has relevance. . . .
one could think of it as a very efficient pump priming. The unilateral
reductions announced by Mr. Gorbachev last December[1] . . . have
already been, to a certain extent, carried out. We see them moving
forward and, indeed, very much according to the schedule that they
have announced. . . .

QUESTION: Mr. Ambassador, I am wondering whether you
can tell us something about what goes on informally around the
negotiations in Vienna.

Is there, for example, a greater tendency for some of the smaller
East European countries to have independent points of view in informal talks outside the CFE formal negotiations?

AMBASSADOR LEDOGAR: We are seeing a great deal more
diversity and differentiation within the Warsaw Treaty bloc than ever
before in my experience. The old days of the Soviet Union calling
the shots and the East Europeans following along in lock step dupli-
cation are gone and that is a good thing and it is something that
interestingly the Soviet Union tolerates and makes no attempt to
hide.

It makes the negotiation, I believe, much more interesting and
the chances for a fruitful progress are greater when we are dealing
with the full dynamic of the interests of all twenty-three parties.

QUESTION: Mr. Ambassador, can you throw light on why President Bush in his proposal brought the number of troops back into
the negotiations when the Western side originally had wished only to
talk about heavy armaments?

Can you also in this respect explain the philosophy behind setting equal limits for Soviet troops in Eastern Europe and US troops
in Western Europe? . . .

AMBASSADOR LEDOGAR: . . . in March when we put down
our original NATO proposal, it was based on the concept that if we

could get a handle on three types of heavy equipment, equipment that is most applicable to the ability to launch surprise attack and to sustain large-scale offensive activity, that would be an effective and yet a manageable group of what we call "units of account" or "treaty limited items". . . .

After all, in modern warfare, infantry does not walk into battle anymore. They ride on troop carriers. It is the only way the modern heavy units would be deployed. Now, the East made a big push of the importance in their view of having troops included, as well as aircraft, beside our proposed three units of account.

Our problem with troops, however, is that it is extremely difficult to verify especially in an Atlantic to the Urals context. We frankly have less than optimal confidence in our intelligence about the units that are far back, Soviet units that are far back in the Soviet Union, in the foothills of the Urals, and so on and so forth. . . .

We certainly [can] verify Soviet troops in Eastern Europe and, of course, US troops anywhere in Europe.

So, the proposal of 275,000 US and Soviet forces deployed outside the Soviet Union, and obviously outside the United States, is designed with those considerations in mind. . . .

QUESTION: Mr. Ambassador, coming back to the time schedule of the negotiations, the NATO side seems to be very optimistic. Again, do you really think it will be possible to finish the negotiations [by] 1990 and to realize the agreement [by] 1993?

Secondly, which timing do the Soviets seem to favor?

AMBASSADOR LEDOGAR: Yes, I think it is possible. The Soviets have made it clear that they also think it is possible. We are not trying to finish the negotiations, we are trying to finish the first agreement in this negotiation.

The negotiation could very well go on to a second phase, where additional security would be sought by, perhaps—including other types of equipment, bridging equipment, anti-tank weapons and so forth, or by concentrating on measures that will go along with the limitations and reductions so as to enhance the effect of reductions. . . .

QUESTION: . . . Do you consider the Eastern side as stable partners, even in case of a time which one might call a time after Gorbachev?

AMBASSADOR LEDOGAR: . . . Let me say first that the Eastern negotiators are speaking for their governments, and I do not think they are independently reflecting, for example, the views of the conservative or the liberal Hungarians. I mean, I think there is a Hungarian view, there is a Polish view.

Now, of course, within the seven members of the Warsaw Treaty Organization there is a differentiation because in real life these days the approaches of those seven governments to some of the fundamental political, economic and defense questions is rather diverse. . . .

. . . you see, for example, the Polish official, I assume operating on instruction, who is willing to tell us that they have only limited interest in having Soviet forces in Poland, and do not want any more there than are necessary for what they see as their collective security. . . .

The same is true for Hungary, for example. . . .

QUESTION: Can we ask you something . . . more political and less technical? You show that you saw a change in the negotiating attitude of the Soviet delegation in Vienna, how and why did these people change, in your opinion, on the terms of their position? . . .

AMBASSADOR LEDOGAR: Yes, well, I can try to give you . . . how things have changed, but I just do not know why. I can guess as to why.

There is no doubt that things have changed, in terms of the collective perception of the Eastern leadership. They have changed in the following way—and I used to represent my country in the earlier attempt at conventional arms control, the so-called MBFR talks.

Now, in those talks we, in the West, were constantly saying, "There is a major problem in the disparity of forces." The East was collectively telling us, "There is no problem." We were saying, "Yes, you have more than we do. You are going to have to do most of the reducing."

The East was saying, "Well, no, the forces are just about equal." We were saying, "We are going to have to have asymmetrical reductions." They were saying, "No, equal reductions."

We were saying, "We have to have verification." They were saying, "No, verification is nothing more than an attempt by you at espionage."

Now all of that has changed. The East came to these negotiations admitting there is a problem, admitting there are disparities, most of which are on their side, admitting the best way to get at them is to go promptly to equal levels on both sides, below the level of the lower party.

This is extraordinary, in terms of a change. They have said that any proposal you have with regard to verification that is reasonable and applicable equally to both sides, we will accept. Now, that is an enormous change. It is a revolutionary change in their attitude.

Why? I do not know. It may be because Mr. Gorbachev wants to try to transfer resources from his military sector to his economic sectors. It may be because the East collectively has concerns about the Western technological lead and their inability to keep up with the rate at which our conventional weapons are developing.

There are a variety of "why" questions that I frankly do not know the answers to, but I can tell you that the fact is that things have changed. The attitude is very businesslike. There is a total lack of propaganda and polemics.

We are moving along promptly. They are not making wild concessions. They are sticking to their positions of importance, but it is a totally different atmosphere.

NOTE
1. See Document 29.

TWO VIEWS OF TWO NEGOTIATIONS

38. *from* **Statement by Pertti Torstila, head of the Finnish delegation. Plenary Meeting of the CSCE Negotiations on Confidence- and Security-Building Measures, Vienna, September 29, 1989.**

We have two sets of negotiations going on in Vienna. It is very important that both of these negotiations take place within the framework of the CSCE. The process of enhancing security and building confidence must not be limited to the military alliances and their members only. It is our conviction that this process of seeking and finding solutions to the security problems of our continent can and must continue as a process among the 35 participating States. . . .

. . . we have recognized and stressed the interrelationship and interdependency between the two negotiations. In conceptual terms, it can be argued whether disarmament can onlẏ succeed in an atmosphere of confidence or whether disarmament itself is a confidence-building measure *par excellence*. Whatever the answer is, the two processes need each other now and support each other also in the years to come. . . .

One of the areas where the two negotiations seem particularly close to each other is the exchange of military information and a system of verifying that information. . . .

. . . The two negotiations have separate tasks but the same general goal, security and stability in Europe.

Instead of engaging ourselves in an endless discussion on the merits of this or that measure belonging to this or that negotiation, we could make concrete progress by joining our efforts to clarify concepts and identify distinctly separate areas.

39. *from* Speech by Rudolf Perina, deputy head of the US delegation to the CSBM conference. Texas A & M University, January 4, 1990. In North Atlantic Assembly, Sub-committee on Confidence- and Security-Building Measures, Geneva and Vienna, *Draft Interim Report,* by Johann Einvardsson. AH 81 PC/CSBM (90) 2, May 1990, p. 15 (Brussels: North Atlantic Assembly, 1990).

Our general assumption last year was that the CSBM negotiation would conclude before the CFE. But with the impetus of a presidential and NATO summit initiative behind it, it now seems more likely that the CFE agreement will be reached before a CSBM agreement. This is, of course, a positive development. But it means that the central (NATO) proposal (on information exchange) in the CSBM negotiation will be significantly reduced in importance (as even more detailed information would be exchanged pursuant to a CFE treaty.)

The effect of all this has been to prompt many of us to question what is the proper role for confidence-building negotiation at a time when arms control (CFE) is making rapid headway. More particularly, many of us in the negotiations are wondering whether all the proposals currently on the table in Vienna push confidence-building forward, in keeping with its pioneering tradition, or whether the CSBM forum has fallen behind the pace of advance in the security and arms control fields.

What we are currently negotiating may be quite different from the responsibilities we should be shouldering. . . . The CSBM forum should delve into broader security problems posed by the new European realities.

The London Forum:
Crumbling Information Barriers

WHAT FREEDOM OF SPEECH MEANS

40. *from* Speech by Margaret Thatcher, prime minister of the UK. CSCE Information Forum, London, April 18, 1989 (London: London Press Service).

That is what freedom of speech means: freedom to express thoughts and views with which others do not agree.

But our purpose here is not to criticize. Rather the aim of the Forum is to be constructive by encouraging everyone to adopt the basic Helsinki standards for free exchange of information. There will only be a common European Home if the occupants can mingle and talk freely.

But the aim of implementing the Helsinki commitments is, on its own, too modest. We need to set our sights higher and see if we can agree on *additional* measures which will serve as a beacon for the new spirit of glasnost and openness.

That would make this Forum a genuine landmark in the process of building trust and confidence between East and West.

Freedom of thought, freedom of expression, freedom of choice, freedom to acquire and disseminate information are at the heart of democracy. We have never believed that policies have to be accepted without discussion. Our tradition is of fierce debate, of testing ideas on the anvil of argument, of assembling the facts to enrich and inform discussion.

It is not only a question of differing ideals and philosophies. It is also very much a practical matter. We would never have had the great surge of technological advance that has revolutionized our standard of living without the creative discussion which leads to scientific discovery and its application.

It is not a matter of luck that the West has led the way in scientific advance, in computers, in medicine, in agriculture, in protecting the global environment, and in many other areas. Nor would we have had that personal enterprise which has been vital for our prosperity if people had not been free to make their own decisions based on best information.

The central command system under which people are instructed what to do has quite plainly failed.

That is not just my conclusion. It is clear from the changes which are being made in the Soviet Union and other countries in Eastern Europe. It is clear, too, from the priority which General Secretary Gorbachev is giving to political change and greater openness—in which we wish him every success.

Now, with the microchip, we are fast moving into a new age of information technology. We have ever more rapid access to ever more information. Countries which try to insulate their people from these developments, which try to limit access to information, to control the use of photocopiers, to restrict contacts with foreigners, do not just fail to live up to their commitments to the Helsinki Accords: they condemn their people to lower standards of living and a second-rate existence.

Freedom of expression has always meant, in our system, freedom within the law—a law passed by a democratically elected Parliament and administered by independent and impartial judges.

Yes, there *are* occasions when the law *does* restrict freedom, in this country and in others. For instance, we have the laws of libel and slander to protect people from defamation. We have laws against incitement to violence, racial abuse and obscene publications. We protect the ownership of copyright and other intellectual property—the fruit of creative individual effort. We also restrict freedom of expression in order to protect national security and to prevent terrorists from using the media to promote their aims.

And I make no apology for measures taken to prevent men of violence using television and the radio to spread fear and to create an illusion of authority. Terrorists have no respect for freedom. They exploit freedom only to undermine it.

Every restriction on freedom of expression has to be carefully weighed to ensure that the remedy is not worse than the disease. And the case has to be made by those who propose a new restriction and every proposal is subject to the most searching examination by Parliament. What must *never* be permitted is arbitrary denial of freedom at the whim of government. . . .

Your aim at this meeting should be to increase the opportunities for *all* European peoples to hear differing ideas, views and opinions, so that they can make up their *own* minds on the great issues affecting their lives. That is what freedom is about.

MEDIA AS AN INSTRUMENT OF GLASNOST

41. *from* Address by Vladimir F. Petrovsky, Soviet deputy minister of foreign affairs. CSCE Information Forum, London, April 1989.

The present Forum brings the European process to a qualitatively new level, lends it a new dimension, makes it meaningful. Indeed, in every aspect of the European process information has top priority. Information is a starting point for discussing specific matters. The latest testimony to that effect is the negotiations on the reduction of conventional arms and armed forces in Europe, which began on March 6.[1] It is generally recognized that real disarmament can be achieved only where there is full information and reliable knowledge of what is subject to reduction and elimination. . . .

In fact, information is also necessary for discussing human rights, for improving economic cooperation, for common ecological under-takings, and, for that matter, in all other areas. So, in our view, this Forum is important because it has to broaden the horizons of coop-eration in the field of information, ensure wider mutual access to information, provide conditions for its free circulation, openness and lack of ambiguity, and at the same time accelerate the entire Euro-pean process. . . .

In his address to the United Nations, Mikhail Gorbachev stressed that "today the preservation of any kind of 'closed' society is hardly possible. This calls for a radical review of approaches to the totality of the problems of international cooperation as a major element of universal security." The readiness of Soviet society for communica-tion in the widest possible terms with the international community, and its consistent policy of glasnost and democratization, form the foundation of our political strategy.

To us it is truly symbolic that a frank and honest European dialogue on the freedom of information should start in April. It marks the end of the fourth year of glasnost reborn, the fourth spring of revived socialist democracy and Lenin's ideas of an open, democratic and free society.

It is logical that we should be speaking of the spring of glasnost. It is our understanding that glasnost is not just freedom of speech. Glasnost is an indispensable prerequisite for expressing the democratic essence of a socialist system which gives priority to the human being and to integrating individuals in all activities of the society and the state. Glasnost means that every citizen should have the right to receive complete and reliable information on any public issue—provided it is not a state or military secret, and their right to express their views on any socially important question openly and freely.

Glasnost and the freedom of information are also the vitally needed oxygen for the normal development of society in general. With full information on the state of affairs of various fields at its disposal, a society would be in a position to react in time to negative tendencies and to define more clearly the prospects and priorities of its efforts. We recognize that we can already see the first results of this rapidly increasing public activity. It is due to the activities of informed people that we have focused our attention on the urgent problems in the economy, the functioning of our political system, environmental protection, health, education, and other social spheres.

The mass media are a most important instrument of glasnost. As a powerful institution of a democratic citizens' society, the mass media serve the purpose of ensuring genuine pluralism of views and precluding not only the dictates of the minority but also the dictates of the majority at the same time, providing, on the basis of the Constitution, real possibilities for all representatives of society to be able to express themselves and protect their own interests. . . .

It is our general view that there are no limits to improving reporters' working conditions. They will continue to be improved alongside the growth of cooperation, international trust, and further diversified international contacts. . . .

. . . we can state with absolute responsibility that the existing obstacles and restrictions in this area will be removed as the overall democratization process in the USSR further unfolds, technological capabilities broaden and economic progress accelerates. Our fundamental policy, which we shall be consistent in pursuing, seeks to achieve the highest standards of glasnost and wide access to information, and also to translate all provisions of international instruments to which the Soviet Union is party into reality and concrete actions. . . .

The Soviet Union proposes that, through common effort, *an information and cultural TV program be established and regularly broadcast to all European countries,* which could in the initial stages be prepared by Intervision and Eurovision.

The establishment of an appropriate mechanism would promote cooperation and enrichment of the creative European potential in the field of information. We are proposing that Europe consider the idea of *establishing a European Information Council.* Its sessions could be convened in different capitals of the CSCE countries for regular discussions on the pressing issues of cooperation in the field of information, on eradicating misinformation and the enemy stereotype, on specific issues and mutual complaints that may arise. Moscow is prepared to host the inaugural meeting of the Council.

The European bank of ideas has already accumulated quite a number of interesting initiatives aimed at enhancing cooperation in the information area. One such initiative was advanced by Great Britain, which has proposed a joint publication by the CSCE countries of a magazine devoted to security and cooperation in Europe and to sharing cultural values between nations. We believe that the level of dialogue achieved so far makes it possible to turn to detailed consideration of this idea. We, on our part, believe that such a magazine could be published under the auspices of the European Information Council which we are proposing.

NOTE
1.   See Document 34.

ROMANIAN NOTIONS OF RESPONSIBILITY IN INFORMATION

42. *from* **Proposal by the Romanian delegation. CSCE Information Forum, London, May 9, 1989. RFE/RL B-Wire, CN063.**

To extend cooperation in all fields among the participating states and to establish a climate of confidence and détente on the continent, the exchange of information must be correct and based on an analysis and understanding of the realities of each country: It should also reflect the economic, social and cultural development of each nation and focus on the major problems, which, at a particular stage, are of concern to peoples ⸱:d on their aspirations to well-being, security and peace.

A genuine knowledge of the life and concerns of peoples implies that information cannot be restricted to narrow, marginal and trivial features which are not always of real importance.

Given the special part played by the media in the education and training of the rising generation in the spirit of humanism and high moral values, the exchange of information must necessarily instill in young people a respect for work, material and spiritual creation in each country and the ideals of peace, cooperation and friendship.

A systematic effort should be made to accentuate the responsibility of the governments of the signatory countries of the Final Act with regard to respect for their national legislatures, which do not permit actions to be taken that are hostile to other countries and peoples.

It would be highly encouraging if every government undertook to ensure that, on the territory of the country concerned, information and news about other countries would be objective and would in no way interfere with the relations of friendship and cooperation among the states.

To that end, governments and the media have a special responsibility for the correct presentation of questions relating to the history of each people and strict respect for historic truth, since any distortion or deviation could have serious repercussions on relations between states and mutual cooperation and understanding, as well as jeopardizing peace and security on the continent.

CZECHOSLOVAKIA PROTESTS DISINFORMATION

43. *from* Speech by Dušan Spáčil, chief Czechoslovak delegate. CSCE Information Forum, London, May 11, 1989. RFE/RL B-Wire, CN078–80.

In our conference there were good and positive moments and also moments which our delegation would have preferred to miss, moments of one-sided and biased discussions. In our forum we met, among other things, to discuss possibilities and to prepare conditions for the free flow of information. I think, we have devoted enough time to this problem from different angles, what we, however, have not done enough, was more to stress the other side of the medal. That is to prevent the free flow of disinformation.

To demonstrate it, I will mention a general problem: Perestroika is certainly "in" and every journalist follows the development in socialist countries with great interest. But why do you, distinguished journalistic colleagues, write only what just you consider to be right, and why do you not report truthfully of all aspects?

In the general evaluation of perestroika by Western journalists there are some countries considered to be very much ahead, very much reformed and because of this, worth lavish praise. Other countries, which do not correspond to the pre-programed picture of perestroika, which do it their way, respecting their own conditions are considered backward, conservative and anti-perestroika.

This pertains also to my country. When I read the Western correspondence about us I do not recognize the country where I live. So let me substitute for the lack of information in the Western media and give you some general facts in this connection.

The government and the Communist Party of Czechoslovakia supported the new thinking, perestroika and glasnost from the very beginning. And Czechoslovakia has decided to realize a perestroika in our own conditions to a full extent.

We are doing it not because we want to strike out everything we have reached in 40 years of our socialist development. On the contrary, we are proud of the results we have achieved in many areas of our life. But we are reforming and changing ourselves because the grade of our knowledge and experience has been showing us that we have to change ourselves and also that we are aware of mistakes we have made.

We felt it already for some years, but the impulse to actually do something came to us from Moscow. But we felt that we had to do it in our own way according to our conditions, which are specific and different from those of our socialist friends. After all, they too do it their way.

Especially in the political sphere great changes and reforms are going on. We are a pluralistic society. Our people are participating in governing the country within the National Front, which is an umbrella organization where five political parties, among other people's organizations such as trade unions, are taking part.

The new element in it is that those organizations feel that they have to be more active and this is the policy which we are following.

But why should we change this setup only to please some Western observers? Yes, we want to revitalize this existing setup in accordance with the principles of new thinking. Part of it will be also a preparation of elections on the basis of several candidates for each respective seat.

Glasnost has entered our press and changed it considerably. The reflection of it is for instance the fact that the most important newspaper, *Rudé Právo*, with its more than one million copies is sold out by the newsstands early in the morning.

You might have read, or heard in the discussion of our conference, that our press informs broadly on the different aspects of internal and international life, brings uncommented reprints from foreign newspapers and very critical articles oriented to all sides, including government and other ministers.

We try to put our reforms and all the changes on a legal basis, which means that we have prepared and are preparing new laws which are being considered in broad discussion with our population.

These are all very important things for the future and we don't want to overspeed them, we don't want to replace the existing system with a new one which will be worse than the previous one.

Therefore we decided to have a preparatory, transitory period in which we experiment to get experiences which will be applied generally. The new system in all spheres should come into force starting January 1, next year.

I could tell you much more, but I have already indulged on your patience telling you facts which seemingly don't correspond with our agenda.

I was obliged to do so because, despite all my positive appreciation of the results of this conference, this aspect—preventing disinformation, or one-sided information—has not been sufficiently aired in our conference.

RIFT BETWEEN THE NEW AND THE OLD

44. *from* William Rees-Mogg, "Signs of the Psychological Iron Curtain Being Drawn Back," *The Independent* [London], May 16, 1989.

The rift between the new and the old regimes is now so wide that the Warsaw Pact countries do not even try to reach a common line. The West still made an attempt at coordination; there was a European Community caucus, and a separate NATO caucus.

The procedural problem of having two caucuses is obvious. The European Community, with Spain currently in the chair, produces the EC line. That then goes on to the NATO meeting, where the United States and other NATO countries outside the EC are also present, but Ireland is not. The other NATO countries feel they are being presented with a fait accompli; the United States is too powerful a nation to enjoy rubber-stamping European decisions, let alone having to wait in the lobby while those decisions are made. The London Information Forum was not the place to settle the relationship between the EC and NATO, but it did point to a problem that has to be resolved.

Everything now starts from glasnost. There has been a historic change. At the Information Forum the psychological iron curtain was drawn back. That came out in many ways. Soviet diplomats chatted freely about Trotsky. When I was giving interviews to Russian journalists I no longer felt that such an interview was different from an interview with any other journalist.

This change in relationship was enhanced by the presence of large numbers of journalists as delegates. The journalists worked together to argue for effective press freedoms; if they had a common characteristic, it was that the government they most criticized was their own. The British government came in for a good deal of criticism.

The issue of press ownership came up more than once. Independent Russian journalists emphasized the importance of journalists' cooperatives in creating new and independent magazines. British journalists raised the question of concentration of press and media ownership and criticized the limitations of private as well as public monopoly.

It was the Russian journalists who were least certain that glasnost is irreversible. They are the most conscious of the limitations on freedom of expression that still exist in the Soviet Union. They warned of the crisis in the economy, of the forces hostile to glasnost. But the experience of the conference was one of a historic shift of consciousness, and that shift has already revolutionized European opinion.

Glasnost is inevitably seen as an opportunity by the European Community, but as a threat to NATO. Already there is hopeful talk about a European Community which includes all the European nations. The European Community—and particularly Germany—is the obvious source of much of the investment that the Soviet Union and East Europe need if glasnost and perestroika are to succeed. This alone makes the EC a real element of world power for the first time.

But if the Cold War is regarded as over, defense becomes a lower priority, a matter only of reinsurance. If that is true, NATO and the

Warsaw Pact will gradually wither away. The Russian liberals, Mrs. Thatcher and Washington all welcome glasnost but share the fear that we cannot be sure of its future success. The realpolitik view is that . . . the West would be mad to throw away proper defenses against a possibly hostile post-Gorbachev Soviet Union. The West German foreign minister, Hans-Dietrich Genscher, believes that there is a new opportunity for Europe. European public opinion tends to agree.

The temptation of this view is very great. An expanding European Community, perhaps rising to a population of 500 million over the next quarter century, would be a focus of world wealth and world power greater than any other. The twenty-first century, though very differently from the nineteenth, would be another European century, free of the civil wars that destroyed twentieth-century Europe. In this all the European powers would play their part, and there would be a natural reassertion of the values of European culture. This is what Dr. Genscher is offering the Germans, and indeed it is what Michael Heseltine[1] is offering the British.

Mrs. Thatcher's view, that we ought to support glasnost but keep our powder dry, has such obvious common sense that it is likely to prevail for the present. Apart from anything else, the communist economies are in a disastrous state, which is both the main reason for glasnost and the main threat to its success. Yet the appeal of glasnost combined with Europe is extremely strong and NATO and the Western governments ignore it at their peril. The London Forum was an interesting minor piece of détente diplomacy, but it certainly showed how contagious and how exciting the marriage of glasnost and Europe can be.

NOTE

1.   UK defense minister.

The Paris Meeting:
Added Human Dimension

MEASURING THE PACE OF IMPROVEMENT

45. *from* Statement by William E. Bauer, head of the Canadian delegation. CSCE Conference on the Human Dimension, Paris, June 5, 1989.

I commented at some length during the plenary last Thursday on the situation in the Soviet Union. I will not reiterate my remarks here this afternoon, other than to repeat how encouraging and hopeful I found our Soviet colleague's presentation. . . .

. . . I was interested in the statement made by our colleague, the Head of the Delegation of Czechoslovakia, on Friday in which he described the reforms underway in Czechoslovakia in terms that bore a remarkable similarity to those used by our Soviet colleague the day before. He said the constitution would be rewritten and the legal system overhauled with the full participation of nongovernmental organizations and individuals. He used the words *glasnost* and *perestroika* several times. If these words and other recent events such as the release of Václav Havel are true indicators of change, we may indeed hope that the government that brutally attacked peaceful marchers during the conclusion of the Vienna Meeting, that put those who led these demonstrations on trial in the face of world opinion, may indeed be taking the first halting steps along the path to fulfillment of its voluntary CSCE commitments in the human dimension. We hope so, because Czechoslovakia in the past had a proud tradition of freedom.

The words are encouraging, but I would like to have heard more. I wish he had said, as our Soviet colleague did several times, that in important areas, practices were running ahead of legal reform. I wish he had said that the laws under which Havel and some other dissidents in Czechoslovakia, such as Tomáš Hradílek, had been charged and convicted, laws such as "incitement" (for the crime of laying flowers in a public square), "damaging state interests abroad" and other equally outmoded reasons for punishing people for doing what we said at Vienna that they should be able to do, would henceforth *never* be applied. . . .

I wish he had assured us that when the new laws and constitution are being discussed, the voices of independent groups, such as Charter 77 and the Helsinki Committee, will be heard and that those who attempt to exercise the rights in the Vienna Concluding Document (which has been so widely distributed in Czechoslovakia) will not be punished. I wish that he had said that the right to leave one's country and return would apply to Jiří Hájek,[1] who, we understand from the press, was pulled off a train to Paris by security authorities, and was therefore unable to read a paper at an important parallel meeting at the Assemblée nationale this past weekend.

Ambassador Doležel told us about the greater freedom of Czechoslovak citizens to travel. This is indeed an encouraging sign. . . .

But again, I wish he had said more. He said that among the reforms in the new constitution would be that it would no longer be a criminal offense to leave the country without permission of the authorities. I wish that he had told us that it would not be an offense at all; that *no* permission would be required. . . .

. . . it would be an understatement to say that I found the statement of our colleague from the GDR on Friday considerably disappointing. It was, frankly, a reiteration of what has by now become a rather shopworn refrain; particularly his attempt to suggest that Western countries ignore social and economic rights, while in his everyone is guaranteed a good living standard. I shall not waste time here refuting these statements, nor engage in analysis of whether the GDR truly fulfills the expectations of all its citizens. I will only ask one question; if people in the GDR are so free, if their standard of living is so high, why is a wall required to keep them in? . . .

"Secure frontiers," said Ambassador Steglich, "are no obstacle to free travel." But the Berlin Wall does not secure any frontier against a threat from without; it secures it against a threat from within. The man who lost his life there last February was not an invader or a threat to any state or well-founded ideology. We see signs elsewhere of barriers coming down; the removal, for example, of barbed wire along the Hungarian border with Austria. There is every indication that the Vienna negotiation will help reduce military tensions and the level of armaments on the European continent. We may well ask, therefore, whether those who so strongly and frequently advocate the lowering of our defenses against each other might begin to contemplate lowering their defenses against their own people.

There was no mention in Ambassador Steglich's speech of *glasnost* or *perestroika* or any other word that means the same thing. . . .

With regard to Romania, . . . I want to state clearly to this meeting and to our Romanian colleague that no one has set out to isolate or persecute Romania. There is no great plot, in the West, among the neutral and non-aligned, in the East, to single out Romania and make it the pariah of the CSCE. The Romanian government has done this to itself, by its actions in the human dimension. Our criticisms will be tempered with encouragement when there is any sign of improvement; they will stop when abuses stop.

For the moment, however, it would be a betrayal of the CSCE and its aims and achievements not to signify in no uncertain terms our serious concern when a participating State that signed the Helsinki Final Act and agreed to all the subsequent CSCE documents continues with a program of rural systematization that could profoundly affect the cultural and economic survival of large numbers of its people; when it persists in measures directed against significant ethnic minorities; when it harasses any who dare to question or criticize—including a former foreign minister now believed to be in ill health as a result of house arrest, constant questioning and harassment, as well as five other party elders, one of whom is 94; when it harasses and persecutes a teacher of languages who writes an open letter against human rights abuses, and refuses to allow her to leave the country; when it represses poets and writers who do the same; when it threatens and bullies priests, ministers and churches attempting to serve the spiritual needs of their people and to enter a dialogue with government; when diplomats and visiting parliamentarians are harassed, threatened and prevented from undertaking their lawful activities; then we are faced with a regime whose defiance of the norms of conduct we have set for ourselves, and the direction in which most of the rest of Europe is moving, is such that if we do not call it to account, we allow the European ideal to be tarnished and the CSCE process to be diminished. . . .

Finally, with regard to Bulgaria, my minister has already alluded to our concern about the treatment of the Turkish minority in that country. This has been a long-standing issue in the CSCE to which, regrettably, the response of successive Bulgarian delegations has simply been to deny its existence. We hope for concrete steps toward the resolution of this problem. We would also like to hear some indication from the Bulgarian delegations that such organizations as the Party of the Green Masses, the Independent Society for the Protection of Human Rights in Bulgaria, the Independent Labor Union of Intellectuals, the Committee in Defense of Religious Rights, Freedom of Conscience and Values of the Spirit, and the Club in Support of Glasnost and Perestroika will be legalized and permitted, as provided for in the VCD,[2] to meet openly and speak freely in promoting human rights. . . .

. . . as my minister said in his opening statement, only four months have gone by since the VCD was adopted, and we can at present only measure trends. Our balance sheet is an interim one. There has been great progress in some countries. In others, there is room for improvement, but there is time for improvement. There are signs that real progress may be possible in some of the countries I have had occasion to mention today. We will watch carefully and sympathetically, and measure progress in the areas where it counts, and can best be verified, in the lives of the people. It is my hope, and that of my government, that when we meet again in Copenhagen[3] we will be able to say that all the problems I referred to today have been solved or are on their way to resolution. We can, indeed, hope for signs that this process will begin as our meeting proceeds.

NOTES
1. Leading dissident and former foreign minister.
2. Vienna Concluding Document.
3. See Documents 70–85.

HUMAN DIMENSION MECHANISM IN ACTION

46. *from* Statement by Antonio Armellini, deputy head of the Italian delegation. CSCE Conference on the Human Dimension, Paris, June 13, 1989.

Analyzing the functioning of the new mechanism on the human dimension agreed upon by the 35 member countries in the Vienna Concluding Document, we have verified the progress made, which is in various ways encouraging. But we must be aware of the many problems yet to be solved. . . .

Today, it is in this spirit of constructive cooperation that Italy wishes to draw the attention of the Conference—on the basis of Stage 4 of the mechanism—on the case relating to the refusal by the authorities of the Socialist Republic of Czechoslovakia to the granting of an exit visa to Alexander Dubček.

I take the liberty to briefly sum up the facts. Alexander Dubček, personally invited by the Italian Communist Party to attend as a guest its National Congress last March, saw his request for an exit visa unexpectedly rejected by his country's authorities. This circumstance was indeed quite peculiar, since Alexander Dubček had been allowed to come to Italy only a few months earlier to receive the degree "Honoris Causa" bestowed upon him by Bologna University in the course of a solemn ceremony.

Recognizing in this episode a violation of the obligations agreed upon in Vienna . . . , the Italian government has resorted last March 24 to the first stage of the mechanism with a specific request for information to the Czechoslovak authorities. In their reply, orally formulated on May 15, they stated that (a) the refusal of the visa was in conformity with administrative regulations already existing, since it was not a humanitarian case; (b) the third paragraph of the First Basket, Principles, laid down the right of each state to "determine its own laws, regulations and political practices"; (c) Czechoslovak laws and practice are in conformity with international law and are in principle in accordance with the Vienna Concluding Document; (d) a process of legislative harmonization is taking place at the moment in Czechoslovakia to bring Czechoslovak laws in full conformity with the obligations taken in Vienna.

Since the reply did not contain, in the judgment of the Italian government, any element of substance relating to the question posed, the Italian government decided to ask, on May 15, for a bilateral meeting on the basis of stage 2 of the mechanism. Such meeting was held in Prague on May 25.

In the course of this meeting, the Czechoslovak authorities showed once again a full and friendly disposition, confirming both from the standpoint of procedures and of the expression of will—many times repeated—the intention to give maximum impulse to the implementation of the mechanism, as an instrument of cooperation and not of confrontation in the context of the CSCE. We acknowledge this fact and, on our part, we do so with pleasure.

As for the substance of the problem, the Czechoslovak delegation has confirmed that the refusal opposed to Alexander Dubček was entirely legitimate, based on decree n.114/1969, still in force. The difference in treatment, with reference to the permission previously granted to travel to Bologna, should not come as a surprise, the delegation said. In the case of the Bologna trip, as a matter of fact, the invitation had been addressed by a private organization and Dubček "like any other Czechoslovak citizen" could travel freely abroad for private reasons. On the other hand, in the case of the Congress of the Italian Communist Party, this was an event of official nature and of political relevance, and the participation of Czechoslovak citizens to similar events had to be examined in Czechoslovakia case by case. As regards Dubček, a citizen who is not a member of the party and "who has no representative function whatsoever," the competent authorities deemed that his presence at the Congress of the Italian Party, where an official Czechoslovak delegation had been equally invited, would be inappropriate as it would bring embarrassment to Czechoslovakia. . . .

. . . In our reply, we stated that the above explanations were completely unacceptable. . . .

The Czechoslovak delegation having at this point declared their wish to further examine the matter, in the light of information which had come out of the discussion, the two sides agreed to temporarily suspend the meeting, convened under stage 2, with the view to set up a further and conclusive session of the meeting in the very near future. The latter, requested by the Italian side on May 30, took place in Paris on June 12, again in a friendly and mutually cooperative atmosphere. On this occasion, the Czechoslovak delegation reaffirmed its intention to maintain without modification its previous statement with regard to the public nature of the trip as a criterion for determining the refusal of the exit visa to Dubček, and repeated that it considered such a decision entirely legitimate. . . . At the same time, the Czechoslovak delegation declared that its government had started a thorough process of legislative revision, taking into account the Vienna obligations, and that such a process would be completed in the shortest possible time, taking into account the technical time required for such adaptations as well as the evolutionary character of the process in question.

On our part, we replied confirming the absolute implausibility of what had been declared to us. . . .

Law n.63/1965 specifies that a travel document can be denied (a) when the trip is not in accordance with the State's interests; (b) when the person is the object of penal proceedings; (c) when the person has been convicted of penal charges in the past; (d) when there is anticipation that the person might be involved abroad in activities that could harm the good name of Czechoslovakia. . . .

If I took some further minutes of your patience to illustrate in an extensive way the above provisions, it is because I think reading them is not without interest.

To the eyes of the Italian government the provisions in question are in contrast not only with several fundamental points of the Vienna Concluding Document—introducing, as the Czechoslovak authorities apparently are doing, those political discriminations that the Vienna Document specifically aims to eliminate—but also with the precise obligations of international law. . . .

We are sorry that the Czechoslovak delegation did not deem it necessary to reply, in the stages of the mechanism so far experienced, to the requests for information and clarification made by the Italian side. . . .

In drawing the attention of the conference, according to stage 4, to the Dubček-Czechoslovakia case, I would like to emphasize once more the character of cooperation ("problem solving" and not, indeed, "problem creating") that Italy attaches to the human dimension mechanism. . . .

. . . Italy offers its contribution to the multilateral discussion in the framework of stage 4 of the mechanism. We wish that also the Czechoslovak delegation, from which we are separated by a clear difference of opinion on the case under examination, but which has declared to share with us the desire to see mutual cooperation based on the mechanism come true among the 35, will not fail to bring new, constructive contributions for a positive solution of the problem, which is crucial indeed, of the freedom of movement of its citizens, as it was agreed upon by all of us in Vienna.

THE RIGHTS OF HUNGARIANS IN ROMANIA: POINT/COUNTERPOINT

47. *from* Speech by André Erdös, head of the Hungarian delegation. CSCE Conference on the Human Dimension, Paris, June 13, 1989. RFE/RL B-Wire, CN030–31.

According to the Vienna Concluding Document, the participating states are obliged to create conditions conducive to promoting the ethnic, cultural and linguistic and religious identity of the national minorities on their territory.

In 1984, Hungarian-language television broadcasts in Romania designed for the Hungarian minority were stopped. Provincial radio broadcasts, including the two local broadcasts in Hungarian, were also eliminated. . . .

Between 1983–87 the number of primary schools dropped by almost a quarter. The number of pupils by almost a half. The number of teachers also by almost one-half.

In the same period—1983–87—the number of secondary schools dropped by almost three-quarters. The number of students by more than a half. The number of teachers by three-quarters.

The number of vocational schools and students has dropped by 60 per cent. The last high school where all education was given in Hungarian closed its doors three years ago. . . .

After 400 years, the city of Kolozsvár (Cluj) no longer has a Hungarian-language university. This national minority of more than two million people no longer has a single Hungarian-language institution of higher education. . . .

In recent years systematic efforts were made to eliminate the network of educational institutions in the service of minorities. One of the most common methods of doing away with Hungarian-language teaching is to transfer Romanian teachers to schools in regions with a Hungarian majority. For example, in the province of Hargita, which is 85 per cent Hungarian, only eight per cent of the school principals are of Hungarian nationality.

Another means used is the "exchange" of students between vocational schools. This means Hungarian students leave their homes and parents and are sent to Romanian regions. They are replaced for the duration of their studies by students of Romanian nationality.

Speaking in Hungarian in educational institutions varies from province to province. To illustrate the situation, we note the case of schools in Nagyvárad (Oradea) where the principal inspector simply prohibited the speaking of Hungarian outside the classroom. In Tirgu Mureş, where 60 per cent of the population is Hungarian, the procedure adopted is different. A day of the week is chosen in advance as the "Patriotic Day" during which the students commit themselves to speak only Romanian. School ceremonies all over the country must be held exclusively in Romanian. . . .

Since 1988, it is no longer permitted to use minority-language names for localities in the press or official documents. This applies even to publications written in the minority languages.

Since 1988, children no longer are given names which do not have equivalents in Romanian. Thus a large number of Hungarian first names have become illegal.

The influx of refugees into Hungary from Romania continues. The number of non-Hungarians previously represented about ten per cent of the total. The latest information indicates a considerable increase. It has reached two-thirds of the total number of refugees coming from Romania. The number of arrivals is about 300 people a week. . . .

In our view, the first step toward improving the situation would be to guarantee the national minorities freedom of association.

We would proclaim loud and clear that national identity is a characteristic peculiar to a community, to a group of persons. That the existence of a minority cannot really develop except within such a community. We should say quite unambiguously that affiliation with your own national identity and the use in private and social life of a national language constitutes an inalienable right.

48. *from* Statement by Teodor Meleşcanu, deputy chief of the Romanian delegation. CSCE Conference on the Human Dimension, Paris, June 13, 1989. RFE/RL B-Wire, CN033–38.

Ambassador Erdös has referred to the situation of the Hungarian minority in Romania. In regard to the minorities you should keep in mind two basic principles which guide the policy of my country.

The first principle is that of national treatment. I would beg you to keep in mind always that nationalities living together in Romania benefit from equal treatment with the Romanian population.

The second principle I would like you to keep in mind when interpreting figures, data or statements is that Romania rejects any policy for our national minorities similar to an apartheid policy as in South Africa. That is, the creation of bantustans or separate communities.

The master idea of our policy is to give an equal chance to all and not to create artificial restrictions—no barriers for citizens of an origin other than Romanian.

Ambassador Erdös says that after 400 years there is no longer a Hungarian-language university in Romania. I am sure you are shocked by this example, but what is the real situation?

There is no university which is exclusively in the Magyar language. In the town of Cluj there is a university where certain lectures are in Magyar. I ask you to understand the meaning of this. It gives students who wish to make their higher education in Hungarian the possibility to do so.

But if everyone is compelled to have their university studies in

Hungarian only, they will suffer discrimination because they cannot work in a business where everyone speaks Romanian. Of the total of 49,000 students in Romania, there are 7,712 who are of Magyar nationality.

Ambassador Erdös has referred to the registering of children's names and that parents are prevented from registering some names. He suggested that this was discrimination against Hungarian Christian names and they cannot be used.

Here, as in many other fields, we have followed the French example. Some 15 years ago, regulations were introduced in order to stop parents naming children Maradona[1] or Unesco or things like that. We have a very broad collection of names, as is the case in France, and recommended that parents use names from that list. We wanted to prevent fashions in which someone gave a child a name of the hero in a television serial. This sometimes created difficult situations for the child at school and in life and sometimes led to an interminable procedure of changing names.

Ambassador Erdös also referred to supposed refugees. Hungary is a neighboring country with which we have had long relations through the centuries. Any Romanian citizen of Magyar descent who wishes to leave for Hungary for good has to request permission to go. These requests are handled with all possible speed.

As far as we are concerned, there is no problem. If a Romanian citizen of Magyar descent wishes to go to Hungary for a temporary visit or in order to leave for good, there is no difficulty on the part of my government.

Once he is in Hungary he is not our concern. If the Hungarian authorities count tourists who remain in Hungary after the expiration of their visas as refugees, that is their problem, not ours.

I would just say it is not possible to declare oneself a refugee. A refugee is not a national status. It is not a country which grants it, but the [United Nations] High Commissioner for Refugees.

NOTE
1. A popular soccer player.

49. *from* Statement by André Erdös, head of the Hungarian delegation. CSCE Conference on the Human Dimension, Paris, June 16, 1989. RFE/RL B-Wire, FF152–53.

At the beginning of the week, I presented some details about the problems facing the Hungarian national minority in Romania. I return to the subject today to respond to the Romanian answer to my statement.

He [Romanian representative Teodor Meleşcanu] offered two basic principles which guide the country in its policy toward minorities. The first principle says there should be equal treatment for all citizens. That does not cause any controversy. We only wish the Romanian government would apply this principle to everyday life.

But the second principle has surprised me. He said Romania rejects any minorities policy of separate development and likened this to South Africa's racial policy of apartheid or the creation of South African-style puppet states or "bantustans."

To liken respect for the Hungarian minority in Romania and its desire to maintain its cultural identity to South Africa's apartheid or the creation of "bantustans" of separate communities seems to me to be totally absurd.

How can the desire to speak one's own language, to have an education in one's mother tongue, to use family names and geographic names of one's choice in any way recall the segregation policies of South Africa or the policy of establishing puppet territories such as Ciskei or Transkei?

Our Romanian colleague says it is difficult to establish on the basis of surnames whether a person is a Romanian or is of Hungarian origin. He mentioned this in connection with the question of education in Romanian or Hungarian-language schools. I cannot understand the uncertainty. There is a very simple way of resolving any doubt. That is to ask people what is their nationality and let them act in accordance with their choice.

Well, in the 1970s lectures in Romanian and Hungarian were really taught at the University of Cluj, in the chairs [departments] of world history, philosophy, mathematics and physics and chemistry. Today there remains only one chair—that of Hungarian language and literature in which there are seven students.

The Romanian delegate also referred to travel conditions. He said those who wished to go to Hungary could do so easily and without any problems. In practice, however, a Romanian is entitled to apply for a passport only once every two years. The individual must also provide a recommendation from his employer. Once a passport has been used it must be returned to the authorities within 24 hours. The individual is not allowed to keep possession of his passport.

With regard to the problem of refugees, our Romanian colleague says it is Hungary's problem if it wants to count as refugees those Romanian tourists whose visas have expired. Indeed, it is the problem of the Hungarian government to find housing and employment for those tens of thousands of "tourists" who come with no intention of being tourists but want to remain for good. And then there are those who risk everything to secretly cross the border between Romania and Hungary and ask for asylum. I suggest my Romanian colleague ask them whether they consider themselves tourists or refugees.

He refers to the procedures of the United Nations High Commissioner on Refugees and says that unless the High Commissioner is involved, we cannot speak of refugees. I would like to inform you that on June 12, Hungary became a party to the 1951 UN Convention on Refugees and the 1967 additional protocol.

Delegates from the UN High Commission have visited Hungary to investigate the situation in regard to refugees and visit places where they have settled. Negotiations are now in progress to open an office of the High Commissioner in Hungary to assist our government in its activities for refugees. Because of the growing number, we are to open three refugee centers.

We question the very future when we recall that in November 1984 it was declared at the highest [Romanian] level: "We have solved the question of nationalities once and for all."

Or when we read a report of the official news agency, Agerpres, in February 1987 which says: "It is well known that Romania is *not* a multinational state" because 89.1 percent of the population are Romanians, another 7.8 percent are Romanians of Hungarian nationality, 1.8 percent are Romanians of German nationality and 1.6 percent are Romanians of other nationalities.

This statement is an obvious contradiction of the spirit and the letter of the Helsinki process.

THE EXPULSION OF BULGARIAN TURKS

50. *from* Statement by A. Mesut Yılmaz, Turkish minister of foreign affairs. CSCE Conference on the Human Dimension, Paris, May 31, 1989.

The 1.5 million-strong Turkish minority in Bulgaria is faced with and has been resisting since 1984 a massive campaign of forcible assimilation designed to eradicate the distinct ethnic, cultural and religious identity of this national minority. The problem is not simply a bilateral issue between Bulgaria and Turkey, but one between Bulgaria and all individuals, institutions and governments respectful of human rights and fundamental freedoms. . . .

We have recently invoked the human dimension mechanism provided by the CSCE Vienna Concluding Document and requested the Bulgarian government to restore the fundamental rights and status of the Turkish minority, and to provide information on ethnic Turks subjected to arbitrary arrest, incarceration, torture and other degrading treatment. We have also proposed to the Bulgarian side to hold a bilateral meeting. However, I regret to say that the Bulgarian government has reacted to this request in an obstructionist way by distorting the facts and putting preconditions. Thus, we have been unable to obtain any positive results. The Bulgarian government has demonstrated her unwillingness to honor the commitments she has undertaken only a few months ago under the Vienna Concluding Document. The latest incidents in Bulgaria, which so deplorably resulted in the killing of several ethnic Turks during peaceful demonstrations provide further evidence in this respect. . . .

. . . The Bulgarian government must understand that it cannot be permitted, at the threshold of the 21st Century, to assimilate a national minority of 1.5 million in sheer defiance of its contractual obligations, including its CSCE commitments. . . .

We have noted that the foreign minister of Bulgaria, yesterday, devoted a good portion of his statement to the problems engendered by the oppressive policies pursued against the Turkish minority in his country. In this context, he also referred to a declaration President Zhivkov made only a few hours before the opening of this conference and said, inter alia: "In the name of the Bulgarian Muslims and in my own name as the president of the state council, I call on the Turkish authorities to open the border to all the Bulgarian Muslims who would wish to go to Turkey on a temporary basis or to settle there."

Obviously . . . , not all Bulgarian citizens of Muslim faith are of Turkish origin. But, I hope that this sufficiently explicit admission by President Zhivkov will enable Bulgarian representatives no longer to argue, in this forum or elsewhere, whether there exists in Bulgaria a Turkish minority whose population was 780,928 according to the 1965 Bulgarian census and whose birthrate is nearly 3 percent.

51. *from* Statement by Oktay İşçen, Turkish representative. CSCE Conference on the Human Dimension, Paris, June 23, 1989. RFE/RL B-Wire, FF126.

My delegation and several other delegations pointed out at various times that the plight of the Turkish minority in Bulgaria is one of the gravest human rights violations in recent times.

The situation has worsened during the Paris meeting. So far more than 50,000 people have arrived in Turkey in a mass exodus. . . .

Unfortunately, Bulgaria continues to defy international public opinion. In our deliberations here in Paris, the Bulgarian delegation has persistently tried to evade the real question by raising irrelevant allegations.

The truth lies with the people who have fled . . . or are fleeing Bulgaria with Bulgarian names inserted in their passports. What other proof do we need to show the truth . . . ?

The expulsion of ethnic Turks began just before the start of the Paris meeting. The figure was only a couple of hundred at the beginning of our conference but now it is around 50,000. These people are expelled to Turkey on short notice of a few hours, leaving behind family members and all that they own.

I repeat here the proposal of the Turkish prime minister, Mr. Özal, for immediate negotiations with Bulgaria to conclude a comprehensive immigration agreement compatible with the nature of the issue and in accordance with international norms.

It is also imperative that the rights of those members of the Turkish minority who might remain in Bulgaria be fully restored and that the Bulgarian government honor its international commitments.

EUROPEAN LEGAL SPACE

52. "Proposal Submitted by the Delegations of France and the Union of Soviet Socialist Republics and those of Austria and the Federal Republic of Germany." CSCE Conference on the Human Dimension, Paris, June 16, 1989. CSCE/CDHP.17.

The participating states of the Conference on the Human Dimension of the CSCE,

Mindful of their common history and recognizing that the existence of elements common to their traditions and values can assist them in developing their relations;

Confirming that they will respect each other's rights freely to choose and develop their political, social, economic and cultural systems as well as their right to determine their laws, regulations, practices and policies;

Seeking to ensure that, in the exercise of these rights, their laws, regulations, practices and policies conform with their obligations under international law and are brought into harmony with the provisions of the Declaration on Principles and other CSCE commitments;

Being in favor of relations based on dialogue rather than confrontation, on law rather than force, and desiring to deepen the human dimension of the CSCE;

Have established as their long-term objective the creation of a common legal area based on the Europe of states in which the rule of law prevails;

Are prepared in this connection to proceed, within the framework of the CSCE, to a comparative analysis of legislation, regulations and jurisprudence, and also of the parliamentary, executive and judicial institutions of the participating states, with a view to the subsequent adoption of practical measures aimed at bringing them closer together and harmonizing them, where advisable and feasible;

Consider that, as the first step in that direction, the participating states which wish to do so might by mutual agreement undertake such a comparative analysis on a bilateral or other basis;

Affirm that they intend to seek out areas of relations between the participating states in which it would be possible to begin to formulate or codify common legal norms.

The Collapse in Eastern Europe

THE UNSPOKEN "BASKET FOUR"

53. *from* John J. Maresca, "The People Have a Right to Choose," *International Herald Tribune,* June 21, 1989.

> All peoples always have the right, in full freedom, to determine, when and as they wish, their internal and external political status, without external interference, and to pursue as they wish their political, economic, social and cultural development.
>
> Helsinki Final Act, 1975

How does this commitment apply to the situation in the Baltic republics? Or in Eastern Europe? Or in Armenia or in other parts of the Soviet empire? This is one of the must disturbing but fundamental issues posed by Helsinki, an issue that has remained dormant because of the recognition in the West of its potential explosiveness. But this issue, the unspoken "Basket Four" of Helsinki, is now before us. The West must consider what its position on self-determination will be as the Soviet Union faces a rising tide of nationalism.

The Helsinki document treats the issue in a principle of "equal rights and self-determination of peoples," which follows the principle of human rights, the basis of Helsinki's famous "Basket Three." The heart of the self-determination principle is the language cited above, but the Helsinki document is an interrelated whole in which each principle must be interpreted "taking into account the others." There are clauses on nonintervention in internal affairs, and respect for the sovereignty of (existing) states. These bar pursuit of self-determination through state-sponsored initiatives aimed at undercutting existing governments.

But there are also important statements addressing situations like those in the Baltic countries, which assert that ". . . no such occupation or acquisition will be recognized as legal." This language was inserted in the Final Act by the West partly to maintain the principle that Stalin's annexation of the Baltic states[1] will not be recognized. The Final Act also accepts that peaceful changes in frontiers are possible.

Other provisions of the Final Act underscore the signatories' commitments to carry out their Helsinki obligations which, though not "legally binding," were undertaken at the highest level and therefore have a politically and morally binding character.

Since Helsinki, the West has concentrated its efforts on human rights. The Western objective has been incremental improvement in the situation in the Soviet Union and Eastern Europe, and not a sudden destabilizing and politically impossible conversion to democratic systems.

This was reflected in the narrowly focused provisions of Basket Three. Though the principle of human rights was established as a matter of inter-state responsibility—a landmark accomplishment of Helsinki—the specific improvements sought were evolutionary. Human rights were of immediate political concern in the West, where the plight of refuseniks, the treatment of political prisoners, and the drama of dissidents occupies center stage. Helsinki offered, for the first time, a way to deal with these difficult questions.

Moreover, self-determination in the Soviet Union and Eastern Europe has been an issue of enormous potential explosiveness. It challenges the very legitimacy of those governments, and present Soviet frontiers. At Yalta, the United States and Britain obtained a Soviet commitment to permit free choice of governments in all of liberated Europe.

Although the Soviets have never carried through on this commitment, it has generally been accepted in the West that to press them to do so was confrontational, counterproductive and dangerous. Even when Eastern Europeans manifested a clear desire for a different form of government—in Budapest and Prague before the Helsinki Final Act, and in Warsaw after it—the West has been circumspect.

But recent events have made it difficult for Western statesmen to avoid the question of self-determination. Eastern Europe is in ferment because of the implications of glasnost and perestroika for Soviet domination of the area. The West cannot now back away from the principles for which it stands. Helsinki's slumbering Basket Four has rather suddenly become a matter for attention.

We can no longer separate the human rights issues that we have pursued so energetically from the implications of self-determination.

The Helsinki human rights principle required governments to "promote and encourage the effective exercise" of political rights and freedoms. Surely this means the ability of citizens to choose freely the type of government they want.

Despite the "new thinking" in the Soviet Union, the issue of self-determination remains a delicate and potentially provocative one. Offsetting the West's principled interest in human rights is an equally strong need to avoid instability and possible bloodshed in the East. But there can be no question that the West should stand forthrightly for the inherent right of people to self-determination, just as it stands forthrightly for human rights. These positions of principle are our great strength at a time when Mikhail Gorbachev's steps toward liberation have caught public attention. It is up to us to point out that "free elections" are a sham when only one political party is permitted, and that the Baltic people have every right to choose their own path.

If we are to maintain Western moral leadership, it will be by revitalizing fundamental attitudes toward the individual and his place in society.

More difficult is the question of how the West can encourage and assist an evolution toward self-determination by those who strive for it. First, we must begin to discuss the issue, as we did with human rights in the context of the Helsinki process. This is the principal framework accepted by all concerned for dealing with delicate East-West differences of view, and we should use it. This forum includes the European countries, the United States and Canada, which helps to cushion criticisms. And we should enlarge the discussion of human rights to include citizens' right to choose their government. . . .

Our effort need not be confrontational; it will be more effective if it is not. It should be expressed rather as a generally felt Western concern that the obvious desires of the peoples must be respected. But to avoid the issue at a time of nationalist demonstrations in the Baltic states and efforts toward increased democracy elsewhere would be to abdicate the Western responsibility to uphold the shared concept of human beings and their relationship to the state. Each generation has its responsibilities before history, and this is clearly one of ours.

NOTE
1. In 1940.

THE FRUITS OF HELSINKI

54. *from* Udo Bergdoll, "Früchte von Helsinki," *Süddeutsche Zeitung*, September 19, 1989. Translated from German by Jeannet Frössinger.

In Hungary, the rusty barbed wire of the once iron curtain is truly suitable only as a souvenir. The words used by the communist leader in Budapest to justify allowing the "GDR-tired" Germans free passage would have sounded familiar in the Folketinget,[1] the Bundestag or the French National Assembly. After liberating themselves from the tutelage of the Eastern superpower, Hungarians and Poles are anxious to catch up with Western Europe.

For Budapest, the guarantee of human rights, as stated in the Helsinki Final Act, and the commitments of the subsequent Vienna meetings, are valued as a higher law than the contracts made with their socialist alliance partners.

The opening and the continuance of open borders by Hungary will be the "empirical" test of whether the Helsinki Final Act, during a crisis, is worth more than the paper on which it was signed in 1975. Budapest has followed the spirit and the letter [of the Final Act], knowing that it would be subject to the anger of those neighbors who are unwilling to implement reforms. The Soviet Union doesn't intervene anymore. This is not a small step, but a major jump ahead on a path that was chosen at the time of the Eastern treaties[2] with recognition of the status quo that resulted from World War II. Without these treaties, the Helsinki Conference would not have been possible. The Moscow of "stagnation" wanted to see its security interests guaranteed. The West coupled this with the questions of human rights and cultural contacts. This trade was neither dangerous nor optimistic.

The Americans were not pushed out of Europe. The dominated people on the other side of the Iron Curtain could call upon the commitments that their governments had signed. This was often done, from Sakharov to the unknown demonstrator in Leipzig or Prague.

In the spring, the states of the Warsaw Pact signed in Vienna the right to free travel. The conference on conventional stability in Europe began. Security issues and human rights were indeed brought into harmony.

NOTES
1. The Danish parliament.
2. A series of treaties between the FRG and the USSR and its East European allies in the early 1970s.

ECOLOGY PLAYS POLITICS IN SOFIA

55. *from* US Congress, Commission on Security and Cooperation in Europe, "The Sofia CSCE Meeting on the Protection of the Environment, October 16–November 3, 1989," *Implementation of the Helsinki Accords,* Hearing before the Commission on Security and Cooperation in Europe, 101st Cong., 1st sess., September 28, 1989 (Washington, DC: US GPO, 1990), pp. 123, 132–33.

From October 16 to November 3, 1989, the thirty-five states participating in the Conference on Security and Cooperation in Europe (CSCE) convened in Sofia, Bulgaria, for a meeting on the protection of the environment. . . .

While the Sofia environmental meeting provided a useful forum for discussion of environmental issues among the 35 CSCE States, its more important result was to serve as a catalyst for radical political changes in Bulgaria. The major elements of this change were the ouster of long-time, hardline leader Todor Zhivkov and his replacement by party leadership which is at least publicly committed to deep, democratic reforms.

The contribution which the Sofia environmental meeting made to these political developments was to provide a protective cover for unprecedented political protest activity, both on environmental questions and human rights issues. This public activity started with meetings in a park of a relatively small group of private Bulgarian environmentalists called Ecoglasnost and eventually led to the mass demonstrations and behind-the-scenes political maneuvering which toppled the old regime.

The turning point came about mid-way in the meeting when the Bulgarian authorities unexpectedly reversed a policy of relative tolerance toward the activities of Ecoglasnost members. . . .

. . . On October 26, when this group was prohibited from gathering signatures to a petition in a downtown park, the authorities brutally broke up their march to protest their decision, detaining more than two dozen individuals and beating many of them, as well as a British journalist covering the event. In response, the negotiations were brought to a halt as virtually the entire meeting demanded an explanation for the crackdown. The meeting at this point was on the verge of collapse. The next day, the Bulgarian Environment Minister, Nikolai Dyulgerov, apologized to some extent, admitting that the authorities had overreacted. At the same time, he also sought to place some of the blame on contacts between the activists and members of the Western delegations. He assured the delegates that the activities of Ecoglasnost would be tolerated, and the delegates, satisfied with the response, subsequently resumed negotiations. However, in the third week of the meeting, Western and NNA delegations jointly raised concerns about reports of continued harassment which, if true, would threaten to deny the meeting a successful outcome. Minister Dyulgerov again responded positively, and the individuals of concern were permitted to resume their activities and to attend the closing plenary sessions of the meeting.

At the end of the meeting, the largest-ever group of private citizens in Bulgaria up to that time delivered, unhindered, a petition citing ecological abuses to the parliament. The rest is history.

ROMANIA WITHDRAWS RESERVATIONS

56. *from* Statement by the Romanian Ministry of Foreign Affairs, by Sergiu Celac. CSCE Negotiations on Confidence- and Security- Building Measures, Vienna, January 15, 1990. CSCE/WV/Inf.14.

Kept aside against its own will by the old regime from the process initiated by the Helsinki Final Act, the Romanian people, now free to decide on its destiny, is ready, in the new circumstances created by the establishment of a truly democratic society, to associate itself entirely with the all-European process.

The Ministry of Foreign Affairs is authorized to declare officially that Romania withdraws its "formal reservations and interpretative statements," presented on 15 January, 1989,[1] upon instruction by the old regime, in connection with the Concluding Document of the Vienna Meeting of the Conference on Security and Cooperation in Europe and confirms the acceptance by Romania of this document in its entirety.

Romania will act towards the full implementation, in good faith, of all provisions of this Document and is determined to contribute, together with other European states, to the establishment on the continent of a climate of peace and security, and of free cooperation among peoples in different fields.

NOTE
1. See Document 32.

CHAOS AND EUPHORIA

57. *from* Edward Steen, "Threat of Peace, but a Tank is Still a Tank," *The Independent* [London], November 21, 1989.

The Berlin Wall has come crashing down—or large chunks of it— and the noise of falling dominoes can be heard all over eastern and central Europe. Mikhail Gorbachev has hinted at an imminent dissolution of the Warsaw Pact. "A new, peaceful era" is dawning, he said, and it is time to recognize the world no longer consists of "two mutually exclusive civilizations."

But at the Conventional Forces in Europe (CFE) disarmament talks in the Vienna Hofburg, they rigidly pretend the blocs are still as they were, and only hope a treaty can be signed before the political furniture has been entirely rearranged. The December tryst in the Mediterranean between Presidents Gorbachev and Bush is liable to complicate matters if Mr. Gorbachev launches another peace initiative. The deadline negotiators are working to is less than a year away; just now they are working out, *inter alia,* an acceptable definition of a tank. After that, describing an armored personnel carrier should be a piece of cake.

"We simply can't afford ourselves the luxury of thinking: What if Germany reunites, then what?" explained a veteran Western arms negotiator, though he admitted the mass outbreak of peace in Europe was much discussed informally. "But all that's not part of the negotiations, and can't be. If we begin to ask whether it's sensible, whether these treaty organizations [NATO and Warsaw Pact] will continue to exist in the future, then maybe the mandate is up the spout. It wouldn't be a conventional arms negotiation but another Congress of Vienna." However, another senior Western official said yesterday a contingency clause providing for defections from the alliances "will have to be considered."

The CFE talks have long since stopped being a simple confrontation between East and West, and are already complicated by democracy on both sides. . . .

True to its protestations of non-interference elsewhere, the Soviet Union has allowed its allies to argue their own corners. The German Democratic Republic has yet to show how its change of course translates; up to now it has been the most hard-line defender of Soviet strategic interests, along with Czechoslovakia and Bulgaria. But it is likely, like Poland and Hungary, to be keen on getting Soviet troops out—in the GDR's case, 350,000 of them.

The curiosity is that at a time when the West has won the ideological argument, and unilateral disarmament would take place anyway—above all for budgetary reasons—the West is as keen as the East to codify mutual cuts in conventional weapons, and as quickly as possible. . . .

A suitably splendid-sounding treaty would help puncture the arguments of those in the West who question overblown defense budgets. Uncomfortable questions have been asked in the US Congress about the defense budget. Britain's £21 bn [billion] is more and more controversial. The governments of the key Western countries are anxious, as one negotiator put it, "not to rush head-long into total disarmament"—evidently a danger if the peace business got out of hand, as it threatened to do. It was the price of being on the winning side, he said, that the sense of threat disappeared.

With the dissolution of the Soviet bloc, the future was highly unpredictable: "It could become a much more ugly scene." Another Western official spoke of "chaos and euphoria in that part of the world," and the calling into question of Western defense policies in place for the last 40 years. It is all very jolly, but awkward too.

NEW CONTENTS OF THE BASKETS: THE SOVIET AND US VIEWS

58. *from* Speech by Mikhail S. Gorbachev, president of the USSR. Plenary meeting of the Central Committee of the Communist Party of the Soviet Union, Moscow, December 9, 1989 (Washington, DC: Soviet Embassy press release).

For all the specificity of deep changes in socialist countries, one cannot deny the fact that they proceed in the same mainstream as our *perestroika*, although we in no way encouraged those processes.

In some socialist countries the situation has been unconventional. Fraternal parties are no longer ruling in Poland and Hungary. Our friends in the German Democratic Republic and Czechoslovakia have already lost their positions. New political forces have emerged in the arena. They include both those who support the socialist idea and those who seek other ways of social development. . . .

Our principled attitude toward the European socialist countries is invariable. They are not only our allies, but also our friends and neighbors. We seek to ensure progress and stability in every way— stability in these countries themselves, in the Eastern European region, and on the whole continent—as well as the inviolability of postwar borders of all the states in Europe. . . .

We firmly declare that we will see to it that no harm comes to the GDR. It is our strategic ally and a member of the Warsaw Treaty. It is necessary to proceed from the postwar realities—the existence of the two sovereign German states, members of the United Nations. Departure from this threatens destabilization in Europe. . . .

And now a few words about the main recent contacts with capitalist countries. . . .

. . . it is necessary especially to single out the working meeting in Kiev with French President François Mitterrand. . . .

The French president believes that it is now necessary to exhibit maximum caution and to take up a well-considered attitude and that the Helsinki principles—primarily, respect for the present realities and the inviolability of the established borders—should be the basis for the development of all processes in Europe. . . .

. . . our relations with Western European countries acquire both a new format and new content. A more developed infrastructure of links, capable of growing into a kind of common European mechanism of cooperation, is being set up. In fact, the point at issue is a marked advance on the road to building a common European home.

Changes in the East and the West of the continent and the accelerating pace of developments call for increasing the rates and expanding the content of the general European process. Proceeding from this, we have proposed to hold a new European meeting in 1990, not in 1992 as was planned earlier. Such a meeting could be held at the summit level. France and Italy support this initiative. Admittedly, other participants in the European process also view it with interest. We are convinced that its implementation, the holding of the Helsinki II meeting, would give powerful impetus to the construction of the common European home in all of its main parameters. . . .

. . . President Bush and I achieved a reassuring degree of mutual understanding about the need to pursue a well-considered and cautious line in the conditions of deep processes taking place in Western and Eastern Europe.

This also applies to German problems. I think that it is also of importance that we regard all these problems primarily within the context of the CSCE process.

59. from "A New Europe, a New Atlanticism: Architecture for a New Era," Address by James A. Baker, US secretary of state. Berlin Press Club, Berlin, December 12, 1989 (Washington, DC: US State Dept. press release).

Now it's time for the CSCE process to advance further. We can look toward filling each of its three baskets with new substance.

First, we can give the security basket further content through the 35-nation negotiations on confidence-building measures currently underway in Vienna.[1] The agreements under consideration there should help prevent force, or the threat of force, from being used again in an effort to intimidate any European nation. Apart from reducing further the risk of war, new confidence-building measures can create greater openness. They can institutionalize a predictable pattern of military interaction, a pattern that is difficult to reverse and that builds a new basis for trust.

Second, the relatively underdeveloped economic basket can assume new responsibilities. President Bush suggested to President Gorbachev at Malta that we could breathe new life into this CSCE forum by focusing it on conceptual and practical questions involved in the transition from stalled, planned economies to free, competitive markets. When our nations meet in Bonn in May of next year to discuss economic cooperation,[2] I suggest we concentrate on this issue.

Third, the CSCE process has made its most distinctive mark in the field of human rights. One fundamental right, however, has not yet been fully institutionalized. This is the right for people to choose, through regular, free, open, multi-party elections, those who will govern them.

This is the ultimate human right, the right that secures all others. Without free elections, no rights can be long guaranteed. With free elections, no rights can be long denied.

Free elections should now become the highest priority in the CSCE process.[3] In 1945, Josef Stalin promised free elections and self-determination for the peoples of Eastern Europe. The fact that those elections were not free, and that those peoples were not allowed to determine their destiny, was a fundamental cause of the Cold War.

Now this Stalinist legacy is being removed by people determined to reclaim their birthright to freedom. They should not be denied. They will not be denied.

As all or nearly all the CSCE states move toward fully functioning representative governments, I suggest we consider another step: We could involve parliamentarians more directly in the CSCE processes, not only as observers as at present, but perhaps through their own meetings. To sustain the movement toward democracy, we need to reinforce the institutions of democracy.

The CSCE process could become the most important forum of East-West cooperation. Its mandate will grow as this cooperation takes root.

NOTES

1. See Documents 38–39.
2. See Documents 68–69.
3. See Document 85.

Part IV

The Institutionalization of the Helsinki Process, 1990

Roof Over Europe's New Architecture

LIVING WITH UNCERTAINTY

60. *from* Stephen S. Rosenfeld, "Living With Uncertainty," *The Washington Post,* February 23, 1990.

There is a gentle international conspiracy to evade the truly tough question of what kind of security system is to replace the fading old system of the two "Cold War" military blocs. George Bush, again this week Mikhail Gorbachev, the prophetic George Kennan and even the estimable Václav Havel agree with almost everyone else that a new system must be devised. But nobody seems to have the foggiest idea what it might be.

Now, this is not to sound a great alarm. Things generally go well. Gorbachev's turn to domestic reform has been validated by his restraint as both inner and outer Soviet empires loosen and by the ferment verging on chaos he permits to spread at home. Such Soviet threat as it now seems arises not from Kremlin design but from possible default or accident. Political decompression, as in Nicaragua, seems to be Moscow's chosen way to back off Third World revolutions. We have time to think. . . .

. . . At the same time, many people have the uneasy feeling that it is imprudent, unadult and feckless simply to let events take their own course. Hence the question, if not the blocs, then what?

"Two-plus-Four"—the two German states and the Big Four wartime allies now steering toward German unity—is not a concept but a mechanism. The Soviet idea of a "common European house"[1] and the American add-on of a "Europe whole and free" do not directly address security. The American intent to use NATO, the European Community and the all-European Helsinki process to build a new "architecture" similarly falls short. So does the Soviet call to slow the German express.

To replace the two Soviet and American blocs, why not one

European bloc? But that was Hitler's goal, and even though it is inconceivable that such a thing could again come to pass, the memory of Hitler has its continuing life in vague and sometimes not so vague apprehensions about the eventual purpose of a reunited Germany. This is how Poland's prime minister comes to suggest that, yes, Soviet troops should stay on. It is partly why Hungary suggests, yes, joining NATO.

A more benign single bloc might be created by a Europe that had found political harmony and economic integration, resolved border anxieties and ethnic tensions and created something like a unitary superstate. It is a dream Europe—a good-dream Europe built on what Havel calls "the family of man"—but it is not yet the Europe that humans actually live in. A stage of transition is still required.

More feasible would be a European balance of power in which Britain and France, both with nuclear arms, apply some combination of explicit embrace and implicit counterweight to contain Germany, while mannerly Soviets and Americans keep (and keep each other) at a distance. The notion of any sort of balance of power is considered old-fashioned, unstable, Kissingerian; it is also familiar and pragmatic. A Europe that had dissolved blocs and dismissed the great powers from active front-line security participation could come to something like this.

All these possibilities, however, have an undeniable artificial quality to them. Politically, they lack a sharp focus on what the actual shape of a future threat is going to be. Psychologically, they do not meet the craving of small countries to have a reliable protector: not just to be part of an abstract security "system" but to have a real fixed address—for 45 years it has been Washington—to go to in emergencies.

As diverting as it is to bash Bush for lacking "vision," a full year's fruitless global inquiry suggests we are in a situation whose uncertainties need not so much be resolved as recognized and lived with. Perhaps the world does not lend itself to the sort of bold strokes the West took after the war. We can push ourselves toward intricate security designs, but we can also wait, nervously but attentively, for more of the future to reveal itself.

NOTE
1. See Document 23.

FOR A EUROPEAN CONFEDERATION: THREE PROPOSALS

61. *from* Speech by François Mitterrand, president of France. Paris, December 31, 1989. *Le Monde,* January 2, 1990. Translated from French by Martine Gilbert and Roger Malone.

We have been proud to celebrate this year the bicentennial of our revolution to commemorate the role played by France in the combat for liberty and equality and for the defense of man's rights. And here, at a distance of 200 years, the same words that hold the same wishes, have overthrown other Bastilles here in Europe where other dictatorships ruled.

Each one of us knows that the changes that have come about in these past few months in the East European countries go beyond in importance everything that we have witnessed since the Second World War and will be inscribed without any doubt as one of the grand events of history. What was necessary was an economic and political breakdown, the intuition and the will of Mikhail Gorbachev, the strength of conviction and moral courage of the resistance to oppression, and finally the shocking maturity of the people in revolution against tyranny.

Nevertheless, we have witnessed the most explosive victory of democracy. From 1789 to 1989, no one would have dreamt of such a celebration for such a beautiful anniversary, but the Romanian drama reminds us that history is tragic and that liberty can only result after the price of suffering.

Let us not forget what millions have suffered, men and women, after such a long night. Their sudden liberation can only be seen as an illusion. They have in front of them many obstacles to surmount and they need us. Europe, it is evident, will not be the one we have known for half a century. Yesterday dependent on two superpowers, she goes like we would go into our own homes, and she will discover her own history and geography.

New questions will be asked that will not have responses in one day, but they are nevertheless raised: the future of alliances, the Atlantic Alliance and the Warsaw Pact; along what path should disarmament be pursued; under what form and under what conditions will the German people be reunited; what type of cooperation will exist between East and West; the permanence or impermanence of the existing frontiers; and to what extent will nationalism be allowed to be reborn.

Or will we witness a tendency toward exploitation, where we will find again the Europe of 1919—we know what followed? Or will Europe reconstruct itself? This can be done in two steps.

First, because of our community of 12 that must absolutely reinforce its structures, which it recently decided to do, I am convinced that she has by its unique existence, greatly contributed to the impetus to create a change for these people in the East by serving as a reference and an allure.

The second step has yet to be invented. Based on the Helsinki Accords, I plan to witness the birth in the 1990s of a European Confederation in the real sense of the term that will associate all the states of our continent in a common organization with permanent exchanges of peace and security. This will obviously only be possible after the inception in the East European countries of pluralism of parties, free elections, representative systems and freedom of information. At the speed at which things are going, we are not very far from this.

62. *from* "Position of the Government of Poland on the idea of 35-nation CSCE summit in 1990," undated [early 1990].

We think it will be useful if the summit gives a signal to start a step-by-step, pragmatic process of institutionalization of the CSCE and presents the vision of a more united Europe, according to the formula of President Mitterrand's European Confederation (which we have welcomed with interest) or M. Gorbachev's "Common European Home." In this context we see the possibility to discuss also the idea to create a permanent council of European cooperation, proposed by the Polish Prime Minister, Tadeusz Mazowiecki, in Sejm,[1] on January 1, 1990.

Our goal is to initiate thinking about practical means to overcome the division of Europe by creating continental structures of cooperation and integration, which will help to realize further European Confederation.

We are open to discuss the idea of creation of such a forum. It could be a place for strengthening mechanisms of European cooperation, starting from less controversial issues, such as ecology, scientific, educational and technical cooperation, and going step-by-step in more complex areas.

NOTE
1. The Polish parliament.

63. *from* "Memorandum on the European Security Commission" [by the Government of Czechoslovakia, Prague, April 6, 1990]. In *Europe, Equal Security for All: Proposal to Establish European Security Commission* (Prague, 1990), pp. 2–4.

We believe that the best suitable basis on which to build a unified all-European security system is provided by the CSCE process. . . .

. . . Czechoslovakia proposes, in the first stage, the establishment of a European Security Commission comprised of the participating States of the Helsinki process. Its justification is seen by us in the fact that it would provide an until now missing permanent all-European platform for the consideration of questions relating to security on the continent, and for seeking their solution. This European Security Commission would operate side-by-side with the existing two groupings[1] and independently of them.

The formation of an effective system of European security would in the second stage be facilitated by the establishment, on a treaty basis, of an Organization of European States, including the United States and Canada.

The third stage would culminate in a confederated Europe of free and independent States. . . .

The European Security Commission would operate on the basis of consensus. It would initially fulfill consultative, coordinating and certain verification functions and, later on, such functions as would be agreed by the participating States. This would include in particular the following tasks:

- Considering international political correlations of European security and proposing the adoption of appropriate measures;

- Forestalling threats to European peace and security, the rise of exacerbated situations, disputes, military incidents and conflicts and recommending as well as offering means of their settlement—good offices, mediation, fact-finding, conciliation, etc.;

- Dealing with questions of threats to, and violations of, security that are due to economic, ecological and humanitarian causes and assume large proportions and have international implications;

- Creating a scope for direct contacts and negotiations of the two groupings and their members, attended, if need be, also by the European neutral and nonaligned countries;

- Commenting on the conduct of negotiations by the European disarmament and security forums and proposing their further orientation;

- Considering the possibilities of expanding the agenda of the existing disarmament forums and the establishment of new ones;

- Considering reports by verification and consultation centers on compliance with European arms control and security agreements;

- Informing each other on doctrinal, structural, organizational and budgetary changes relating to armed forces of the participating States and on the introduction of new weapons systems by them;

- Informing the United Nations as well as regional organizations on the results achieved in the sphere of European disarmament and security.

The Commission would meet on the level of Ministers of Foreign Affairs and their Permanent Representatives. Regular sessions at the level of ministers would be held at least once a year. Extraordinary sessions could be convened at the request of participating States.

Sessions of Permanent Representatives would be held once a month or more frequently if so requested by a participating State.

Subordinated to the Commission would be a Military Committee composed of representatives of the CSCE participating States. It would be meeting at least once a year and would deal with questions specified by the Commission. For the purpose of the implementation of its tasks the Commission may establish auxiliary bodies. The necessary technical services for the Commission would be secured by a not-very-sizable, operative, permanent Secretariat.

Czechoslovakia offers Prague as the permanent seat of the Commission.

NOTE
1. NATO and the Warsaw Pact.

WHAT THE CSCE CAN DO: THREE VIEWS

64. *from* Speech by Margaret Thatcher, prime minister of the UK. Königswinter Conference, Cambridge, March 29, 1990 (London: British Information Services).

First, the Summit should strengthen democracy by agreeing on a new provision setting out the conditions to be fulfilled for elections to be considered truly free.[1] Britain and the United States put forward an outline proposal, including a suggestion for independent observers, at the Paris meeting last June.[2] We want to see a commitment to free elections become one of the new CSCE principles.

Second, we should do the same for the rule of law and human rights. The CSCE countries should set out the essential principles for a sound legal system, vital for freedom, and should all commit themselves to respect and uphold the rule of law according to these principles.

And third, we should extend political consultation through the CSCE, as a way of involving the widest possible number of countries in discussions about Europe's future. There should be meetings at the level of Foreign Ministers twice a year, and there might also be a procedure for convening extraordinary meetings in times of tension or crisis.

And fourth, we should consider giving the CSCE a conciliation role in disputes rather on the lines that GATT[3] has in the trade field. The CSCE could offer its good offices in any dispute between two or more of its members, for instance in matters concerning minority rights.

And fifth, the Summit should add to the Helsinki principles the right to private property, the freedom to produce, buy and sell without undue government interference. These rights are fundamental to a free and prosperous society. Their importance is now acknowledged throughout Eastern Europe and private property has just been made legal in the Soviet Union. The CSCE should reflect and encourage this.

And sixth, the Summit should solemnly reaffirm the original Helsinki commitments on European borders: that frontiers are inviolable and can only be changed by peaceful means and by agreement, in accordance with international law.

And finally, the Summit should not only sign the CFE Agreement, which we hope will be ready by then, but look ahead to the next steps in arms control in Europe. . . .

Let me stress that I do not believe that the CSCE can in any way take on a defense role. That must remain the task of NATO and the Western European Union. What it can and should do is to strengthen democracy, the rule of law and human rights. If we can get to a stage when they are practiced and observed throughout Europe, that in itself will be an enormous contribution to Europe's security.

NOTES
1. See Document 98.
2. CSCE Conference on the Human Dimension.
3. General Agreement on Tariffs and Trade.

65. *from* "The Future of a European Community," Speech by Hans-Dietrich Genscher, FRG minister of foreign affairs. American Society of Newspaper Editors, Washington, DC, April 6, 1990.

The only element binding the whole of Europe at the present is the CSCE process. The efforts to intensify that process and to render it more permanent by creating new institutions are indispensable contributions to stability in Europe.

The architecture of all Europe is taking shape in the CSCE process. That process must become a framework of stability for the dynamic, dramatic and in some cases revolutionary developments in Central and Eastern Europe, including the Soviet Union.

Regular conferences of foreign ministers and summit conferences will build confidence and mitigate or prevent conflicts.

What institutions can be established in the CSCE process?

1. A pan-European institution for the protection of human rights. The Court of Human Rights and the Human Rights Commission of the Council of Europe should be extended to the whole of Europe.[1]

2. The incorporation of the right to free elections in the catalogue of principles contained in the Helsinki Final Act, including provisions which permit the monitoring of elections.[2]

3. Recognition of the rights of minorities and checks to determine whether these rights are being respected.

4. A European center for the early detection and political settlement of conflicts.

5.   A center for establishing the European legal area and harmonizing European law.

6.   A European environmental agency.

7.   A center for the development of a European telecommunications system, a European transport infrastructure and a European transport policy.

8.   The extension of cooperation under EUREKA [3] to the whole of Europe.

9.   An institution for promoting economic cooperation throughout Europe. This should be the role of a European Development Bank.

These would all contribute to stability throughout Europe. They would help consolidate the process of democratization, increase cooperation in and develop the *one* Europe.

NOTES
1.   See Document 96.
2.   See Document 85.
3.   An initiative by European countries to support high-technology research and development.

66. *from* "The United States and a New Europe: Strategy for the Future," Report by Stanley R. Sloan, senior specialist in international security policy, Research Coordination Office, Congressional Research Service, The Library of Congress. *CRS Report for Congress,* May 14, 1990, Washington, DC.

It is not necessary to argue the case for the emergence of a new collective security system in the future to understand the potential benefits of strengthening the CSCE process today. If the Soviet Union eventually transforms its political and economic system to become a true democracy and join the Western economic system, then some form of collective security system could perhaps be devised based largely on the CSCE framework. In the near term, however, strengthening the CSCE process could provide a way to resolve several dilemmas created by the process of German unification and the disintegration of the Warsaw Pact.

First, a commitment to strengthen the CSCE process could help reassure the Soviet Union that it would be a participant in future European security discussions. This participation is regarded by all European governments as a legitimate Soviet right. It might be one of the keys to ultimate Soviet acceptance of the membership of a united Germany into NATO.

Second, the CSCE provides the means for Germany to accept constraints on its future force levels and nuclear status in a multilateral context. Germany would far prefer to accept such constraints in the CSCE framework than in the "Two-plus-Four" talks or in bilateral negotiations with the Soviet Union.

Third, the CSCE provides a means for the East European countries who want to end their security dependence on the Soviet Union and the Warsaw Pact to do so without provoking the Soviet Union, as ties with NATO would likely do.

The critics of the CSCE have raised a number of important points. The CSCE is still a process, with no legal foundation, and decisions can currently be blocked by a single participant. On the other hand, the CSCE does not have to be invented, it can be strengthened, and it is receiving growing political support in Europe as the one framework that expresses the hope for a future Europe of cooperative relations among all states. Working with this structure and seeking to remedy some of its weaknesses could be much easier technically and politically than starting from scratch with some entirely new institutional concept.

Strengthening the CSCE

The initial goals of the CSCE policy path would be to overcome some of the weaknesses of the CSCE process and thereby to lock in the accomplishments to date of the CSCE and to provide a stronger foundation for further development.

If the CSCE is to be adapted for greater tasks, the first step might be to envision transforming the key principles in the CSCE Final Act into a treaty, amending the Final Act to add features necessitated by German unification and to establish a practical relationship between the CSCE framework and other European organizations and arrangements. This process would help deal with the concerns of countries that are not directly involved in the Two-plus-Four discussions. Incorporating key elements of the Final Act into a treaty would beneficially bypass the process of drafting a peace treaty. The Germans want to avoid being asked to sign anything like a World War II peace treaty, believing that it would place an onus on Germany that should, in all fairness, have been removed by postwar history. Finally, the treaty mechanism would allow the US Congress to play a direct role in establishing future security arrangements, strengthening American political support for those arrangements. A

CSCE summit proposed for late-1990 could mandate the preparation of such a treaty.

The CSCE Final Act lays out a set of guidelines for cooperation among states in promoting peace, economic cooperation, and human rights in Europe. This "declaration on principles guiding relations between participating States," which would be the heart of a new treaty, precludes any changes in European borders except through peaceful means. A critical step would be to amend the Final Act to reflect the outcome of the Two-plus-Four talks—the conditions under which German unity will take place. These terms might include, for example, termination of Four-Power rights in Germany and Berlin and membership in NATO combined with promises not to station NATO forces in Germany's eastern territory and German reaffirmation of its commitment not to become a nuclear power. Such provisions could be drafted in such a way that Germany would not be singularized. For example, the CSCE Treaty could include a pledge by all non-nuclear-weapons states that they will not develop or acquire nuclear weapons capabilities. Similar approaches could be developed on other issues to avoid singling out Germany unnecessarily.

In addition, the provision in the Final Act that notes the sovereign right of states to enter into treaties and other international agreements could be strengthened to acknowledge clearly the legitimacy of all treaties, bilateral accords, and organizations in Europe that contribute to the goals articulated in the Final Act. This "grandfather clause" would spread the CSCE umbrella over a wide range of present institutions, as well as over new institutions deemed necessary in the future. That clause could also make it clear that it will not be necessary or even desirable to do everything at a level requiring all 35 CSCE participants in the future, and that practical cooperation consistent with the goals of the CSCE can take place at a variety of bilateral, regional and transatlantic levels. This approach would also provide the basis for continued adherence of current NATO members to the North Atlantic Treaty, whose principles should be preserved even if the organization itself becomes less relevant to new political realities in Europe.

It would seem wise to avoid creating another large international bureaucracy in the CSCE, at least initially. The CSCE probably will be given a staff to help schedule and coordinate activities, but most of the practical business of managing European affairs could be handled by a variety of other organizations, obviously with overlapping memberships.

Giving the CSCE process legal standing and institutional base could provide a way for the United States and the Soviet Union to remain constructively involved in future European developments—an important consideration—while at the same time supplying the international framework for German unification. Such a framework could make it easier for the Soviet Union to accept membership in NATO of a united Germany, and in other arrangements that have been suggested for a European defense pillar to integrate German military forces with those of its neighbors.

As noted above, a CSCE Treaty would also allow the US Congress to participate through the ratification process in the creation of a new European order. This would help establish a strong domestic foundation for a leading US role in the process of strengthening democratic institutions across Europe and in the construction of a more cooperative European security system. This is not just a parochial American concern. It is useful in this context to reflect on the refusal of the Congress to go along with President Wilson's League of Nations plan following World War I. US abstention from participation in the League seriously limited its potential. Following World War II, the Truman Administration was sufficiently wise to engage the Congress in the treaty commitments and institution-building of the early postwar period. The involvement of the Congress in building the system helped ensure support for its continuation. A new European security order likewise would benefit from a US commitment shared equally by the Republican presidency and the Democratic-controlled Congress.

Merging CSCE and Conventional Arms Control
It would also be important to link the CSCE political commitments to the process of conventional arms control. This linkage could help provide the reassurance required by the Soviet Union concerning ceilings on future German military forces. The negotiation on Conventional Armed Forces in Europe (CFE), already under the CSCE umbrella, provides a mechanism for monitoring military force levels throughout Europe and regulating future military relations among NATO and Warsaw Pact countries. The verification and compliance provisions to be agreed as part of a first stage CFE accord could serve as the core for a future management system for European military forces. These provisions and negotiations are likely to be merged with the on-going discussions of Confidence- and Security-Building Measures (CSBMs) among the 35 CSCE participants.

A second stage CFE could produce substantial reductions for all participants and restructuring of forces to limit the potential and incentives to initiate hostilities between or among any of the participants. The neutral and nonaligned countries, which now participate in the CSCE, could be affiliated with the CFE process through participation in the compliance and confidence-building procedures, if not in the reductions themselves. The process of conventional arms control within the CSCE framework will have to be restructured, away from its current East-West foundations, to encourage stable and peaceful military relations among all participants. Reductions and stabilizing measures will have to be designed to ensure military stability and predictability in bilateral relations among neighboring states, in European subregions, as well as on European-wide scale from the Atlantic to the Urals.

It would be logical, given the blurring of bloc-to-bloc distinctions that is taking place, for CFE-II reductions to be taken on a national basis, with all participants reducing forces on an agreed-upon percentage basis. National limits could serve as a cap on German military forces desired by the Soviet Union without singling out Germany by surrounding those limits with a multilateral context in which all countries accepted limitations on their forces. The Hungarian government has even proposed that the allocation of reductions within NATO and the Warsaw Pact be appended in some way to the CFE treaty to accomplish the objective of national ceilings in the first CFE accord rather than in follow-on negotiations.

Nuclear Arms Control
New negotiations aimed on US and Soviet short-range nuclear weapons seem likely to join the international agenda by 1991. While such negotiations are a necessary ingredient in the process of adjusting military force structures to accommodate new political realities, the negotiations themselves might be conducted outside the CSCE framework, because most such weapons systems are owned by the Soviet Union and the United States. The outcome of the negotiations, however, could be fed into the CSCE framework as part of the outline for a new European security system.

PRACTICAL SECURITY FOR EUROPE

67. *from* Flora Lewis, "Practical Security for Europe," *The New York Times,* July 4, 1990.

East and West are flailing around for a European security system that can transcend the cold war balance of terror without falling back into the dangerous prewar national balance of power.

For the moment, there are two approaches. One is to stick narrowly to existing negotiation tracks based on rival blocs, even though the East bloc is disintegrating. The other is to conjure a state of generalized "mutual security" where everybody guarantees the peace and safety of everybody else and nobody is afraid.

Neither can work as the crucial transition. . . .

. . . The Conference on Security and Cooperation in Europe . . . is offered as the framework for lots of fuzzy ideas to accommodate all interests—East, West and neutral.

It is appealing, but in the same way the League of Nations was appealing after World War I: dependent on the assumption of good will. Getting from here to there takes more than thinking up new institutions.

A Polish communist, at an East-West meeting here, put it succinctly: "Our system collapsed because it was built on a concept. If you base a new security system on a concept, it too will be doomed to collapse."

That doesn't mean that the CSCE can't be useful. It can provide a forum for regular political consultations, an umbrella for regional groups and cooperation on pragmatic issues like pollution, energy and transport.

The US is too timid on accepting a CSCE meeting this year, which the Soviets and all the Europeans want as an earnest of trying to end the East-West divide with nobody excluded. Washington fears it will lead to dissolving NATO. That may be Moscow's hope since its own alliance proved worthless.

There's little risk. Western Europe isn't tempted, especially given new uncertainties about Germany. CSCE is too frail to be a security system and too big for tough negotiations on disarmament, which imply concessions on sovereignty.

A better approach would be to build on practical measures instead of trying to institute concepts. The verification regimes being worked out to support arms control agreements offer a solid base. Most important will be the system to monitor reductions of conventional forces in Europe. . . .

As now being negotiated, the verification regimes contain no constraints beyond exposure. But that is already a powerful deterrent to a secret arms buildup. It is a long-term program, since not only will destruction of existing weapons and withdrawal of troops be monitored, but inspections will continue to make sure that they are not replaced.

When they have gone into effect and states feel they have adequate warning against new threats, broader agreements will be possible.

The European Community is a good example. It started with the Coal and Steel Community. Jean Monnet, who launched the idea, had a grandiose goal—to make another war between Germany and France impossible. By focusing first on vital nuts and bolts, he persuaded governments to accept commitments they would never have dreamed of making on overall national policy.

Step by step, the Common Market grew both in size and responsibility as members saw that the benefits of working together were so much greater than the risk of letting down their guard. And the success of the Community has, in effect, overpowered the partition of Europe.

The goal now is that no nation feel threatened. There are new dangers of ethnic conflict and civil wars that could spread. The verification regimes can begin to bring needed assurance. This concrete program, not high-flown rhetoric, can change the meaning of security in Europe.

Bonn: Toward the Security of the Market

WASHINGTON CHANGES ITS MIND

68. *from* Commission on Security and Cooperation in Europe, *The Bonn CSCE Conference on Economic Cooperation in Europe, March 19–April 11, 1990* (Washington, DC, undated [mid-1990]).

Negotiating History of the Bonn Economic Conference
The FRG had first suggested that a conference on East-West economic cooperation be held within the framework of the CSCE during the preparations for the Vienna meeting. It was introduced as an idea with strong support from both West German Chancellor Helmut Kohl and Foreign Minister Hans-Dietrich Genscher. By the time it was formally proposed in Vienna, in March 1987, it had support of the 12 member States of the European Communities as well as Norway. . . .

From the time it was first suggested to the very conclusion of the Vienna Meeting, the United States expressed serious reservations about the FRG proposal. Among the arguments against the proposal were the fact that the conference would: duplicate work in other multilateral or bilateral fora; provide Eastern countries with a forum to attack COCOM[1] restrictions and other Western trade policies which they did not like; give a political endorsement of East-West trade in general at a time when a differentiated approach was preferable; and turn more into a trade fair for the conclusion of business deals than a meeting to encourage economic reform. The United States and some other Western and neutral countries argued that increased trade would come about in the long run not as a result of Western governmental support or encouragement, such as through a politicized economic conference, but as a result of the restructuring of the Soviet and East European economic systems which would make Eastern goods more competitive in Western markets and foreign investment in these countries more attractive.

These arguments were all presented in the context of the need for balanced progress within the CSCE process and the need to focus less on additional meetings and more on actual implementation of Vienna provisions. Given the heavy emphasis on military-security issues at the Vienna meeting and the plethora of other proposals for follow-up meetings, it was felt that the economic conference, particularly the high-level and elaborate one proposed by the FRG, would further squeeze human rights in the CSCE process. . . .

Nevertheless, in January 1989 the United States dropped its objections to the Bonn proposal in light of the overall positive result that was being achieved at the Vienna meeting. . . .

After giving consensus to the Bonn Economic Conference, the United States remained concerned about its implications while violations of human rights in the Soviet Union and East-Central Europe continued to take place. Following the major political changes in Eastern Europe and further Soviet implementation of its CSCE commitments in 1989, however, the conference was viewed in a new light. With increased economic cooperation now more desirable and economic reform possible, the United States and others now saw the conference as a useful opportunity to focus attention on the need for the development of private/cooperative economic activity in the Soviet Union and Eastern Europe as well as other reform measures. In addition, there was continued interest in emphasizing traditional Basket II items, such as better conditions for business representatives and more and better economic and commercial information, which remain problems in East-West commercial relations. . . .

The US Delegation to the Conference
In line with the mandate for the conference, which called for the presence of representatives of the business communities of the participating States, the US delegation included a number of business people, economists, financial experts and trade lawyers who participated in the conference. Unfortunately, US private-sector participation was not as large as that of many other delegations, and the Department of State originally was hesitant to encourage active involvement of these individuals in the formal discussions. Nevertheless, as the conference progressed and the procedures became more flexible, US private representatives made up for their fewer numbers with their thorough presentations of US business views and concerns.

The General Debate
The Bonn Conference was opened by FRG Chancellor Helmut Kohl, who stressed the importance both of economic cooperation and the

CSCE process in promoting positive change in Europe. Speaking the day after the first free elections in East Germany, he also commented positively on the prospects for German unification. . . .

. . . In his opening statement, US Ambassador Holmer stressed the historic times in which the Bonn Conference was taking place. He noted the relationship between effective economic systems and democratic political systems, the influence of domestic economic measures on international trade activity, and the difficulties involved in the transition from a command economy to one that is mixed or based on free markets. . . . He concluded: "On the heels of the political and economic revolutions of 1989, now is the time not to be timid". . . .

. . . In contrast to the heated exchanges which have transpired in CSCE meetings of the past, the discussions in Bonn had a positive tone to them, reflecting the many encouraging developments that have been taking place. The Soviet and East-Central European delegations detailed their many reform efforts but were candid in admitting that many economic problems remain, to some of which they had few if any answers. Although there were some criticisms of existing COCOM and other Western restrictions on trade, such criticisms were not raised in a polemical way. . . .

In a statement that was welcomed by other delegations, the Romanian delegation used the Bonn Conference to state for the record that it supported the entire draft document of the Sofia Meeting on the Protection of the Environment, which was held in October and November of last year while Ceauşescu was still in power.[2] At that time, Romania was the only country to deny consensus to the document, and it did so because of two paragraphs which dealt with the rights of independent environmental activists to make their ecological concerns known. With Romania's objection removed, the participating States intend to pursue the document's implementation, including in international organizations such as the Economic Commission for Europe.

Proposals

Fewer proposals were introduced at the Bonn conference than at most CSCE meetings. The primary reason for this was that, in the weeks leading up to Bonn, the 12 CSCE States which are members of the European Community (EC-12) prepared and circulated a comprehensive draft concluding document to be adopted by the meeting. . . . This preempted the normal pattern of negotiations in the CSCE, in which specific proposals are first introduced and discussed and then combined in a draft concluding document. Given the shortness of the meeting, the EC-12 effort had the advantage of facilitating the eventual informal negotiations on a final document. At the same time, unlike strongly worded proposals, it presented compromises on some issues even before there was any discussion on what might be acceptable.

The only major proposal introduced at Bonn was by the United States. While supporting the EC proposal for a final document, . . . it tabled a proposal listing 10 principles which complemented the practical measures specified in the EC draft. As stated in the proposal, these principles were:

1.   Multi-party democracy based on free, periodic and general elections.

2.   The rule of law and equal protection of the law based on respect for human rights and effective, accessible and just legal systems.

3.   Economic activity that does not involve forced labor or discrimination against workers on political, ethnic, gender or religious grounds, or the denial of the rights of workers to form and join independent trade unions.

4.   Sound fiscal and monetary policies.

5.   International and domestic policies which support the expansion of free and open trade, investment and unrestricted capital flows, and free transfer of capital and profits in convertible currency.

6.   Free and competitive market economies in which supply and demand determine prices.

7.   Full recognition and protection of the rights of citizens to hold and use private property, including intellectual property rights.

8.   Unhindered exchange of goods and services among companies—whether private or state-owned—and individuals in both domestic and international markets, including direct contacts with customers and suppliers.

9.   Prompt payment of adequate and effective compensation in the event of private property being taken for public use.

10. National economic objectives focused on productivity rather than simply production. . . .

Negotiating a Concluding Document

From the time a CSCE meeting on economic cooperation in Europe was first proposed, the West German government and many other governments indicated their desire to have a document at such a meeting adopted. Others, including the United States, were skeptical about the utility of documents at any subsidiary meetings as long as provisions of the Helsinki Final Act, the Madrid Concluding Document and, most recently, the Vienna Concluding Document, were being blatantly violated. As long as this was the case, it was argued, stress should be kept on a thorough and frank review of implementation at these meetings. In the absence of a major, new human rights document, moreover, a document in the field of economics became even less desirable for some if balanced progress in the CSCE process was to be maintained.

By the time the Bonn Conference convened, however, things had changed so dramatically on the European scene that all countries felt that the adoption of a document was a desired result. There were several reasons for this. First, the progress that has been taking place in the Soviet Union and in East-Central Europe has overtaken some CSCE commitments, making a statement of new goals to be reached not only desirable but necessary. A second and related reason was that such a statement was now possible, whereas consensus on ambitious, new commitments at previous meetings could not be reached. Third, as mentioned earlier, the West German hosts wanted a document which would symbolize a successful conference, especially with trade and economic ministers planning to attend the closing of the conference. Finally, and in some ways perhaps the most immediate reason for some countries, including the United States, to seek agreement to a document was a desire to demonstrate progress in all areas of the CSCE leading up to a summit meeting of the participating States later in the year.

From the start, practically every delegation stated that it could support the EC-12 proposed draft document, which needed only a few amendments. . . . The EC-12 document contained many compromises from the very beginning, and reaching agreement to a text based on this draft was not a difficult exercise. Somewhat more difficult, however, was the insertion of the US-proposed economic principles, which would strengthen the document considerably. Through a series of bilateral discussions, the US was able to get agreement by practically every delegation, including those of the East-Central European countries, to the principles with only a few changes. . . .

The main holdout was the Soviet Union, which had stated early in the conference that it would accept no reference to private property in a final document. Fears of the meeting ending without a document led many delegations to seek to convince the United States that it should withdraw its principles. They argued that it was still too early to press the Soviets on this key issue and that doing so could threaten Gorbachev. The US delegation held firm, maintaining that the Soviets needed to be pressed on this point, which, in fact, would seem to support Gorbachev's proclaimed goals for the USSR.

In the end, the Soviet delegation's position proved largely tactical, and the principles were included in the concluding document.

NOTES
1. Coordinating Committee for Multilateral Export Controls.
2. See Document 55.

THE MAGNA CARTA OF FREE ENTERPRISE

69. *from Document of the Bonn Conference on Economic Cooperation in Europe of the Conference on Security and Cooperation in Europe* (Washington, DC: US Commission on Security and Cooperation in Europe, 1990).

Meeting at a time of profound and rapid change,
   The participating States,
   Confirm their intention to shape a new order of peace, stability and prosperity in Europe based on the comprehensive and balanced concept set out in the Helsinki Final Act and the subsequent documents of the CSCE . . . ;
   Reaffirm the fundamental role of the CSCE in the future of Europe;
   Recognize that democratic institutions and economic freedom foster economic and social progress;
   Share the common objectives of sustainable economic growth, a rising standard of living, an improved quality of life, expanding employment, efficient use of economic resources and protection of the environment;
   Believe that cooperation in the field of economics, science and technology and the environment is an essential element in their over-

all relations, and that it should become even more prominent in the future; . . .

Believe that the success of their cooperation will depend in large measure on prevailing political and economic conditions;

Stress the importance of the political and economic reforms . . . and of a supportive international economic environment, recognize the particular economic interests and concerns of countries as they achieve a market economy, and acknowledge other difficulties, such as indebtedness, which are to be dealt with in the competent fora;

Consider that the process of economic reform and structural adjustment, with increased reliance on market forces, will enhance economic performance, improve efficiency of the public sector, respond better to the needs and wishes of consumers, improve the conditions for closer cooperation and contribute to a more open world trading system; . . .

Recognize that the performance of market-based economies relies primarily on the freedom of individual enterprise and the consequent economic growth;

Believe that economic freedom for the individual includes the right freely to own, buy, sell and otherwise utilize property;

Confirm that, while governments provide the overall framework for economic activity, business partners make their own decisions;

Consider that the progressive convergence of economic policies among the participating States opens new long-term perspectives for the strengthening of their economic relations.

Accordingly the participating States,

Recognizing the relationship between political pluralism and market economies, and being committed to the principles concerning:

- Multiparty democracy based on free, periodic and genuine elections;

- The rule of law and equal protection under the law for all, based on respect for human rights and effective, accessible and just legal systems;

- Economic activity that accordingly upholds human dignity and is free from forced labor, discrimination against workers based on grounds of race, sex, language, political opinion or religion, or denial of the rights of workers freely to establish or join independent trade unions;

Will endeavor to achieve or maintain the following:

- Fiscal and monetary policies that promote balanced, sustainable growth and enhance the ability of markets to function efficiently;

- International and domestic policies aimed at expanding the free flow of trade, capital, investment and repatriation of profits in convertible currency;

- Free and competitive market economies where prices are based on supply and demand;

- Policies that promote social justice and improve living and working conditions;

- Environmentally sustainable economic growth and development;

- Full recognition and protection of all types of property including private property, and the right of citizens to own and use them, as well as intellectual property rights;

- The right to prompt, just and effective compensation in the event private property is taken for public use;

- Direct contact between consumers and suppliers in order to facilitate the exchange of goods and services among companies—whether private or state-owned—and individuals in both domestic and international markets,

Have come to the following conclusions:

A. Development and diversification of economic relations
1. The participating States wish to create favorable conditions for a harmonious development and diversification of their economic relations based on internationally agreed rules and practices. . . . They agree to permit and encourage direct contacts between businessmen . . . , facilitate, on a non-discriminatory basis, the establishment and operation of business offices and firms in their territory, including the renting and purchasing of commercial premises and housing, . . . as well as the unhindered recruitment of local staff. . . . They encourage direct contacts between representatives of commercial and business organizations and economic institutions. . . .
2. The participating States resolve to publish and make available comprehensive, comparable and timely economic, commercial and demographic information. . . . To that effect, they will provide the

United Nations Trade Data Bank (COMTRADE) with up-to-date trade figures to at least the three-digit level of the United Nations product classification (SITC-Rev.2). They will also publish detailed, comparable and up-to-date data on balance of payments and gross national product statistics on at least an annual basis. . . . They stress the need for national statistics and accounting systems to conform with international standards.

3. The participating States will . . . undertake comprehensive co-operation between their respective statistical services. . . . The object of this cooperation is to exchange detailed and complete information on relevant statistical elements available and the techniques and methodology employed, and to correlate statistical data with the aim of achieving comparability of such statistics among participating States. . . .

4. The participating States recognize the particular importance of small and medium sized enterprises in their economic cooperation. . . . To that end they will endeavor to provide the appropriate economic, legal, banking and fiscal conditions that take account of the specific requirements of SMEs. . . .[1]

5. The participating States are prepared, insofar as the appropriate conditions exist, to provide support for the SME sector by promoting: business cooperation networks, which facilitate the search for business partners; access to information services, including publications and data banks; management and expert training and information on availability of technical know-how and innovations.

6. The participating States confirm the importance they attach to marketing and product promotion. . . . They will therefore encourage trade promotion activities including advertising, consulting, factoring and other business services, and the organization of seminars, fairs and exhibitions. They favor the conduct of market research and other marketing activities by both domestic and foreign firms on their respective territories.

7. The participating States recognize the importance, for the economic process, of the development of the human potential. They therefore recognize the value of cooperation in training programs for managers and specialists in marketing, product promotion and other fields. . . .

B. Industrial cooperation
1. The participating States note that the economic, fiscal, legal and social infrastructure and the political conditions in their countries

determine the extent to which the various forms of industrial cooperation, including joint ventures and other means of direct foreign investment, can be envisaged. . . .

2. The participating States . . . will ensure adequate and effective protection and enforcement of industrial, commercial and intellectual property rights. . . .

3. Among the conditions for the development of industrial cooperation the participating States emphasize the need for market-oriented and stable economic policies, an appropriate and reliable legal and administrative framework, consisting of such elements as: fiscal, competition, bankruptcy, and insolvency legislation; company laws; arbitration procedures (taking due account of the UNCITRAL[2] model law and other relevant agreements); protection of industrial and intellectual property rights; investment protection in national legislation as well as in the framework of multilateral and bilateral agreements; free transfer of capital and profits in foreign currency; accounting systems; a free flow of economic data and market information; business facilities; and entrepreneurial autonomy.

4. Possible forms of industrial cooperation . . . will be decided by firms according to the conditions existing and the nature and the objectives of the cooperation.

5. The participating States recognize the importance of comprehensive information on all legal provisions of host countries for foreign investment. . . .

6. The participating States are prepared, insofar as the appropriate conditions exist, to foster a favorable climate for investment and the different forms of industrial cooperation, on a non-discriminatory basis, . . . with particular reference to the transfer of profits and repatriation of invested capital. . . .

C. Cooperation in specific areas

1. The participating States, while acknowledging the role of governments in creating favorable framework conditions, recognize that the initiative of the enterprises directly concerned is of the paramount importance. . . .

2. The participating States consider that they should extend and deepen their cooperation in the field of energy and raw material saving techniques. To that end . . . they will cooperate . . . in the field of hydrocarbon technologies, solid fuels and renewable energies and processes for the separation of waste components and their recycling and upgrading. They will also cooperate in the field of nuclear energy and of the safety of nuclear installations. . . .

3. The participating States are prepared to exchange information on energy and raw material saving techniques and . . . to undertake joint projects to measure energy-combustion-related environmental pollution, to enhance energy efficiency by means of substitution of energy products. . . .

4. The participating States . . . recognize that it is vital to ensure the environmental sustainability of economic development. . . .

5. . . . The participating States consider that among the areas for cooperation are pollution monitoring, major technological hazard and accident prevention, assessment of chemicals, treatments and disposal of toxic and dangerous waste, as well as prevention and reduction of air and water pollution, especially that of transboundary watercourses and international lakes, and transboundary pollution caused by energy production, conversion and consumption. . . .

6. The participating States are prepared, insofar as the appropriate conditions exist, to take the necessary steps in order to stimulate the exchange of know-how [and] to promote the wider adoption of environmentally sound technologies. . . .

7. With a view to improving the quality of life, . . . the participating States intend to cooperate in assessing the impact of environmental stress on the population by exchanging relevant data on the effects of environmental pollution. . . .

8. The participating States affirm the importance of cooperation in agro-industry and food processing. . . .

9. The participating States . . . stress the importance of increasing cooperation in the consumer goods sector and . . . note that conversion from military to consumer production may give rise to new business opportunities.

10. The participating States . . . will promote closer cooperation, and encourage the exchange of information on town planning, including infrastructure (e.g., transport), housing construction, protection of monuments and restoration of the architectural heritage. They will also encourage the exchange of information on, and new approaches to, the economic adaptation of structurally weak regions and the alleviation of environmental damage in urban areas.

D. Monetary and financial aspects

1. The participating States consider that the introduction of undistorted internal pricing is essential to economic reform and a necessary step to currency convertibility. . . . They agree that progress toward full convertibility and efficient allocation of resources requires a functioning price mechanism which reflects market-deter-

mined and undistorted domestic costs, consumer preferences and international prices. . . .

2. The participating States are prepared, insofar as the appropriate conditions exist, to cooperate in establishing conditions for an efficient price mechanism and for progress toward convertibility. This could involve fields such as reform of the banking system, introducing a money market, reform of the investment laws, transformation of public enterprises, taxation, structural adjustment policy, organization of a labor and capital market as well as a foreign exchange market. . . .

3. The participating States acknowledge that a market-oriented financial system facilitates the expansion of economic cooperation and that financial instruments play an important role in that context. While, in the period of transition to a market economy, public financial support to well-defined projects can serve as a multiplier in the framework of economic reforms, such intervention should not distort the emerging market mechanisms. The participating States agree that capital from private sources will progressively become the principal source of external investment.

4. The participating States look forward to the successful conclusion of negotiations to establish the European Bank for Reconstruction and Development. . . .

In view of the profound and rapid changes taking place in Europe, and wishing to maintain the valuable momentum built up at the present Conference, the participating States . . . see a need for discussion of the specificities and longer-term issues of economic changes and reforms in the participating States and related problems of cooperation among them and to share experiences. To this end, they invite the ECE,[3] in view of its annual session, to develop practical measures in priority fields. They invite the OECD[4] to consider hosting meetings of experts from the CSCE participating States and the OECD member States to promote the process of economic reform. They recommend that the objective of such undertakings is full integration of the reforming countries into the international economic system.

NOTES

1.   Small and medium-sized enterprises.
2.   United Nations Commission on International Trade Law.
3.   United Nations Economic Commission for Europe.
4.   Organization for Economic Cooperation and Development.

Copenhagen:
Toward the Security of Pluralism

THE CONSCIENCE OF THE CONTINENT

70. *from* "CSCE: The Conscience of the Continent," Speech by James A. Baker, US secretary of state. CSCE Conference on the Human Dimension, Copenhagen, June 6, 1990 (Washington, DC: US State Dept.).

We are present at the creation of a new age of Europe.

It is a time of discussion of new architectures, councils, committees, confederations and common houses.

These are, no doubt, weighty matters.

But all these deliberations of statesmen and diplomats, scholars and lawgivers, will amount to nothing if they forget a basic premise.

This premise is that "all men are created equal, that they are endowed by their Creator with certain inalienable rights, that among these are Life, Liberty and the pursuit of Happiness."

It is "to secure these rights [that] governments are instituted among them, deriving their just powers from the consent of the governed."

That is why we are here. . . .

As we leave the Cold War behind us, we confront again many age-old national, religious and ethnic conflicts that have so sorrowed our common civilization. CSCE, NATO, the EC and other democratic institutions of Europe must play a greater part in deepening and broadening European unity. We must ensure that these organizations continue to complement and reinforce one another. . . .

The prospects for the fulfillment and protection of human rights have never been greater. It is time for CSCE to take on additional responsibilities—but never at the price of forgetting its fundamental purposes: If CSCE is to help build a new Europe, a Europe different from all those empires and regimes that rose and fell, it must build from the liberty of Man.

Three challenges lie before us:

First, we must ensure that the freedoms so recently won are rooted in societies governed by the rule of law and the consent of the governed.

Second, we must ensure that all peoples of Europe may know the prosperity that comes with economic liberty and competitive markets.

And *third*, we must ensure that we are not drawn into either inadvertent conflict or a replay of the disputes that preceded the Cold War.

CSCE is the one forum where our nations can meet on common ground to channel our political will toward meeting these challenges for the entire continent. CSCE's three baskets are equally suited to today's political, economic and security challenges. Though it lacks military or economic power, CSCE can resonate with a powerful and irresistible voice. It can speak to Europe's collective concerns and interests. It can become, if you will, "the conscience of the continent". . . .

The new social compacts between government and governed now being written in Eastern and Central Europe must be constantly renewed through free elections. As we all know well, democracy—like CSCE—is a *process*. Democracy evolves through give-and-take, consensus-building, and compromise. It thrives on tolerance, where the political will of the majority does not nullify the fundamental rights of the minority.

The free elections proposal that the United Kingdom and the United States tabled last year in Paris[1] has gathered strength from the dramatic events of last fall and the new elections of this spring. In my travels to Eastern and Central Europe, democratic activists enthusiastically supported the proposal. . . .

But free and fair elections alone do not ensure that the new democracies will succeed. The irreducible condition of successful democracy, beyond legitimate elections, is clear: fundamental individual freedoms must be guaranteed by restraints on state power. Where these guarantees are absent, there is no *true* democracy. Indeed, where they are absent, the risk of dictatorship always looms. . . .

Therefore, we strongly support efforts at this meeting to set forth for CSCE the elements of a democratic society operating under the rule of law. In this regard, President Bush told President Gorbachev how highly we value Soviet efforts to institutionalize the rule of law, glasnost, and democratization in the USSR. . . .

I recently shared with colleagues six ideas on how we can work together to improve CSCE as a process by reinforcing CSCE's organization.

First, the United States favors regular consultations among the signatory states. Ministers may wish to meet at least once a year, and their senior officials should convene at least twice a year. Such exchanges will invigorate the CSCE as a forum for high-level political dialogue.

Second, we support the holding of CSCE review conferences on a more frequent basis, perhaps every two years, and with a fixed duration of about three months.

Third, to ensure that the political commitments we make in the CSCE strengthen political legitimacy, we seek adoption in Copenhagen and confirmation at the Summit of the principles of free and fair elections, political pluralism, and the rule of law.

Fourth, we seek confirmation at the Summit of the Bonn Principles of Economic Cooperation.[2] These principles make clear our mutual commitment to the supportive relationship between political and economic liberty. Specifically, 35 nations will endeavor to achieve or maintain the free flow of trade and capital, market economies with prices based on supply and demand, and protection for all property including private property and intellectual property.

Fifth, CSCE can play a major role in dispute management. We therefore hope that the CSCE Summit will reinforce the mandate of the January 1991 Valletta Conference on Peaceful Settlement of Disputes so that it can achieve concrete results. We also believe that CSCE can foster military openness and transparency through innovative proposals in the Vienna CSBM talks, for example, the proposal for a mechanism to request clarification of unusual military activities.

In particular, we believe that CSCE should consider a mechanism to improve communications among member states. Our approach might be similar in essence, if not in structure, to the mechanism we have established in the human dimension area[3] as well as to the one which we plan to establish for CFE. We should find a way of constructively addressing compliance questions with regard to CSCE security obligations. This might include observation and inspections reports in accordance with the Stockholm agreement.[4] We should provide for meetings to exchange information and to discuss the implications of military activities and other unusual occurrences having security implications.

Sixth, I proposed that we begin preparatory work for the possible CSCE Summit through a meeting of officials this summer—so I am, of course, pleased that the 35 nations now have agreed that our officials will meet next month in Vienna.

I am also pleased that the 35 have agreed to our offer to host a CSCE ministerial meeting this fall in connection with the UN General Assembly.[5]

Then, at the CSCE summit, we would expect to sign a CFE agreement,[6] and President Gorbachev last week indicated he shared this view. At the 35 nation Summit, we also would expect to review, record and consolidate progress in all three Helsinki baskets; to strengthen CSCE as a process; and, to plan ahead for the 1992 review conference.[7]

Our work, both before the Summit and during it, must also address the subject of institutionalizing CSCE.

Until now, CSCE has shown a remarkable ability to both reflect and change with the times. I am confident that it will continue to do so, provided we preserve the flexibility that has made it effective. As we consider proposals for CSCE's development—either for adoption at the Summit or for referral by the Summit leaders to other upcoming meetings of the CSCE—the United States will be guided by three key principles.

One, proposals should reinforce fundamental democratic and market values. *Two,* suggestions for new institutions should complement rather than duplicate roles assigned to existing institutions and fora. And *three,* proposals should result in a stronger trans-Atlantic process of dialogue and consultation regarding Europe's future.

NOTES
1. At the CSCE Conference on the Human Dimension.
2. See Document 69.
3. See Documents 18 and 46.
4. See Document 11.
5. See Document 90.
6. See Document 91.
7. See Document 98.

ALBANIA: THE OBSERVER WITH RESERVATIONS

71. *from* "Albania Wants Full Role in CSCE Process." Agence France-Presse report, Copenhagen, June 6, 1990. *Foreign Broadcast Information Service,* FBIS-EEU-90-111, June 8, 1990, p. 3.

Albania wants to join the East-West human rights, security and cooperation process after a short transition period. . . .

Emerging from decades of international isolation, the only European country not in the Conference on Security and Cooperation in Europe was for the first time granted observer status at the Conference on the Human Dimension. . . .

Albanian ambassador in Stockholm Petrit Bushati told journalists: "The aim is that we adopt all the rules of the conference and of course take care to accept what has been accepted by other participating countries."

But asked if Albania would allow opposition parties, Tirana's delegate Bejo Saza said there was no history of opposition and there was "no need to artificially create opposition."

"There has never been any request for political parties," he said. "This government has enjoyed full approval by the people."

Mr. Bushati denied that the 55,000-strong Greek minority in Albania suffered discrimination.

Eighty-five political prisoners were in Albanian jails, but they had sought to use "violence or force to overthrow or change the government." He said there was "no law against religion in Albania" and "no harassment."

"Albania has carried out many transformations in a short period of time," Mr. Bushati said.

PANDORA'S BOX OF MINORITY RIGHTS

72. *from* Roland Eggleston, "Debate on Minority Rights Divides Copenhagen Talks." Report by RFE/RL correspondent, Copenhagen, June 22, 1990. RFE/RL B-Wire, FF032.

The complex question of rights of national minorities became the most divisive issue at Copenhagen.

The conference had before it three proposals for a substantial

statement on the rights of minorities. The strongest was drawn up by
Hungary, Czechoslovakia, Yugoslavia, Austria and Italy. It provided
the source for most of the controversy.

THE FIVE-NATION PROPOSAL

73. *from* Roland Eggleston, "Five Nations Propose Code of Rights for
Minorities." Report by RFE/RL correspondent, Copenhagen, June 8,
1990. RFE/RL B-Wire, FF055.

Proposed rights:
1. National minorities have the right to be recognized as such by the
states in which they live and to exist as a community.

2. Persons belonging to a national minority have the right to
freely adhere to such a minority. No disadvantage may arise for them
on account of the exercise or non-exercise of the rights pertaining to
them as members of such a minority.

3. Persons belonging to national minorities have the right to fully
and effectively exercise their human rights and fundamental freedoms without discrimination of any kind.

4. National minorities have the right to freely express, preserve
and develop their ethnic, cultural, linguistic and religious identity.

5. National minorities and persons belonging to them have the
right to maintain and develop their culture in all its aspects, to profess and practice their religion—in particular to worship, have access
to, possess and use religious materials and carry out religious educational activities in their mother tongue.

6. Persons belonging to national minorities have the right to use
their mother tongue in private as well as in public life.

7. National minorities have the right to maintain their own educational, religious and cultural institutions. For this purpose they also
have the right to solicit voluntary financial and other contributions,
including public assistance.

8. Persons belonging to national minorities shall have access to
adequate types and levels of public education in their mother tongue.

9. Persons belonging to national minorities have the right to
establish organizations within the state in which they live as well as
international organizations for the protection of minority rights.

10. National minorities and persons belonging to them have the

right to establish and maintain unhindered contacts among themselves within their country, as well as across frontiers with citizens of other states with whom they share a common national origin or cultural heritage.

11. National minorities have the right to fully participate in decision-making about matters which affect the preservation and development of their identity and in the implementation of those decisions.

12. National minorities and persons belonging to them have the right to obtain, produce, possess, reproduce, distribute and exchange information in their mother tongue through all means of communication, regardless of frontiers.

Government action:

13. The participating States commit themselves to guarantee the protection as well as the possibility for the effective exercise of the rights of national minorities and persons belonging to them.

14. The participating States will take all the necessary legislative, administrative, judicial and other measures to create favorable conditions and enable such minorities to express their identity, to develop their education, culture, language, traditions and customs.

15. The participating States will take the necessary measures to eliminate prejudices and foster a climate of tolerance and mutual respect among persons belonging and persons *not* belonging to national minorities.

16. The participating States, in their cooperation, will take into account the rights, the legitimate interests and aspirations of the national minorities living in their territories.

17. The participating States, taking into account the specific territorial conditions of national minorities, consider that in addition to the rights mentioned above, such minorities should be given the right to an appropriate form of self-government on the territory in which they live.

18. The participating States will protect the national minorities, through legislative and other measures, against any activity, including propaganda, which in any forms justifies or promotes hatred and discrimination on the grounds of national origin, threatens the existence or identity of national minorities, has an adverse effect on the expression and development of that identity or prevents them in any other manner to enjoy and exercise their universal rights and fundamental freedoms.

In this context, they express their readiness to receive international observers to monitor population census in the territories where national minorities live.

19. None of these commitments may be interpreted as implying any right for any state, national minority or person belonging to such minority to engage in any activity or perform any act which would be contrary to the purposes and principles of the Charter of the United Nations as well as the principles set forth in the Helsinki Final Act.

In exercising their rights, national minorities and persons belonging to them will respect the universal human rights and fundamental freedoms of others.

20. The participating States agree to enhance the role of the mechanism of the human dimension of the CSCE in the context of safeguarding the rights of national minorities.[1]

They will also consider the possibility to set up an appropriate conciliation mechanism to facilitate the settlement of questions related to such minorities.

The participating States will further consider, with respect to the protection of national minorities, the experience and the results which could be obtained within the framework of the Council of Europe.

NOTE
1.   See Documents 18 and 46.

THE GATHERING STORM

74. *from* Roland Eggleston, "Autonomous Administrations for Minorities Suggested." Report by RFE/RL correspondent, Copenhagen, June 11, 1990. RFE/RL B-Wire, FF059.

A new proposal on national minorities presented by Canada, West Germany and the Netherlands suggested that the minorities be allowed autonomous administrations in some circumstances.

75. *from* Roland Eggleston, "Special Meeting Proposed to Discuss Minority Rights." Report by RFE/RL correspondent, Copenhagen, June 14, 1990. RFE/RL B-Wire, FF008.

Switzerland proposed that a special meeting be convened next year, possibly in Bern. The idea was supported by the United States, Canada and most European countries which provide a home for minorities, particularly Austria.

Switzerland made its proposal when it became clear that the problem was too large for solutions to be found in the remaining three weeks of the Copenhagen Conference.

Soviet Foreign Minister Eduard Shevardnadze described interethnic differences as a "gathering storm" when he spoke to the conference.

Turkey's Foreign Minister, Ali Bozer, told the conference he was "apprehensive about the awakening racism and xenophobia against immigrants and minorities in some quarters of Europe." He said no one wanted a "return to the chaotic Europe of pre–World War I which was marked by ethnic strife."

Minority rights already enshrined in many international documents, including the 1975 Helsinki Accords, deal with the *individual* rights of minorities. That covers the basic rights of individuals to use their mother tongue, maintain their minority culture, and practice their religion.

Now minorities and their champions are pressing for recognition of collective rights—in politics, education, culture and other fields. Demand for self-government was one of the goals of some ethnic Hungarians in Romania.

Another example of collective rights was the demand by some minorities for education in their mother tongue from kindergarten to university. This requires special schools, technical institutes and universities.

COLLECTIVE RIGHTS QUESTIONED

76. *from* Roland Eggleston, "Romania Criticizes Some Views on Minorities." Report by RFE/RL correspondent, Copenhagen, June 22, 1990. RFE/RL B-Wire, FF074.

On June 22 Romania told the conference that some concepts circulating around the meeting about minorities had nothing to do with human rights, with democracy or with international law.

Chief Romanian delegate Traian Chebeleu said:

"One of these concepts is the thesis that a state would have the right to protect the rights of minorities in other states with which it shares the same language, culture or ethnic origin."

"This is the 'mother tongue' thesis. Another version of it is that the motherland state would have the right to political representation of the minorities of the same ethnicity in other states.

"Still another version is that the government of the motherland state bears responsibility for the minorities of the same ethnicity wherever they may be. There is also a variant claiming that the problems of such minorities are internal problems of the motherland state. An additional one proclaims minorities in other states as integral parts of the people of the motherland state.

"I wonder how many 'motherland' states would claim the right to pressure the United States Congress and government in order to make sure that the rights and freedoms of the American citizen are guaranteed—taking account of the numerous countries whose citizens have left for America during the past two centuries.

"There is also the opposite situation. If we were to canonize the concept of the motherland state, would we not commit a grave injustice to those ethnic and national minorities in whose case there is no state which could assume the defense of their legitimate rights and freedoms? One example is the Roma.[1]

"There is no need for a demonstration to see the incompatibility of such theses with international law. Nor do they have anything in common with European values of democracy. In today's Europe there is no method to enjoy representation or political responsibility except through free elections. We know of no case of people in an independent country voting for leaders of another independent country.

"Another concept is the one arguing that minorities have collective rights. From the legal point of view this is nonsense.

"It is wrong to speak of minority rights or majority rights. Rights are best thought of as inherent in each human being, irrespective of what kind of ethnic, national, religious or cultural grouping he or she may belong to. At least, this is the spirit of the Universal Declaration of Human Rights which always speaks of the rights inherent in individual human beings and not of group or collective rights.

"The fact that certain rights, given their nature, are exercised collectively or jointly with other members of the group does not make them 'collective' rights. A case in point being the right to education in the mother tongue or the right to use the mother tongue.

"In order to acquire a right and exercise it, one has to have the legal capacity to assume the responsibility to do that. It is a practical impossibility for minorities as a whole to assume such a responsibility. It is not pure chance that minorities, as such, are recognized neither in international law nor in internal law as subjects or legal persons and, therefore, possess no legal capacity to acquire rights and obligations.

"Finally, I would like to say a few words about the concept of 'free adherence' to a national minority, which has been mentioned in some proposals here.

"In our mind, a person either belongs to a national minority or does not. The ethnic origin, the religious or cultural identity of every individual is the one freely stated by the individual concerned. I really cannot see how one person can 'adhere' or 'identify' with a minority to which he or she does not belong.

"One can think, of course, of possible interpretations and consequences of such language. If a person is free to adhere to a minority, it means that he or she is also free *not* to adhere to it.

"From what we have witnessed in the postwar period, that could mean a green light to policies of assimilation of minorities when persons belonging to such minorities have been compelled, through various means of intimidation and constraints, to identify themselves with or 'adhere' to a majority population.

"This is a purpose which should not be given legal and political foundation in CSCE documents."

NOTE
1. Also known as Gypsies.

RE-ENTER MACEDONIA

77. *from* Roland Eggleston, "Macedonian Problem Surfaces at Copenhagen Conference." Report by RFE/RL correspondent, Copenhagen, June 20, 1990. RFE/RL B-Wire, FF080.

The latest problem to surface at Copenhagen was the old dispute over what and where is Macedonia.

Basically it revolved around demands by Macedonian activists in Yugoslavia for Greece to recognize a Macedonian minority in northern Greece. The demands involved about 20,000 Greeks, most of them living in the border region.

Greece's response was that "Macedonia" today was a purely geographical term. It says that people living in the area concerned are ethnologically homogeneous and there is no minority.

Disputes over "Macedonia" have a long history in the region.

The background to the current dispute lies in an effort by Yugoslavia in the 1940s to create a Macedonian Republic. It was to include Macedonians in Yugoslavia and Greece and also the so-called Pirin Macedonians in Bulgaria. For several reasons, the plan never materialized. Yugoslavia was left with its own Macedonian Republic.

In Copenhagen there was a two-pronged attack. The official Yugoslav delegation raised the matter inside the conference. In addition, Yugoslav activists were bombarding diplomats from other delegations with pamphlets asking them to recognize the issue as a human rights problem.

Some of the activists lobbying delegates in the corridors of the conference were among the thousands of Greek children who left during the civil war in 1946–49 and were taken to Yugoslavia and other countries.

The Greek response was that there is no minority question in the region. Greek diplomats repeated this with growing irritation in Copenhagen. They have also found non-diplomatic activists to respond to the "white paper" with pamphlets of their own. Some of them charge the Yugoslav initiative was part of a campaign to revive the 1940s idea of a broader Macedonian Republic.

In addition the Greek delegation has called for a special meeting of experts on the minorities question. Unlike other proposals under consideration in Copenhagen, this has nothing to do with drawing up a code of minority rights. Greece said the meeting should define exactly what constitutes a "national minority."

This is a problem which has baffled experts in the United Nations for years. When reminded of this by reporters, a Greek diplomat commented: "Of course it could take years, but it is where we should begin."

78. *from* Roland Eggleston, "Bulgaria, Yugoslavia Clash over Macedonia." Report by RFE/RL correspondent, Copenhagen, June 22, 1990. RFE/RL B-Wire, CN127.

On June 22, Bulgaria and Yugoslavia clashed over the existence and treatment of ethnic minorities in the two countries.

Yugoslav delegate Vladislav Jovanović said more than 231,000 Macedonians live in Pirin Macedonia along Bulgaria's border with Yugoslavia. He said Bulgaria was grossly violating their human and national rights and denying their fundamental freedoms.

Bulgaria's chief delegate, Ivan Garvalov, replied that Yugoslavia had enough internal political problems of its own and should concern itself with those. He said Yugoslavia could be accused of violating all the human rights agreements he mentioned in regard to Bulgaria.

Garvalov repeated Bulgaria's assertion that it has no Macedonian minority. He said that there is a national consensus on that with all Bulgarian political parties and movements agreeing that "there has never been and is not now such a minority in Bulgaria."

The Bulgarian delegate said that there is in fact a Macedonian problem, but not the one raised by Yugoslavia.

He said: "We want to know about the fate and the rights and the freedoms of the 1,200,000 Bulgarians who are living in the Republic of Macedonia. What happened to these Bulgarians? Where are they? Why have they disappeared?"

Garvalov said: "The answer is that in the past 45 years the Bulgarian population in the Yugoslav Republic of Macedonia has been systematically assimilated and persecuted and its national consciousness has been methodically erased, including the use of the Bulgarian language. The language has been banned."

MIGRANT WORKERS AND GYPSIES

79. *from* **Roland Eggleston, "Yugoslavia, Turkey Seek Rights for Migrant Workers." Report by RFE/RL correspondent, Copenhagen, June 19, 1990. RFE/RL B-Wire, FF082.**

Yugoslavia and Turkey have told the Copenhagen conference it was time for a code of human rights for migrant workers in Europe.

The chief Yugoslav negotiator, Vladislav Jovanović, told the conference there are now more than 12 million migrant workers and their families in Europe.

But unlike national minorities and other large groups there is no general international agreement protecting their rights or ensuring equality in education and other spheres. There is only a variety of bilateral and multilateral agreements.

"It is time to introduce measures to improve the status and ensure the human rights and dignity of all migrant workers," he said.

Yugoslavia and Turkey want the human rights code to be modelled partly on agreements on national minorities which are already accepted in the Helsinki process. These cover educational, cultural, religious and language rights.

They believe that the code should also take up the agreements in the Helsinki process about family reunification for the benefit of other members of the family who wish to join the emigrant worker.

The Helsinki process previously considered the rights of migrant workers but Yugoslavia and Turkey consider the texts to be weak. As an example, they cite the document approved last year at the end of the Vienna Conference reviewing the Helsinki Accords.

One paragraph in it "invites" countries accepting migrant workers "to make efforts to improve the economic, social, cultural and other conditions of life for migrant workers and their families."

Another paragraph says the countries "affirm their readiness" to take measures to ensure equality of opportunity between the children of migrant workers and the children of their own nationals regarding access to all forms of education.

Yugoslavia and Turkey believe these and other statements should be upgraded to "commitments" by governments.

80. *from* Roland Eggleston, "Gypsies Seek Recognition as a Minority." Report by RFE/RL correspondent, Copenhagen, June 28, 1990. RFE/ RL B-Wire, FF051.

Europe's Gypsies took their cause to the Copenhagen conference.

An articulate Romanian Gypsy, Nacelle Gheorghe, said there that Gypsies—or "Roma" as they prefer to be known—are seeking the status of a "non-territorial minority."

According to their figures there are around a million Gypsies in Bulgaria, about 800,000 in Hungary and Czechoslovakia and more than a quarter of a million in the Soviet Union. There are more in Western Europe.

Gheorghe acknowledged that until now the term "Roma" has been unknown in international diplomacy. Minorities are usually known by their motherland—ethnic Hungarians, ethnic Turks and ethnic Germans are examples. But Gheorghe said "non-territorial minority" describes the Gypsy situation of being a minority of many countries but without a motherland.

The organization he represents, the International Roma Union, argues that Gypsies should be granted full minority rights regardless of the country in which they live. They want to be covered by the 1989 Vienna Document on human rights which obliges governments to protect the ethnic, cultural, linguistic and religious rights of national minorities on their territories.

Other paragraphs in the same document oblige governments to

ensure that minorities can maintain and develop their culture, including their language, and receive instruction in it.

Gheorghe and other Gypsy representatives presented their arguments to all the 35 delegations taking part in the Copenhagen conference. They said most are sympathetic but are wary of recognizing the Gypsies as a minority.

However they persuaded diplomats to accept a direct reference to Gypsies in the final document of the Copenhagen Conference. It occurs in a paragraph requiring governments to condemn racial and ethnic hatred, xenophobia and discrimination against anyone.

DOCUMENT DELAYED

81. *from* "Copenhagen." RFE/RL report, Copenhagen, June 28, 1990. RFE/RL A-Wire, CN0104.

Final agreement on the document of the Copenhagen conference was delayed because France, Greece, Bulgaria, Romania and some other countries had reservations about the chapter on national minorities. Agreement was reached after the chapter was revised.

82. *from* Roland Eggleston, "Bulgarian Statement on Human Rights." Report by RFE/RL correspondent, Copenhagen, June 28, 1990. RFE/RL B-Wire, CN0114.

Bulgaria's delegate, Ivan Garvalov, said: "The applicability of those provisions on minorities which are of a political rather than a humanitarian nature is exclusively the competence of each participating state, as it stems from the adopted document."

He said these were provisions related to organizations and associations, the use at hearings before public authorities of languages other than the official languages, local or autonomous arrangements, financial and other contributions and public assistance.

The Bulgarian delegate added: "While confirming its readiness to implement fully and effectively the agreed provisions on an equal footing with all participating states, Bulgaria declares that this shall not in any way prejudice the right of the freely and democratically elected parliament in Bulgaria to consider those provisions, and to determine the appropriate legal and other means for their implementation in accordance with the sovereign will of the Bulgarian people."

Bulgaria also made another comment which delegates said was aimed at countries which claimed they had no national minorities on their territory.

It said: "In the absence of any definition, the use of the term national minorities in the document as well as the provisions related to the rights of persons belonging to such minorities—whenever they exist—and covering other similarly identifiable groups cannot be construed *either* as exempting any participating state from compliance with the international standards on human rights and fundamental freedoms, *or* as contrary in any way to the relevant principles of sovereign equality, inviolability of frontiers and the territorial integrity of states."

83. *from* "Human Rights Conference Stumbles Over Minority Rights Issue." Reuters report, Copenhagen, June 27, 1990. RFE/RL B-Wire, FF144.

France, concerned about its Breton and Corsican speakers, objected to a draft declaration clause saying national minorities should be taught in their own language.

84. *from* Roland Eggleston, "Copenhagen Agreement Stresses Rule of Law, Free Elections." Report by RFE/RL correspondent, Copenhagen, June 28, 1990. RFE/RL B-Wire, FF114.

[France] felt [such clauses] could encourage demands by activists in Brittany.

Because of its objections several texts on national minorities were changed in the final version of the Copenhagen document. Among them was a paragraph about possible autonomy for certain national minorities.

The original version "welcomed" efforts toward local or autonomous administration as a means of promoting the identity of certain minorities. The new text drops the reference to "welcoming" these moves and describes local or autonomous administrations as only one of the possible means to protect the identity of minorities.

One of the authors of the document, the Austrian ambassador, Helmut Türk, told the conference the paragraph on autonomy was included because it represents the actual situation in certain European countries.

He added: "It is *not* meant to imply any commitment for any state to follow such a course of action." His comment was intended to reassure France, Greece and other countries opposed to autonomy demands, but was less welcome to Hungary which strongly supports the aspirations of the Hungarian minority in Transylvania.

In a later speech, Finland's delegate, Peter Stenlund, went out of his way to say that his country was satisfied with its experience in granting a large degree of self-government to those living in the Åland Islands and is preparing similar measures for the Sami people of Lapland.

But despite these changes, diplomats said the final Copenhagen text on national minorities is an advance on previous documents in the Helsinki process. It is the first time there has ever been any sort of reference to autonomous administrations or the use of mother tongue in dealing with public authorities. Some other texts also improve on previous references.

As Sweden told the conference, the discussions on national minorities are only the first step in trying to resolve the tensions generated by this issue.

BLUEPRINT FOR A DEMOCRATIC EUROPE

85. *from* Thomas Buergenthal, "The Copenhagen CSCE Meeting: A New Public Order for Europe," *Human Rights Law Journal* 11 (1990).

The Document of the Copenhagen Meeting (DCM) is divided into five chapters.[1] The first chapter deals with the rule of law and free elections. Certain other basic rights are proclaimed in Chapter II, which also considers measures designed to outlaw and prevent torture, capital punishment, alternative service for conscientious objectors to military service, and a whole range of other issues, including states of emergency. Chapter III deals with democratic values and institutions. The rights of national minorities are considered in Chapter IV. The final chapter amplifies the four-step human rights mechanism that the Vienna Concluding Document established. Annexed to the document is a so-called "Chairman's Statement," which deals with the access of non-governmental organizations and the media to the CSCE human dimension meetings.

The flavor and spirit of the Copenhagen meeting can be gauged by the language of the introductory or preambular part of the DCM. In it, the participating States "welcome with great satisfaction the fundamental political changes that have occurred in Europe" since the May-June 1989 Paris meeting. They also "recognize that pluralistic democracy and the rule of law are essential for ensuring respect for all human rights and fundamental freedoms, the development of human contacts and the resolution of other issues of a humanitarian character." Concepts such as "pluralistic democracy" and "the rule of law" had not been previously mentioned in CSCE documents. . . . True, these are merely words, but no such words would have been allowed into any CSCE document between 1975, when the Helsinki Final Act was signed, and June 1990, when the DCM was adopted.

A. The Rule of Law and Free Elections
What distinguishes this chapter of the DCM from earlier CSCE documents is the willingness of the participating States to move beyond the repetition of certain human rights guarantees found in all major international instruments on the subject. . . . What is new on the conceptual plane is the recognition by the participating States that their new Europe must be free, democratic and pluralistic, a Europe in which all government is subject to the rule of law. In short, this chapter commits the participating States to the establishment of a democratic *Rechtsstaat,* a democratic *état de droit.*

The commitment to the democratic *Rechtsstaat* finds expression in paragraph 3 of the DCM, where the participating States "reaffirm that democracy is an inherent element of the rule of law." To ensure that the rule of law does in fact apply to and control all state activity, . . . the DCM stipulates that "the activity of the government and the administration as well as that of the judiciary will be exercised in accordance with the system established by law." It provides for effective remedies to challenge administrative decisions, and it requires an independent and impartial judiciary. The participating States also commit themselves to "a clear separation between State and political parties, and to the principle that the military and the police must be under the control of and accountable to civil authorities. . . .

. . . Chapter I of the DCM also articulates some basic due process principles embracing rights designed to protect the individual against possible abuses by the justice system. These rights do have their counterparts in the International Covenant of Human Rights. Some of them also repeat, rephrase and amplify provisions found in the Vienna Concluding Document. This is true, for example, of the right to a fair hearing and the right to counsel. . . . One important due process provision that the DCM proclaims has no precise counterpart in the Covenant or the European Convention . . . : "No one will be charged with, tried for or convicted of any criminal offense unless the offense is provided for by a law which defines the elements of the offense with clarity and precision."

Chapter I also deals with elections, a topic not addressed by earlier CSCE documents. The overarching premise here is that "the will of the people, freely and fairly expressed through periodic and genuine elections, is the basis of the authority and legitimacy of all government." To translate this principle into specific commitments, the participating States undertake, *inter alia,* to "hold free elections at reasonable intervals," to "guarantee universal and equal suffrage to adult citizens," and to "respect the right of citizens to seek political or public office, individually or as representatives of political parties or organizations, without discrimination." They also commit themselves to "ensure that candidates who obtain the necessary number of votes required by law are duly installed in office." This chapter also contains a somewhat ambiguous provision designed to facilitate the presence of foreign or domestic election observers. . . .

B. Human Rights and Fundamental Freedoms

Chapter II of the DCM is a grab bag of provisions dealing with a variety of human rights matters. In part, the focus here is on substantive human rights rather than on the due process of law rights found in Chapter I. This list includes rights that are already guaranteed by international human rights treaties, such as freedom of expression, freedom of assembly and association, freedom of thought, conscience and religion, and the right of everyone to leave his country and return to it. Some of these provisions restate, albeit with greater precision, commitments relating to rights proclaimed in earlier CSCE documents. A number of DCM commitments are not, however, found in these earlier documents. The most significant among these is a provision dealing with the right to property. In this provision the participating States "reaffirm" that "everybody has the right to enjoy his property either on his own or in common with others". . . . the International Covenants on Human Rights contain no provision ensuring the right of property. Since the Soviet Union and its former allies strongly opposed the inclusion of the right-to-property guarantees in the Covenants, its adoption in Copenhagen is an important indicator of changed attitudes.

This chapter also contains provisions which seek to bridge the gap that frequently exists between the proclamation of rights and the existence of conditions or practices necessary to ensure the exercise of these rights. . . .

Chapter II also contains a number of important provisions concerning efforts to prohibit torture. It addresses other issues as well, including the death penalty, conscientious objections, efforts to promote the free movement of people, and the protection of rights of migrant workers. The chapter concludes with a carefully drawn provision designed to limit the powers of government to suspend human rights guarantees during a state of public emergency. . . . Here special emphasis is put on the requirements that "the imposition of a state of public emergency must be proclaimed officially, publicly, and in accordance with the provisions laid down by law" and that "measures derogating from (international law) obligations will be limited to the extent strictly required by the exigencies of the situation."

C. Democratic Values and Institutions

The basic premise of Chapter III is "that vigorous democracy depends on the existence as an integral part of national life of democratic values and practices as well as an extensive range of democratic institutions." To this end, the DCM encourages the participating States to cooperate for purposes of sharing ideas and expertise regarding constitutional reform, electoral legislation, the establishment and management of courts and legal systems, and a whole range of other issues that bear on the proper functioning of democratic societies.

An important provision in this chapter is paragraph 28, which relates to the role the Council of Europe might play in promoting democratic values and institutions within the CSCE framework. . . .

The Council of Europe has not only pioneered the most effective system for the international protection of human rights through the adoption, elaboration and implementation of the European Convention of Human Rights; it has also played a major role in the promotion of human rights and human rights education in Europe. Paragraph 28 of the DCM . . . suggests, albeit somewhat cautiously, a future role of the Council of Europe in advancing the human dimension objectives of the CSCE.[2]

This caution may be due to two factors. One has to do with the fact that the CSCE has yet to make a decision whether to establish its own institutional framework. If it does, it would presumably wish to assume some of these functions itself or in cooperation with other institutions. The second factor relates to the problem that the membership of the Council of Europe comprises thus far only Western European nations. While its membership will no doubt be augmented by the entry of various newly democratic Eastern European States, it is unlikely that the Soviet Union will become a member of the Council of Europe in the very near future. Moreover, since the US and Canada are extra-European States, their status as far as the Council of Europe is concerned presents its own set of complex problems. Thus far no one on either side of the Atlantic appears to have seriously analyzed the relevant options. Although none of these problems is insurmountable, it is clear that it will take time to resolve the question whether the Council of Europe should or can assume a special role within or in relation to the CSCE. . . .

D. *Minority Rights and Intolerance*

. . . the international law of human rights traces its origins to international efforts to protect the rights of minorities. . . . The post–World War I period saw the institutionalization of minority protection within the League of Nations. But the abuse by some minority groups of their status to advance irredentist interests between the two world wars and the efforts by a number of countries in Eastern Europe to rid themselves of their obligations under minorities treaties, regarded by them as unfairly imposed at the Versailles Conference, explain the absence of any references to minority rights in the Charter of the United Nations. Post–World War II human rights law, as reflected in the UN Charter and subsequent treaties, with minor exceptions, eschewed minority protection in favor of the principle of non-discrimination and the protection of individual rights. Over the years it has become increasingly apparent, however, that the Charter approach, while a significant advance, needed to be supplemented by some form of minority protection. Little progress was made in this regard until the Helsinki Final Act and the process it initiated began to address minority rights issues.

Principle VII of the "Declaration on Principles" of the Helsinki Final Act . . . recognizes that individuals belonging to national minorities have, in that character, "legitimate interests" that are entitled to protection. The Madrid Concluding Document strengthened this proposition by stressing "the importance of constant progress in ensuring the respect for and actual enjoyment of the rights of persons belonging to national minorities." The Vienna Concluding Document devotes two paragraphs to minority rights issues. The first requires the participating States to "exert sustained efforts to implement" the aforementioned provisions of the Helsinki Final Act and the Madrid Concluding Document. . . . The second provision amounts to a major departure from the earlier commitments. Here the participating States declare that "they will protect and create conditions for the promotion of the ethnic, cultural, linguistic and religious identity of national

minorities on their territory." This language constitutes the first explicit recognition within the CSCE of the principle that a national
minority, as distinct from individuals comprising the group, is entitled to protection and to the benefit of conditions promoting its
identity. . . .

By the time the Copenhagen Conference convened, serious civil
disturbances and armed clashes involving national minorities in some
Central Asian areas of the Soviet Union and in the Balkans attracted
worldwide attention. Ancient animosities and conflicts that many
thought had dissipated long ago reemerged with some of the fervor
of bygone days. . . . It is therefore not surprising that the DCM
devotes almost an entire chapter . . . to minority rights issues. Its
scope and content make this chapter the most far-reaching international statement on the subject to date.

There are a number of themes that characterize the DCM commitments concerning minorities. The first is that "to belong to a
national minority is a matter of a person's individual choice and no
disadvantage may arise from the exercise of such a choice." This
proposition is coupled with the principle of equal protection and
non-discrimination in the enjoyment of basic rights. The second theme
is that the participating States recognize that "the questions relating
to national minorities can only be satisfactorily resolved in a democratic political framework, based on the rule of law, with a functioning independent judiciary. . . ." The third proposition is that persons
belonging to national minorities "have the right to freely express,
preserve and develop their ethnic, cultural, linguistic and religious
identity and to maintain and develop their culture in all its aspects,
free of any attempts at assimilation against their will." The exercise
of this general right presupposes the recognition of a whole range of
specific rights. The list includes the right to use one's mother tongue
in public and to disseminate information in that language; the right
to establish special educational, cultural and religious institutions and
to conduct religious educational activities; the right to maintain contact with other members of one's minority group, inside the country
or abroad; and the right to work with international non-governmental organizations.

The fourth theme in the chapter dealing with minority rights
shifts the focus from specific rights of individuals who are members
of minority groups to measures designed to protect the minority
character of the group. . . . the participating States declare that they
"will protect the ethnic, cultural, linguistic, and religious identity of
national minorities on their territories and create conditions for the

promotion of that identity." Another, rather ambiguous and somewhat confused provision, suggests the possibility of establishing "appropriate local or autonomous administrations corresponding to the specific historical and territorial circumstances of such minorities and in accordance with the policies of the State concerned." Some of these propositions are balanced with restrictions and limitations designed to make clear that the protection of minority rights and of minorities as such must not result in discrimination against others. Moreover, no doubt motivated by concerns that the national minorities not be used as political pawns by governments in their international relations, as was so often the case in the past, the participating States emphasize "the particular importance of increasing constructive cooperation among themselves on questions relating to national minorities". . . .

One remaining section of Chapter III was influenced in large measure by the hate campaigns against certain minority groups, the outbreak of antisemitic acts of vandalism, and the racist violence that shocked Europe in the fall of 1989 and the spring of 1990. On this subject, the participating States wanted to be on record that they "clearly and unequivocally condemn totalitarianism, racial and ethnic hatred, antisemitism, xenophobia and discrimination against anyone as well as persecution on religious or ideological grounds". . . . Efforts at earlier CSCE conferences to condemn "antisemitism" by name failed in part because of Soviet opposition. In Copenhagen the USSR did not object to doing so. Another first was the willingness of the DCM to address the "problems" of the Romany people, although it did so only very much in passing. It is likely that future conferences will pay greater attention to this issue and to the discriminatory treatment encountered by migrant workers in certain CSCE States. . . .

E. Human Rights Mechanism
Chapter V of the DCM amplifies the human dimension mechanism which was established by the Vienna Concluding Document. . . .

F. Chairman's Statement
The third meeting of the conference on the Human Dimension of the CSCE is scheduled to be held, according to the timetable established by the Vienna Concluding Document, from September 10 to October 4, 1991, in Moscow. To ensure that NGOs[3] and the media have unimpeded access to the meeting, the Chairman's Statement, consistent with earlier precedents, lays down various rules bearing on "the practices of openness and access" for NGOs and the media. . . .

Conclusion

The Document of the Copenhagen Meeting reflects the geopolitical transformation of Europe in a dramatic way. The concept of a democratic, pluralistic society subject to the rule of law—a principle to which all participating States committed themselves in Copenhagen —makes for a very different Europe from the Europe that existed in 1975 when the Helsinki Final Act was adopted. Of course, no one is so naive as to believe that the acceptance of the concept of a democratic *Rechtsstaat* automatically transforms all 35 European nations into such States. Even if all of them had the very best intentions of complying with these commitments, which is something that remains to be demonstrated, it would still take years for some countries to accomplish this goal. It must be acknowledged, however, that the acceptance of the concept would not have been possible even a few years ago; its acceptance now must, consequently, by viewed as tremendous progress. The mere existence of the instrument is also very important in itself. There has always been a long and often arduous time gap between the adoption of those human rights instruments that became the great milestones on the road of human freedom and the day, if ever, when they are fully complied with. This has been true of the Magna Carta, of the French Declaration of the Rights of Man, of the American Declaration of Independence, and of the Universal Declaration of Human Rights.

The contents of the DCM, with its emphasis on the rule of law, on pluralism and free elections, and on the protection of minorities, make it a landmark international charter.[4] Unlike other contemporary human rights documents, such as the Universal Declaration, the Covenants or the European Convention, the DCM focuses on issues relating to the form and nature of government and the role of individuals and groups in society without, however, neglecting traditional human rights concerns. It is thus a document which, in its political scope and significance, is unmatched by other international human rights instruments. The fact that it is not a legally binding instrument but a political commitment does not really affect its long-term potential significance. After all, neither the Magna Carta, the American Declaration of Independence, the French Declaration of the Rights of Man nor the Universal Declaration were adopted as legally binding instruments. They became the historic milestones they are today because, over time, they captured mankind's imagination as eloquent expressions of universal hopes and aspirations about human rights and freedom. That aspect, not their legal character, explains their overriding political and moral impact and their influence.

Whether the DCM will acquire a similar status remains to be seen. What cannot be doubted, however, is that the DCM does contain a substantial body of significant commitments capable of setting a moral and political tone for the new European political order. That Europe would eschew totalitarianism, authoritarianism and any other form of political oppression. It would be a democratic Europe in which human rights would be respected and in which racial, ethnic, religious, national and cultural groups could live and work together in peace. Only time will tell whether all this is but one more utopian dream or the dawning of a new political era.

NOTES
1. For full text, see *Document of the Copenhagen Meeting of the Conference on Human Dimension of the CSCE, June 1990* (Washington, DC: Commission on Security and Cooperation in Europe, 1990).
2. See Document 96.
3. Nongovernmental organizations.
4. Author's note: One major European newspaper hailed its adoption as the promulgation of a "Constitution": "Die KSZE-Staaten geben sich ein Grundgesetz," *Süddeutsche Zeitung,* June 30–July 1, 1990.

The Road to the Summit

NO SUBSTITUTE FOR CFE

86. *from* Manfred Wörner [secretary general of NATO], "We Still Need a Conventional Forces Treaty," *The Washington Post,* March 6, 1990. RFE/RL B-Wire, FF034.

Recent commentaries on both sides of the Atlantic questioning the value of the conventional forces negotiations in Vienna bring to mind the wag's remark that arms control agreements become possible at the moment they are no longer needed. Indeed, some are suggesting that an agreement in Vienna will actually legitimize an unwanted Soviet troop presence in the countries of Central and Eastern Europe. This thinking is far from the mark. Indeed, the pace of East-West relations—and of political change in the East—has made the conventional forces agreement more rather than less necessary.

A CFE agreement is the basis for opening the way to a new European order, politically and militarily. The negotiating table in Vienna is where the interests of the NATO allies, the newly emerging democracies in Central and Eastern Europe and the Soviet Union come together in an effort to create a stable and secure situation in Europe, at much lower levels of forces.

We have welcomed Soviet unilateral reductions and will continue to do so. We welcome also the fact that the members of the Warsaw Pact, in an exercise of free self-determination, can decide whether they wish to have Soviet troops on their territory. Where they do not, the Soviets should leave; and we are gratified by the indication they are now going to do so. But this is not the basis for the durable peace we seek.

A CFE treaty has at least four major advantages. First, only by treaty can we establish the obligation that withdrawn equipment must be destroyed and troops must be demobilized. Under this treaty, we will obtain the destruction of nearly 40,000 Warsaw Pact tanks, enough to pack a highway from Paris to Bonn. More than an equal number of other items under negotiation—artillery, helicopters, personnel carriers, aircraft—must also be destroyed.

Second, only under the CFE treaty will such reduction be subject to rigorous verification. Indeed, the extensive verification regime created by the treaty will in and of itself be one of the most important achievements of the negotiations. In addition to verifying compliance, the regime will entail the periodic inspection of 6.5 million square kilometers from the Atlantic to the Urals. This will have a crucial deterrence and confidence-building effect, and prevent to a great degree any attempts to mask significant military activity.

Third, it is essential to keep in mind that only by a CFE treaty can we constrain Soviet forces inside the Soviet Union. Actions taken by the Warsaw Pact governments, and the withdrawals of forces under the now-accepted proposal by President Bush for a Soviet ceiling of 195,000 troops in Europe, will not affect the Soviet forces in the Western Military Districts, except as the Soviets themselves so decide.

And fourth, a CFE agreement will increase Soviet confidence that its legitimate security interests are being respected. The security situation in Europe will be a matter of contractual obligation rather than unilateral action subject to reversal. The framework we have established will also ensure—and this is often forgotten because of our tendency to focus on events in Central Europe—that the reduction of military forces in the central area does not result in accentuation of confrontation on the flanks of this alliance.

Finally, I can only describe as disingenuous the argument that, by negotiation we are conferring on the Soviet Union the right to maintain forces in Central and Eastern Europe which it otherwise would not have. The negotiations will establish ceilings, and it will be up to the participants in the negotiations, including basing countries, to decide how to implement the results. The real question for the Warsaw Pact is whether the Soviet Union is willing to respect the expressed desires of the other members. There is nothing in the treaty ceiling that will prevent a host nation's seeking withdrawal of forces stationed on its territory. And there is of course no requirement in the treaty or otherwise for countries involved to maintain forces at the ceiling that will be set. What the treaty *will* do is ensure that all parties are obligated not to return to the postwar imbalance of forces that threatened our security in Europe.

We have before us opportunities this year to change the face of East-West relations in a concrete and lasting way. I expect that we will have a summit of the Conference on Security and Cooperation in Europe this year that will look to the future, and that this epoch-making agreement will be signed there. I also expect that we will see a united Germany, and a redoubled effort by the members of the alliance to build the free, peaceful and undivided Europe we have sought for so long, in cooperation with our neighbors to the East. The CFE agreement is an essential cornerstone for this historic task.

TRANSFORMED NATO NURTURES CSCE

87. *from* "London Declaration on a Transformed North Atlantic Alliance," *NATO Review* 38, no.4 (August 1990).

The member states of the North Atlantic Treaty Alliance propose to the member states of the Warsaw Treaty Organization a joint declaration in which we solemnly state that we are no longer adversaries and reaffirm our intention to refrain from the threat or use of force against the territorial integrity or political independence of any state, or from acting in any other manner inconsistent with the purposes and principles of the United Nations Charter and with the CSCE Final Act. We invite all other CSCE member states to join us in this commitment to non-aggression.

In that spirit, and to reflect the changing political role of the alliance, we today invite President Gorbachev on behalf of the Soviet Union, and the representatives of the other Central and Eastern European countries . . . to establish regular diplomatic liaison with NATO. This will make it possible for us to share with them our thinking and deliberations in this historic period of change.

To reduce our military requirements, sound arms control agreements are essential. That is why we put the highest priority on completing this year the first treaty to reduce and limit conventional armed forces in Europe (CFE) along with the completion of a meaningful CSBM package. These talks should remain in continuous session until the work is done. Yet we hope to go further. We propose that, once a CFE treaty is signed, follow-on talks should begin with the same membership and mandate, with the goal of building on the current agreement with additional measures, including measures to limit manpower in Europe. With this goal in mind, a commitment will be given at the time of signature of the CFE treaty concerning the manpower levels of a unified Germany.

Our objective will be to conclude the negotiations on the follow-on to CFE and CSBMs as soon as possible and looking to the follow-up meeting of the CSCE to be held in Helsinki in 1992. We will seek through new conventional arms control negotiations, within the CSCE framework, further far-reaching measures in the 1990s to limit the offensive capability of conventional armed forces in Europe, so as to prevent any nation from maintaining disproportionate military power on the continent. NATO's High Level Task Force will formulate a detailed position for these follow-on conventional arms control talks. We will make provisions as needed for different regions to redress disparities and to ensure that no one's security is harmed at any stage. Furthermore, we will continue to explore broader arms control and confidence-building opportunities. This is an ambitious agenda, but it matches our goal: enduring peace in Europe. . . .

New negotiations between the United States and the Soviet Union on the reduction of short-range nuclear forces should begin shortly after a CFE agreement is signed. The Allies concerned will develop an arms control framework for these negotiations which takes into account our requirements for far fewer nuclear weapons, and the diminished need for sub-strategic nuclear systems of the shortest range.

Finally, with the total withdrawal of Soviet stationed forces and the implementation of the CFE agreement, the Allies concerned can reduce their reliance on nuclear weapons. These will continue to fulfill an essential role in the overall strategy of the Alliance to prevent war by ensuring that there is no circumstance in which nuclear retaliation in response to military action might be discounted. However, in the transformed Europe, they will be able to adopt a new NATO strategy making nuclear forces truly weapons of last resort. . . .

The Conference on Security and Cooperation in Europe (CSCE) should become more prominent in Europe's future, bringing together the countries of Europe and North America. We support a CSCE Summit later this year in Paris which would include the signature of the CFE agreement and would set new standards for the establishment, and preservation, of free societies. It should endorse, *inter alia:*

- CSCE principles on the right to free and fair elections;

- CSCE commitments to respect and uphold the rule of law;

- CSCE guidelines for enhancing economic cooperation, based on the development of free and competitive market economies; and

- CSCE cooperation on environmental protection.

We further propose that the CSCE Summit in Paris decide how the CSCE can be institutionalized to provide a forum for wider political dialogue in a more united Europe. We recommend that the CSCE governments establish:

- A program for regular consultations among member governments at the Heads of State and Government or Ministerial level, at least once each year, with other periodic meetings of officials to prepare for and follow up on these consultations;

- A schedule of CSCE review conferences once every two years to assess progress toward a Europe whole and free;

- A small CSCE secretariat to coordinate these meetings and conferences;

- A CSCE mechanism to monitor elections in all the CSCE countries, on the basis of the Copenhagen Document; [1]

- A CSCE Center for the Prevention of Conflict that might serve as a forum for exchanges of military information, discussion of unusual military activities, and the conciliation of disputes involving CSCE members states; and

- A CSCE parliamentary body, the Assembly of Europe, to be based on the existing parliamentary assembly of the Council of Europe, in Strasbourg, and include representatives of all CSCE member states.

The sites of these institutions should reflect the fact that the newly democratic countries of Central and Eastern Europe form part of the political structures of the new Europe.

NOTE
1. See Document 85.

CSCE BEYOND THE MEDITERRANEAN?

88. *from* Giuseppe Jacoangeli, "La Riunione della CSCE sul Mediterraneo e le Prospettive di Cooperazione fra i Paesi della Regione," *Lettera Diplomatica* (Circolo di Studi Diplomatici, Rome) 22, no. 631 (November 12, 1990). Translated from Italian by Luigi Giovine and Roger Malone.

Ever since the first days of the application of the Helsinki Accords, which gave birth to the CSCE, it was agreed that the conference should not limit itself to the promotion of East-West relations, but rather extend its attention to the strengthening of dialogue among all countries of the Mediterranean area, including those of the southern belt of the region that did not participate in the CSCE. This was not only in consideration of the fact that about one-third of the signatories of the Helsinki Accords are Mediterranean countries, but also because the often complex events of this area have ended up having decisive effects on Europe.

Italy has always upheld the need for strengthening, on a unilateral basis, the inter-Mediterranean dialogue, which was by the way also favored by France, by Spain and by other countries of Mediterranean Europe, in the conviction that an important contribution to the political stability of the region can only be provided through a renewal, on a new basis, of the cooperation between European countries and the countries of the southern belt.

If this view of the problem was valid during the past years, when the two meetings in Valletta and Venice took place, it has become even more valid after the political events in Eastern Europe, which in a short time have led to intensified relations between Western Europe and the new East European democracies, thereby stimulating in particular the interests of our entrepreneurs for those markets in transition from centralized to market economies.

Such evolution has given rise to considerable apprehension in all Third World countries, including those in the southern zone of the Mediterranean region, because of the fear that the flux of public funds for development and the flux of private investment—up to then directed to them—would ultimately be diverted, at least in part, toward Eastern Europe.

From this, the need has risen for the CSCE to send a signal of solidarity and availability to the countries of the southern and eastern Mediterranean, confirming its willingness not only to preserve, but also to intensify relations among the countries of the region in the various fields of economics, culture, ecology, technology, and the transfer of technologies.

At the meetings of Valletta and Venice, only Israel and Egypt were present, whereas at Palma the invitation was accepted formally by all, with the sole exception of Lebanon: This although some of the countries invited only made brief appearances, like Libya and Syria, and others, like Algeria and Egypt, were only present during the initial and final phase of the proceedings. Nevertheless, the other delegations present, in particular those of Tunisia and Morocco, followed the deliberations most assiduously, making a relevant contribution to its conclusion.[1]

Still, from the beginning of the Conference, the hesitation of other Western countries to participate and undertake the path to an increased effort in the Mediterranean region was evident, especially in relation to making more financial resources available, and this preoccupation has dominated all the deliberations surrounding the formulation of a concluding document, in which many delegations insisted on avoiding all mention of the opportunity of increasing the efforts intended to favor certain forms of cooperation.

Undoubtedly, the present international political juncture has considerably influenced the attitude of some of the delegations during the deliberations. In the first place, the Gulf crisis, with its many political and economic implications, then the bloody clashes in Beirut and Jerusalem—which took place precisely during those days—accentuated the tendency of a group of countries not to raise the profile of the conference, mainly in order to prevent it from becoming a forum for a political debate of unpredictable consequences.

It is certainly inevitable that in the conception of a policy for the Mediterranean, there be in the realm of the CSCE a difference in view between the coastal countries and the others. The persistence of unsolved problems, such as that of the Palestinians, of Lebanon, of Cyprus, and of the Gulf crisis itself, certainly does not favor the creation of better conditions toward launching a constructive debate on the future prospects of the Mediterranean among all interested parties.

The foreign ministries of Italy and Spain, at the opening of the meeting in Palma de Mallorca, proposed to initiate as soon as possible a Conference for Security and Cooperation in the Mediterranean, which should be inspired by the very principles of the CSCE and operate as a catalyst between the factors involved in integration and as an identifier and multiplier of the factors involved in stabilization.

Drawing from the positive experience of the CSCE, the Conference for the Mediterranean should operate along the same lines of security, economic cooperation, cultural cooperation and in the field of the human dimension, with the fundamental objective of insuring a picture of political stability and of better living conditions for the populations of the region.

In the meantime, also in order to create an initial embryo of cooperation among Mediterranean countries, Italy has taken the initiative to gather the first group of states, formed by France, Italy, Portugal, and Spain for the northern region, and by the five member states of the Union of Arabic Maghreb, with the objective of strengthening, through various forms of intervention, the ties of interdependence, which already exist among them, and of accumulating experiences which, in the future, will serve expanded cooperation with the rest of the Mediterranean basin.

NOTE

1. For the official summation of the Palma de Mallorca meeting, see *Document of the Meeting on the Mediterranean of the Conference on Security and Cooperation in Europe, October 1990* (Washington, DC: Commission on Security and Cooperation in Europe, 1990).

HELPFUL TO GERMAN UNIFICATION

89. *from* Tom Heneghan, "Instead of Sealing German Spilt, CSCE Helped to Overcome It." Report by Reuters correspondent, Bonn, November 15, 1990. RFE/RL B-Wire, FF097.

Originally a Soviet plan to cement the continent's division, the CSCE played such a key role in uniting Germany that Bonn has become one of its firmest backers.

Helmut Schmidt and Erich Honecker, leaders of the two Germanys then split by walls and barbed wire, first met over a cup of coffee at the 1975 European Security Conference in Helsinki.

Bonn, bound by its constitution to reunite the German people, had patiently tested any peaceful way it could find to change the postwar stalemate in Europe.

"If there hadn't been a CSCE, we would have had to invent it now," quips Hans-Dietrich Genscher, the Bonn foreign minister present at the creation and now set to celebrate the CSCE's 15th anniversary at its summit in Paris.

"The task was to create a basis for change in Europe," he told a radio interviewer recently. "Our expectations have been fulfilled; we are now living in a fundamentally changed Europe."

East Germany was all but sealed off in 1975. Only 16,000 people were allowed to emigrate to the West that year—a total passed in a week during the mass exodus early this year.

The collapse of communism in the East also toppled many of the hurdles in the way of trade and investment, two key concerns for Germany's powerful economy, although the region's economic crisis and lingering bureaucracy have made it less attractive than it looked when the Final Act was signed.

Genscher, who was born in the East of the country, says he

always believed Germany would one day be reunited. But he adds: "Nobody can claim to have had a schedule in his head."

Coming on the heels of former-Chancellor Willy Brandt's *Ostpolitik*, some of Bonn's NATO allies viewed the opening to the East with suspicion and the CSCE became for West Germany a way to work for change without upsetting its neighbors.

It also drew a blueprint for remodelling NATO and the Warsaw Pact in a way that the Soviet Union could accept.

"The CSCE turned out to be especially useful in smoothing the path for the Soviet Union to accept German unity," the weekly *Die Zeit* said.

"As unification turned out to be inevitable, Bonn and other capitals thought up new CSCE institutions to help the Soviet Union accept German unity without losing face."

Never shy about testing out new ideas, Genscher thought aloud about CSCE bodies to promote pan-European cooperation in everything from environmental protection to high technology.

Genscher has spoken so glowingly of the "CSCE process" that he occasionally has to point out that Bonn does not see it as the successor to the NATO and Warsaw Pact alliances.

"NATO will have a role within these more cooperative structures in Europe, but not become superfluous," he said last week. "It will continue as part of these structures."

UNHELPFUL TO BALTIC INDEPENDENCE

90. *from* Sonia Winter, "Baltic States Press for Rights in Baker, Helsinki Meetings." Report by RFE/RL correspondent, New York, October 3, 1990. RFE/RL B-Wire, FF064.

The Baltic question received unexpected attention at yesterday's close of a two-day Helsinki Conference of the 35 foreign ministers in New York.

As soon as the concluding ceremony ended, US Secretary of State James Baker hurried to an unscheduled meeting with the three Baltic foreign ministers—Lennart Meri of Estonia, Janis Jurkans of Latvia, and Algirdas Saudargas of Lithuania.

Their talks lasted nearly an hour, producing clear assurances of US support for the Baltic states but little promise of satisfying their requests for broadened international recognition.

The ministers came to New York to renew a request for observer status in the CSCE. The first Baltic application, at a Helsinki meeting in Copenhagen in June, was blocked by Soviet opposition.

A US State Department official says informal polling of the views of the other Helsinki members showed the Soviet Union was the only one to object in Copenhagen. Under CSCE rules of decision by consensus, that was enough to sink the request. The Soviet Union apparently has not softened its position since.

Baker told reporters that the US has "advocated observer status for the Baltic nations as a first step toward full membership"—but without success. "Consensus has not been obtained through this conference," he says, adding that "as things now stand, it is not likely that there will be a consensus at the Paris conference." [1]

The three Baltic presidents sent a statement to the New York meeting asking that the Baltic question be included on the agenda of the CSCE summit to be held in Paris next month. The statement said that it is the sovereign will of the peoples of the Baltic states to regain their independence and to return as "legal and equal members of the community of world and European nations."

At a joint news conference earlier, the Baltic foreign ministers said there is growing support for their aspirations among the Helsinki members. The ministers were able to attend the New York sessions as guests of the Scandinavian delegations.

Statements by the Nordic Helsinki members over the past two days suggest they may have decided a public campaign is more effective than quiet diplomacy in advancing the Baltic cause.

Swedish Foreign Minister Sten Andersson says Baltic representatives ought to be able to communicate as much as possible with the rest of the world. "We would welcome a Baltic information office in Stockholm," he said, noting that Sweden has already established consular branch offices in Estonia and Latvia.

Foreign Minister Uffe Ellemann-Jensen says Denmark would very much like to welcome the Baltic states as observers, and is "convinced that they already fulfill the conditions for full membership."

Iceland's foreign minister, Jón Baldvin Hannibalsson, says his government has pledged "unreserved support for membership of the Baltic states in the CSCE." He says Iceland also wants to expand contacts and cooperations with the Baltic republics.

Norwegian Foreign Minister Kjell Magne Bondevik says his country regards Estonia, Latvia and Lithuania as qualified to fully participate in CSCE proceedings. "They should now be allowed to attend CSCE meetings as observers," he said, adding that "Norway regrets the Baltic problem remains unsolved."

Poland's Foreign Minister, Krzysztof Skubiszewski, also spoke up for the Baltics, declaring that his country will support any arrangements "whereby these old European peoples [would] be associated with the Helsinki process."

NOTE
1.   The November 1990 CSCE Summit; see Document 98.

CONVENTIONAL ARMS AGREEMENTS REACHED

91. *from* Colin McIntyre, " 'Swords-to-Plowshares' Accord Set to be Signed in Paris." Report by Reuters correspondent, Vienna, November 14, 1990. RFE/RL B-Wire, FF056.

After 21 months of talks, the 16 members of NATO and the six remaining states of the Warsaw Pact [signed] a treaty in Paris drastically slashing their conventional weapons arsenals.[1]

The treaty will limit each alliance to 20,000 tanks, 30,000 armored cars, 20,000 artillery pieces and 6,800 combat aircraft, spread between four European zones. Just to meet the new tank limit, Moscow will have to take 19,000 out of service.

More than any other international negotiations the Conventional Forces in Europe (CFE) talks have been transformed by the dramatic changes in Eastern Europe last year.

"One of the main Western objectives at the start of the talks was to squeeze Soviet forces out of Eastern Europe," a senior Western diplomat said. "The changes in the region have done that for us."

Under growing pressure from countries rushing to embrace democracy after throwing over their communist governments, the Soviet Union was forced to start pulling out troops and tanks from its former allies even before the talks were concluded.

"In many ways, this is the first arms treaty in history to be implemented before it is signed," another Western envoy remarked.

The 200-page treaty will be signed during next week's CSCE summit in Paris.

To avoid getting bogged down in troop figures, participants agreed to focus instead on weapons that can be used to seize and hold another country's territory in a surprise attack.

The two sides did address the question of troops stationed abroad when Moscow and Washington agreed [in May 1989] to limit their contingents in Central Europe to 195,000 each.

But even this greatly reduced figure soon became irrelevant as the Soviet Union stepped up its disengagement from the region.

The wider personnel issue raised its head only in relation to the German question, after Moscow threatened to block a CFE treaty unless there were specific limits on the size of united Germany's armed forces.

The two Germanys pledged to cut their combined armed forces to 370,000 within three or four years. To avoid the impression that Germany is being singled out, the other participants [committed] themselves not to increase their forces, and to start talks on reducing them in further CFE talks.

These talks, to start a week after the Paris summit, are expected to concentrate on personnel and specific issues such as aerial inspection rights.

With arms limitations now less of a burning issue than before, many delegates see the main focus of the treaty shifting to topics such as information exchange and verification.

Under the treaty signatory countries will for the first time have to provide detailed information on the size and location of their military forces, and to notify others of any changes.

The treaty permits hundreds of inspections of military installations on both sides during the 40-month period during which the cuts must be completed. There will also be regular inspections once the ceilings have been achieved.

NOTE

1. For full text of the treaty, see *Treaty on Conventional Armed Forces in Europe, Paris, November 19, 1990* (Washington, DC: US Information Agency, 1990).

92. from "CSCE Countries Adopt Document on Security-Building Measures." Agence France-Presse report, Vienna, November 18, 1990. RFE/RL B-Wire, FF002.

The 34 member countries of the CSCE adopted an accord on security-building measures, clearing the way for its signature by the 34 CSCE leaders at their summit in Paris.

The document, negotiated by the Conference on Security-Building Measures (CSBM), provides for new and concrete measures to increase sharing of military information with the aim of reducing the risks of an accidental outbreak of war.

The accord comes two days after the approval of the Conventional Forces in Europe (CFE) Treaty, providing for sharp cuts in NATO and Warsaw Pact forces.

The 50-page CSBM document, the result of 20 months of negotiation, ran into last minute difficulties over questions of exchange.

The accord provides for exchange of information, the creation of a communications network and the establishment of a consultation and cooperation mechanism to handle questions of "unusual military activity."

A center for conflict prevention is to be established in Vienna immediately after the Paris summit, and will serve as a headquarters for the functioning of the consultation and verification processes provided for under the agreement.

The document also provides for contacts between military leaders and visits to air bases, which had previously been off-limits.

Both the CSBM and CFE negotiations are to start up again on November 26 in Vienna, and are scheduled to merge into a single negotiations process after the 1992 CSCE summit in Helsinki.

Part V

Clouds
Over
the
New
CSCE,
1990–1991

The Different Kinds of Challenges

DON'T BUILD TOO MUCH ON IT

93. *from* "A CSCE Club For All Europe," *The Economist,* November 17, 1990.

The Paris summit will mark the changes that a year ago brought down the Berlin Wall and toppled communist regimes all over Eastern Europe. The 34 leaders will give their blessing to German unity. They will look on as Europe's two opposing alliances, NATO and the Warsaw Pact, sign an arms-cutting treaty that will rid Europe of many weapons that have helped keep the peace since 1945. But dismantling the old order is one thing, building a durable new one is another.

The temptation, as the champagne corks pop, will be to think big and go for the Grand Design that has eluded Europe all century. Better to let those of Europe's institutions that have proved their worth build on what they do best.

The base on which the Grand Designers want to build is the 34-nation Conference on Security and Cooperation in Europe (CSCE). What started in 1975 as a round of cautious contacts between East and West on human rights, trade and military matters is to be "institutionalized." That means more summits, a secretariat (a modest one, but multiply whatever number you think of by 34), a "conflict-prevention center" and a parliamentary wing, the Assembly of Europe. And why stop there? Grand Designers talk of a Confederation of Europe, of European peacekeeping forces and of an all-Europe security system to replace NATO and the Warsaw Pact.

In grimmer days before the Wall came down, the CSCE kept moral pressure on the communist regimes to treat their people better. It did a bit for economic contacts. It has produced bright ideas for preventing armies from alarming each other into war. It can do more: check that nobody is cheating on the new arms-cutting agreement, write stiffer words about human rights and democracy into its declarations, be a forum for officials from Vancouver to Vladivostok to swap all sorts of ideas over cocktails and canapés. But it cannot be the foundation stone of a new Europe.

The fatal weakness of the CSCE is what its boosters see as its main strength: it is a regional club that everybody can join. Nobody can be thrown out; everybody has a veto. Like other regional clubs, it works at the pace of the slowest. Superimpose the plans for the CSCE on to Europe's existing institutions and its flaws are apparent.

The real standard-setter for human rights is the Council of Europe. Countries have to qualify for membership by taking on binding commitments, not just by making pious declarations (Hungary is in, Poland and Czechoslovakia soon will be). If they backslide, they can be thrown out (Greece in 1969, Turkey all but in 1981). What a pity, then, if there has to be an Assembly of Europe, that it is to be grafted on to the council's parliament. Today's non-qualifiers and tomorrow's backsliders will all have a seat. Even if the council keeps up its high standards, there will be less incentive to meet them.

Nor can the CSCE wipe out the poverty line that still divides East from West. The economic hub that the Hungarians, Czechs and others desperately want to attach themselves to is the European Community. They are not much interested in declarations about all-European cooperation, or even a little local cooperation with their neighbors in the east. Meanwhile, there are plenty of other institutions to join, from the IMF[1] to the new European development bank.

When it comes to talking about security, the CSCE includes the two big powers, America and the Soviet Union, that are bound to have a large say in Europe's future. But high-flown ideas about an all-European security system only expose the CSCE's greatest flaw. Collective security does not work: if everybody is allied to everybody else, nobody is allied to anybody. With 34 votes, on a continent that for all the recent Europhoria is still riven with political, economic, ethnic and military tensions, such a system is a blueprint for collective insecurity, if not disaster. Which is why there will still be a need in the West for an organization—call it NATO or something else, change its political profile and its military structure where need be, maybe add new members eventually—of collective self-defense. When it comes to real security, common values are the surest foundation.

That still leaves the CSCE with plenty of room to do what it does best: building confidence in arms control, cheerleading for democratic politics and open markets, prodding offenders over human rights. The hope will always be that the political and economic values that have been shown to work in Western Europe and America will eventually take root in every part of Europe. Just don't build too much on it.

NOTE

1. International Monetary Fund.

THE MIGRATION PROBLEM GONE FULL CIRCLE

94. *from* **Annika Savill, "The Russians Are Coming, But We Won't Talk About It,"** *The Independent* **[London], November 15, 1990.**

The curious aspect about this [CSCE] summit is what there won't be: discussion of a concern that is likely to grow more urgent than most others in the post–Cold War era—Soviet migration.

Throughout the CSCE process, the West attacked Moscow for its non-exit policy. Now, even as East and West meet in Paris, new Soviet legislation facilitating both entry and exit is at the committee stage of parliament; the law is expected to be passed in January [1991]. And what will happen then? In the midst of growing political and economic chaos, some Soviet officials have predicted an exodus westward of some three million within a year. One thing is clear: the Russians are coming, if in numbers as yet unknown.

Finland, the neighboring country potentially at the receiving end of this, is already tightening its borders against illegal crossings. Sweden might do its bit by housing 300,000 Russians on the island of Gotland (which aptly enough is noted among Swedes for one curiosity—its area is calculated to be exactly large enough to provide standing room for the population of the world). The serious scenario is a mass exodus to Czechoslovakia, Hungary and above all Poland—where the economy is crippled already and where, incidentally, unemployment is expected to double between June and December this year [1990]. As one Polish official said: "We are so used to people wanting to flee the country, we have no mechanism in place for trying to keep people out."

Somebody will have to help the Poles share the burden; the Soviet Union will not want to take back the people it has finally let out; Germany, although already committed to accommodate two million ethnic Germans from the Soviet Union, and although it conceivably has the border controls to keep others out, will be obliged eventually to take in large numbers as an emergency measure; the chain of mass movement westward will have begun.

There is, as the international community knows full well, a lamentable lack, if not total absence, of international bodies to deal with this sort of problem; the office of the United Nations High Commissioner for Refugees is there for what its name implied, political refugees, and although its mandate has been updated to take in refugees from, say famine, it by no means includes economic migrants.

Since a burden-sharing plan is needed with some urgency, and since the CSCE was the pressure body for Moscow to let people out in the first place, [the Paris] summit would have seemed a logical forum as a start. It emerges, however, that no Western country wants to bind itself by dealing with the matter in a high-profile multilateral context where talk of quotas would eventually come up. "At this stage, we would rather the discussions were kept to a bilateral level," said one Western diplomat. Some West European officials have even taken the line that the Soviet Union is deliberately exaggerating estimates of a future exodus to frighten the West into providing more aid and investment so that the Russians can be employed at home. (Compare the approach of the southern EC countries to North Africa, where Italy, France, Spain and Portugal are using aid as a trade-off to stem huge immigration.) So, the Soviet migration issue is being delegated to a January [1991] meeting of the Council of Europe—less effective—and deferred to another CSCE meeting at a lower level in Moscow [in 1991]—too late.

Those with foresight raised the question years ago: if the Soviet Union yielded to Western demands to let people out, would the West do its bit and let them in? Now, said one migration expert, "the West is in an impossible political and moral dilemma: is it going to admit to the Russians that it has effectively been lying all these years?"

RESURGING CONFLICTS OF BYGONE DAYS

95. *from* Alan Riding, "Eastern Leaders Warn Against New Socioeconomic Division." *New York Times* report, Paris, November 21, 1990. RFE/RL B-Wire, FF005.

Dampening the euphoria surrounding the 34-nation summit meeting called to celebrate the end of the Cold War, Eastern European leaders warned of the threat to stability if the ideological separation of Europe is replaced by an economic and social divide.

Prime Minister Tadeusz Mazowiecki of Poland was among those expressing such concerns.

"Our common future may be darkened by the sinister clouds of the resurging conflicts of bygone days," he told the leaders attending the meeting, "unless the split into a rich and a poor Europe, an 'A' class and a 'B' class Europe, is overcome."

While announcing plans to seek formal dissolution of the six-nation Warsaw Pact, Hungary's prime minister, József Antall, cautioned Western European leaders that "a new welfare wall may arise in place of the Iron Curtain, which has now been removed."

The former Eastern bloc's economic plight cast a dark shadow across the second day of the three-day conference, and leader after leader also spoke somberly of the related dangers of ethnic, nationalist and border disputes in the region.

With the Soviet president, Mikhail Gorbachev, sitting beside him, President Borislav Jović of Yugoslavia, a country already being torn apart by nationalist strife, recalled "that in situations of political and economic instability and national bigotry, democracy falls as the first victim."

Antall made no reference to Hungary's own problem of minorities, but he also recognized that "despite the changes that have taken place in the direction of democracy, we now see ethnic or nationality problems emerging in Europe, sometimes with greater intensity than in the past."

Outside the glittering wall of the Kléber International Conference Center near the Arc de Triomphe, the mood was no more cheerful as talk of a war in the Persian Gulf continued to dominate the private conversations of President Bush, Gorbachev and other European leaders.

The West German chancellor, Helmut Kohl, who has taken the lead in organizing food and other aid for the Soviet Union, said breakthroughs of the past year in human and minority rights "must not be undermined by new discord between neighbors or nationalities."

"Following the opening of national borders," he went on, turning to economic needs of the East, "there must be no borders which perpetuate the prosperity divide. The ideological gulfs that have been overcome must not be torn open again by social gaps."

Recalling Germany's own "moral and political responsibility" for Europe's convulsed history this century, Kohl pledged that "peace alone will emanate from German soil" and he promised to continue supporting the process of economic, political and social change in Eastern Europe.

Other territorial disputes were also raised, with Spain's prime minister, Felipe González, noting that, in the case of the British enclave of Gibraltar in southern Spain, "one European country still has a colony inside the territory of another European country."

President George Vassiliou of Cyprus, which is partially occupied by Turkish forces, said his was "the only European country facing occupation by a foreign army with its citizens denied the exercise of their fundamental freedoms."

COUNCIL OF EUROPE BIDS FOR A ROLE

96. *from* Joel Blocker, "Council of Europe Asks for Major Role in Future CSCE Process." Report by RFE/RL correspondent, Paris, November 20, 1990. RFE/RL B-Wire, FF136.

The Council of Europe, which is rapidly opening its doors to reforming Central and East European countries, made a bold offer to play a major role in the implementation of the Helsinki process and suggested that its parliamentary assembly could become the "basis" for a future pan-European parliament.

Council General Secretary Catherine Lalumière told the Paris summit meeting of the Conference on Security and Cooperation in Europe that the Strasbourg-based organization was rapidly becoming an important organ for "pan-European cooperation."

She recalled that two weeks ago Hungary had become the council's 24th member state and said two other Central European nations, Poland and Czechoslovakia, were likely to gain full membership in 1991. In addition, she noted, five East European countries—the Soviet Union, Bulgaria and Yugoslavia as well as Poland and Czechoslovakia—now had guest status in the council's parliamentary assembly, which enables them to participate in debates without a vote.

In regard to human rights, Mrs. Lalumière said that the CSCE now had to move beyond general principles "and do everything possible to implement them. The Council of Europe can make a contribution to this end," she added, citing its possession of what she called "perfected instruments," such as the European Convention of Human Rights and its implementation mechanism, the European Human-Rights Court. The court, in particular, provides collective safeguards for ensuring respect for human rights in legislation and practice of contracting states, she said.

The 35-year-old European Human-Rights Court in fact allows individual citizens to protest human-rights violations over the heads of their governments, which are pledged to respect the court's decisions. All Council of Europe members must sign the human-rights convention and obey its stipulations.

The council's desire to become what Lalumière called "the safest reference point for realizing the Helsinki human rights process" has generally been approved of by its member states. But the idea of extending the authority of the European Human-Rights Court to the CSCE's two trans-Atlantic members, the United States and Canada, has met with great skepticism in North America. US officials doubt that the Congress would ever approve of a scheme that would allow American courts to be overruled by a "higher" European tribunal.

The council's ambition of seeing its parliamentary assembly form the core of a future CSCE "Assembly of Europe" has also failed to spark much enthusiasm in North America. Lalumière noted today that the assembly, with its five special guests, already includes 29 out of the 34 CSCE member states and pleaded for the use of "existing institutions" rather than the creation of new ones. But US and Canadian parliamentarians have expressed fears that they would be "swallowed up" by their European counterparts in any such grouping, and Washington generally wants the CSCE to "go slow" in creating substantial new institutions.

Accordingly, the summit meeting's final document[1] pushes the question of the European assembly's constitution off to an unspecified later date. It calls merely for consultations with the parliaments of all 34 member states and subsequent discussion at a mid-1991 CSCE meeting. Similarly, the document carries no endorsement of the Council of Europe's desire to engage itself actively in the CSCE's human-rights provisions.

Lalumière told our correspondent today she "had reason to believe our US and Canadian friends" could be persuaded that their interests and rights would be protected if they joined the Europeans on both issues. But for the time being, it appears that the question of the council's role in the future of the CSCE has become another issue dividing the European and American members of the organization.

NOTE

1. See Document 98.

LITHUANIAN PARLIAMENT WARNS CSCE

97. *from* Statement from the Supreme Council of the Republic of Lithuania to the CSCE, Munich, November 22, 1990.

The leadership of the USSR is becoming more insistent in its attempts to interfere with the restoration of the rights of the Baltic peoples, which were trampled upon fifty years ago as a result of the criminal pact between Stalin and Hitler. Some political leaders and the mass media are attempting to create the impression that the Soviet Union is a democratic government under law that seeks peace and cooperation, but its relations with Estonia, Latvia and Lithuania prove just the opposite. The Soviet Union is now moving towards a rupture of economic relations with the Baltic countries, which will be even more ruthless than that of the blockade of Lithuania, while simultaneously usurping their sovereign right to establish independent contacts with the rest of the world across their borders. Thus, the Soviet Union is planning to artificially create an economic catastrophe and social conflicts in a closed environment, in order to overthrow freely elected democratic structures and to restore communist dictatorship and Kremlin absolutism in Estonia, Latvia and Lithuania. Unlawful acts of violence by occupational forces, which were obviously performed with impunity, as well as evil and threatening statements from individual leaders and leading circles in the USSR are employed as psychological pressure.

We, the Baltic peoples, are on the brink of a new danger of destabilization and massive misfortune, even though this region of Europe has, up to now, been relatively peaceful. The Soviets want to turn our Baltic path of peace into a path of conflict, burning barricades and a new disaster zone. We will oppose such a turn of events, but this aggressive state has significantly more resources and we do not see who will stay its hand. All the same, despite previous disappointments, we look hopefully to the democratic countries of the world, where law is respected and where human freedoms are protected. We await actions that would avert our despair and the dilemma of whether to take desperate steps in the name of liberty, honor and survival.

One such supportive action would be the immediate inclusion of the question of the independence of the Baltic countries on the agenda of all the working groups of the CSCE. The principle of consensus must not be converted to concession to lawlessness. To prevail upon the lawless to accept the consensus of the lawful is something entirely different.

THE CHARTER OF PARIS

98. *from* Charter of Paris for a New Europe, Paris, November 21, 1990.

A New Era of Democracy, Peace and Unity
We, the Heads of State or Government of the States participating in the Conference on Security and Cooperation in Europe, have assembled in Paris at a time of profound change and historic expectations. The era of confrontation and division of Europe has ended. We declare that henceforth our relations will be founded on respect and cooperation. . . .

The Ten Principles of the Final Act will guide us towards this ambitious future, just as they have lighted our way towards better relations for the past fifteen years. . . .

We undertake to build, consolidate and strengthen democracy as the only system of government of our nations. . . .

Human rights and fundamental freedoms are the birthright of all human beings, are inalienable and are guaranteed by law. . . .

Democratic government is based on the will of the people, expressed regularly through free and fair elections. Democracy has as its foundation respect for the human person and the rule of law. . . .

We affirm that, without discrimination, every individual has the right to: freedom of thought, conscience and religion or belief, freedom of expression, freedom of association and peaceful assembly, freedom of movement;

No one will be: subject to arbitrary arrest or detention, subject to torture or other cruel, inhuman or degrading treatment or punishment;

Everyone also has the right: to know and act upon his rights, to participate in free and fair elections, to fair and public trial if charged with an offense, to own property alone or in association and to exercise individual enterprise, to enjoy his economic, social and cultural rights.

We affirm that the ethnic, cultural, linguistic and religious identity of national minorities will be protected and that persons belonging to national minorities have the right freely to express, preserve and develop that identity without any discrimination and in full equality before the law. . . .

Freedom and political pluralism are necessary elements in our common objective of developing market economies towards sustainable economic growth, prosperity, social justice, expanding employment and efficient use of economic resources. The success of the transition to market economy by countries making efforts to this effect is important and in the interest of us all. . . .

Preservation of the environment is a shared responsibility of all our nations. . . .

We reaffirm our commitment to settle disputes by peaceful means. We decide to develop mechanisms for the prevention and resolution of conflicts among the participating States. . . .

The unprecedented reduction in armed forces resulting from the Treaty on Conventional Armed Forces in Europe,[1] together with new approaches to security and cooperation within the CSCE process, will lead to a new perception of security in Europe and a new dimension in our relations. In this context we fully recognize the freedom of States to choose their own security arrangements.

Guidelines for the Future
. . . Being aware of the urgent need for increased cooperation on, as well as better protection of, national minorities, we decide to convene a meeting of experts on national minorities to be held in Geneva from 1 to 19 July 1991. . . .

In accordance with our CSCE commitments, we stress that free movements and contacts among our citizens as well as the free flow of information and ideas are crucial for the maintenance and development of free societies and flourishing cultures. . . .

. . . We undertake to continue the CSBM negotiations under the same mandate, and to seek to conclude them no later than the Follow-up Meeting of the CSCE to be held in Helsinki in 1992. We also welcome the decision of the participating States concerned to continue the CFE negotiation under the same mandate and to seek to conclude it no later than the Helsinki Follow-up Meeting. . . .

We call for the earliest possible conclusion of the Convention on an effectively verifiable, global and comprehensive ban on chemical weapons, and we intend to be original signatories to it. . . .

We unreservedly condemn, as criminal, all acts, methods and practices of terrorism and express our determination to work for its eradication both bilaterally and through multilateral cooperation. We will also join together in combating illicit trafficking in drugs.

Being aware that an essential complement to the duty of States to refrain from the threat or use of force is the peaceful settlement of disputes, both being essential factors for the maintenance and consolidation of international peace and security, we will not only seek effective ways of preventing, through political means, conflicts which may yet emerge, but also define, in conformity with international law, appropriate mechanisms for the peaceful resolution of any disputes which may arise. . . . We stress that full use should be made in this context of the opportunity of the Meeting on the Peaceful Settlement of Disputes which will be convened in Valletta at the beginning of 1991. . . .

We reaffirm the need to continue to support democratic countries in transition towards the establishment of market economy and the creation of the basis for self-sustained economic and social growth, as already undertaken by the Group of Twenty-Four. . . .

We are determined to give the necessary impetus to cooperation among our States in the fields of energy, transport and tourism for economic and social development. . . .

. . . We pledge to intensify our endeavors to protect and improve our environment in order to restore and maintain a sound ecological balance in air, water and soil. . . .

In order to promote greater familiarity amongst our peoples, we favor the establishment of cultural centers in cities of other participating States as well as increased cooperation in the audio-visual field and wider exchange of music, theater, literature and the arts. . . .

We recognize that the issues of migrant workers and their families legally residing in host countries have economic, cultural and social aspects as well as their human dimension. . . .

We are concerned with the continuing tensions in the [Mediterranean] region, and renew our determination to intensify efforts towards finding just, viable and lasting solutions, through peaceful means, to outstanding crucial problems, based on respect for the principles of the Final Act. . . .

New Structures and Institutions of the CSCE Process
We, the Heads of State or Government, shall meet next time in Helsinki on the occasion of the CSCE Follow-up Meeting 1992. Thereafter, we will meet on the occasion of subsequent follow-up meetings.

Our Ministers for Foreign Affairs will meet, as a Council, regularly and at least once a year. These meetings will provide the central forum for political consultations within the CSCE process. . . .

The first meeting of the Council will take place in Berlin. . . .

In order to provide administrative support for these consultations we establish a Secretariat in Prague.

Follow-up Meetings of the participating States will be held, as a rule, every two years to allow the participating States to take stock of developments, review the implementation of their commitments and consider further steps in the CSCE process.

We decide to create a Conflict Prevention Center in Vienna to assist the Council in reducing the risk of conflict.

We decide to establish an Office for Free Elections in Warsaw to facilitate contacts and the exchange of information on elections within participating States.

Recognizing the important role parliamentarians can play in the CSCE process, we call for greater parliamentary involvement in the CSCE, in particular through the creation of a CSCE parliamentary assembly, involving members of parliaments from all participating States.

NOTE
1. See Document 91.

THE NEW INSTITUTIONS

99. *from* Supplementary Document to Give Effect to Certain Provisions Contained in the Charter of Paris for a New Europe, Paris, November 21, 1990.

A. The Council
1. The Council, consisting of Ministers for Foreign Affairs of the participating States, provides the central forum for regular political consultations within the CSCE process.

2. The Council will:

- consider issues relevant to the Conference on Security and Cooperation in Europe and take appropriate decisions;

- prepare the meetings of the Heads of State or Government of the participating States and implement tasks defined and decisions taken by these meetings.

3. The Council will hold meetings regularly and at least once a year.

4. The participating States may agree to hold additional meetings of the Council. . . .

B. *The Committee of Senior Officials*
1. The Committee of Senior Officials will prepare the work of the Council, carry out its decisions, review current issues and consider future work of the CSCE. . . .

2. In order to prepare the agenda of the meetings of the Council, the Committee will identify the issues for discussion on the basis of suggestions submitted by the participating States. . . .

4. . . . Meetings will be convened by the Chairman of the Committee after consultation with the participating States.

Meetings of the Committee will be held at the seat of the Secretariat and will not exceed two days, unless otherwise agreed. . . .

5. . . . the first meeting of the Committee will be held in Vienna from 28 to 29 January 1991. . . .

C. *Emergency mechanism*
The Council will discuss the possibility of establishing a mechanism for convening meetings of the Committee of Senior Officials in emergency situations.

D. *Follow-up meetings*
Follow-up meetings of the participating States will be held as a rule every two years. Their duration will not exceed three months, unless otherwise agreed.

E. *The CSCE Secretariat*
1. The Secretariat will:

- provide administrative support to the meetings of the Council and of the Committee of Senior Officials;
- maintain an archive of CSCE documentation and circulate documents as requested by the participating States;
- provide information in the public domain regarding the CSCE to individuals, NGOs, international organizations and non-participating States;
- provide support as appropriate to the Executive Secretaries of CSCE summit meetings, follow-up meetings and inter-sessional meetings. . . .

3. In order to carry out the tasks specified above, the Secretariat will consist of the following staff:

- a Director, responsible to the Council through the Committee of Senior Officials;

- three Officers who will be in charge of organization of meetings, . . . documentation and information, financial and administrative matters . . . ;

- administrative and technical personnel. . . .

F. The Conflict Prevention Center (CPC)

1. The Conflict Prevention Center (CPC) will assist the Council in reducing the risk of conflict. . . .

2. During its initial stage of operations the Center's role will consist in giving support to the implementation of CSBMs such as:

- mechanism for consultation and cooperation as regards unusual military activities;

- annual exchange of military information;

- communications network;

- annual implementation assessment meetings;

- cooperation as regards hazardous incidents of a military nature.

3. The Center might assume other functions and the above tasks are without prejudice to any additional tasks concerning a procedure for the conciliation of disputes as well as broader tasks relating to dispute settlement, which may be assigned to it in the future by the Council of the Foreign Ministers.

4. The Consultative Committee, composed of representatives from all participating States, will be responsible to the Council. As a rule, these representatives will be the Heads of Delegation to the CSBM negotiations until the Helsinki Follow-up Meeting. The Consultative Committee will:

- hold meetings of the participating States which may be convened under the mechanism on unusual military activities;

- hold the annual implementation assessment meetings;

- prepare seminars on military doctrine . . . ;

- supervise the Secretariat of the Center;

- provide the forum for discussion and clarification, as necessary, of information exchanged under agreed CSBMs;

- have overall responsibility for the communications network within the mandate of the CPC.

5. The Consultative Committee will . . . determine its own work program and may decide to hold additional meetings. . . .

6. The Secretariat will carry out the tasks assigned to it by the Consultative Committee to which it will be responsible. In particular, it will establish and maintain a data bank, for the use of all participating States, compiled on the basis of exchanged military information under agreed CSBMs and will publish Yearbooks on that basis.

7. The Secretariat will consist of the following staff:

- a Director;

- two officers in charge of organization of meetings, . . . communication, documentation and information, financial and administrative matters;

- administrative and technical personnel. . . .

8. The first meeting of the Consultative Committee . . . will be convened on 3 December 1990. . . .

G. The Office for Free Elections

1. The function of the Office for Free Elections will be to facilitate contacts and the exchange of information on elections within participating States. The Office will thus foster the implementation of paragraphs 6, 7 and 8 of the Document of the Copenhagen Meeting of the Conference on the Human Dimension of the CSCE. . . .[1]

2. To this end, the Office will:

- compile information, including information provided by the competent authorities of the participating States, on the dates, procedures and official results of scheduled national elections within participating States, as well as reports of election observations, and provide these on request to governments, parliaments and interested private organizations;

- serve to facilitate contact among governments, parliaments or private organizations wishing to observe elections and competent authorities of the States in which elections are to take place;

- organize and serve as the venue for seminars or other meetings related to election procedures and democratic institutions at the request of the participating States. . . .

H. Procedures and Modalities Concerning CSCE Institutions
Staffing Arrangements
　　1. The director of each institution will be of senior rank, seconded by his/her government, and appointed by the Council to a three-year, non-renewable term, on a basis of rotation. . . .
　　2. The officers will be seconded by their governments. Their terms of office will normally last two years. . . .
　　5. No participating State will have its nationals occupy more than one seconded position in the CSCE institutions, unless no other participating State is willing to second its national to a vacant position. . . .
Costs
　　The costs:

- of seconded personnel will be borne by the seconding country;

- of installation of the CSCE institutions will be shared according to CSCE procedures;

- of operation, including cost of official travel of staff once appointed, will be shared according to CSCE procedures;

- of the premises of the institution as well as the necessary security arrangements including those of meetings held at the seat of the institution, will be borne by the host country. . . .

　　The first director of each institution will be nominated by the first meeting of the Committee of Senior Officials and confirmed by the Council. . . .
　　15. The CSCE Secretariat, the Conflict Prevention Center and the Office for Free Elections are accountable to the Council, which is empowered to determine their tasks and methods of operation. Arrangements relating to the procedures, modalities and the locations of these institutions may be reviewed at the Helsinki Follow-up Meeting.

I. Communications
The Council, acting upon recommendation of the Consultative Committee and of the Committee of Senior Officials, as appropriate, may decide that the communications network, established as part of the agreement on additional CSBMs, be used for other CSCE-related purposes.

NOTE
1.   See Document 85.

US AND USSR: THE DISAPPEARING SUPERPOWERS

100. *from* Fred Kaplan, "Europe Choreographs New World Order, But Bush is Out of Step." Commentary in *The Boston Globe,* Paris, November 21, 1990. RFE/RL B-Wire, FF137.

President Bush came to the European [CSCE] summit to talk about the Persian Gulf, but the Europeans came to talk about Europe and now seem on their way to building their own "new world order" without the United States at the helm.

Bush has tried to maintain US influence over the continent by rallying the European leaders to the cause of the liberation of Kuwait, by military means if necessary, but he has met with much less success than he had hoped for.

This was not how Bush had planned it six months ago, when this summit . . . was first scheduled.

Bush and his secretary of state, James A. Baker 3rd, were closely involved back then in "the new architecture" of Europe, devising a central, stabilizing role for the United States even as the Soviet military threat, the main rationale for the US presence on the continent for the past 45 years, was vanishing.

Then came August 2 and Iraq's invasion of Kuwait. The new Europe was relegated to the sidelines of US diplomatic discourse.

Bush and Baker have spent most of their energies at this summit trying to gain advance approval for a resolution, to be placed before the UN Security Council, authorizing the use of force to push Iraq out of Kuwait.

In speeches here and, before the summit, in Germany and Czechoslovakia, Bush has urged Europe not to turn inward but to accept new global responsibilities—meaning, the context is clear, to do whatever is necessary to turn back the aggression of President Saddam Hussein of Iraq.

The Europeans have replied with good wishes for Bush, a few with vocal or whispered support, but not with the firm manifesto Bush had desired or with any evident inclination to turn the new "Europe free and whole" into a holding-company for US military policy.

Britain has most clearly endorsed Bush's call for support, a situation that would not be altered even if Prime Minister Margaret Thatcher were ousted from power in the Conservative Party's runoff balloting.

The Soviet Union and France publicly hedge on the matter, though their officials might say privately they will come through, ultimately, in support of a resolution for force.

In the meantime, however, these powers and others at the summit consider the gulf a separate issue from their determination to move ahead in shaping the new contours of Europe. . . .

In his statement at the summit . . . , Bush noted [that] "Europe is entering unknown waters" and hailed the CSCE as "ideally suited to help its members navigate."

But in contrast with his and Baker's enthusiasm for such tasks a few months ago, Bush offered no focus, much less firm ideas on the subject.

Meanwhile, the only tangible basis for a continued US presence, much less dominance, on the continent—the need to offset the Soviet army in Eastern Europe—is evaporating.

In fact, the summit has accelerated this disappearing act. The 22 nations of NATO and the Warsaw Pact signed a treaty cutting each alliance to equal levels of armaments. They also formally declared they are "no longer adversaries" and pledged never to use or threaten force against one another.

The Hungarian Prime Minister, József Antall, announced that the Warsaw Pact will formally disband by 1992. Soviet officials have said recently [that] they will pull all their troops out of Eastern Europe by 1995.

The North Atlantic Treaty Organization, under these circumstances, seems to have little purpose in life. There may still be "instabilities" in European politics, such as ethnic conflicts in the Soviet Union, Czechoslovakia, Romania, Hungary, but NATO is ill-suited to deal with these problems.

At the NATO summit in July [1990] in London, Bush and other Western leaders pledged to reorient the Atlantic Alliance to deal with these new politics. An administration official said last week that the Paris summit would "demonstrate NATO's adaptability to change."

Yet in fact, the future of NATO has not been mentioned. Gorbachev proposed that a conflict-prevention center, which is being created as part of CSCE, might evolve into an "All-European Security Council."

Such a prospect, and the idea has appeal to many Europeans, would supersede NATO altogether. And that would raise the question in many European minds: What is the United States still doing here?

Developments have not yet reached that point. Most of the European leaders say they want the United States to stay, that they value America's presence as a ballast in fast-changing times.

But what happens if the Europeans are able to provide their own stabilizing influences and show, to themselves and others, that they can do so without the active aid of outsiders? Bush's main failure at this summit may ultimately be seen not as the failure to wrap up the controversy over another UN resolution on the Persian Gulf, but rather the failure to secure the United States a first-class ticket aboard the new Europe.

101. *from* "Gorbachev, While Praised, Cuts a Lonely Figure at Summit." Reuters News Analysis report, Paris, November 21, 1990. RFE/RL B-Wire, FF055.

As Mikhail Gorbachev strode into the hall for the final session of the European security conference,[1] for a few moments he looked like a man alone among a crowd of strangers.

Heading towards his seat at the huge white-sycamore table, the Soviet president glanced right and left but leaders and delegates from the 33 other countries deep in animated discussions at first failed to greet him.

The brief scene appeared to symbolize a subtle switch in the perception of the man who was long an international superstar but in Paris seemed more the odd-man-out—a relic of an age which he himself had helped consign to history.

"He is a man in decline," said Michel Tatu, a leading French specialist in communist affairs.

Looming as a distracting backdrop for the summit's formal burial of the Cold War were Gorbachev's mounting domestic problems which many Western leaders fear could tear his country apart and create a new region of high tension in the East.

In the wings of the conference, delegates and officials were in intense discussion on how the Soviet Union—which for decades had proclaimed it had created an ideal society of plenty—could be helped through a grim winter ahead.

Gorbachev himself recognized the problem by, according to Canadian Prime Minister Brian Mulroney, providing the Western states with a list of food needs, while insisting that he did not want hand-outs.

But in his own speech at the conference, the Kremlin chief, the only leader from the former Soviet bloc in Paris who still proclaims his belief in Marxism-Leninism and the communist future, warned the West against using aid to pressure him.

In language more reminiscent of an earlier age, he took a clear swipe at his own rebellious republics, declaring that "unbridled na-tionalism and mindless separatism" were a threat to the new Euro-pean security order.

Three of the republics—Baltic Latvia, Lithuania and Estonia—sent foreign ministers to Paris in a bid to cement their drive for a return to their pre-war independence by gaining admittance to the conference as observers.

They were expelled after a few hours following what summit officials said was a Soviet protest, and the ministers told a news conference the action showed Gorbachev's limited understanding of non-Russian national feelings.

The Balts, to their delight, won public support in conference speeches from Norway, Sweden, Denmark, Iceland, the Vatican and Moscow's one-time docile allies of Poland and Czechoslovakia.

"The West in general is still ready to send Gorbachev flowers, but they are letting him know that he is expected to find a reasonable solution to the Baltic issue," Tatu, who writes for the newspaper *Le Monde,* told Reuters.

The East Europeans, all represented by leaders put in power by the anti-Marxist revolutions that swept through the old bloc last year, signalled that they would be pushing for a total wrap-up of its once-mighty Warsaw Pact by 1992.

And Czechoslovakia's president, Václav Havel, a former jailed dissident, delivered a bitter valedictory on the military grouping whose Soviet-led forces stormed into his country in 1968 to end a cautious democratic experiment.

The West's NATO alliance, he said, as Gorbachev and his uni-formed and bemedalled defense minister, Marshal Dmitry Yazov, looked on stony-faced, "has proved itself to be a guarantee of free-dom and democracy. The Warsaw Pact is an outdated remnant of the past."

Diplomats at the conference expressed surprise that the Soviet president felt compelled to bring Yazov, regarded in Moscow as a conservative, and seat him prominently at his side as the only military man around the table.

"Perhaps this was Gorbachev's recognition that the army could pose a threat and has to be associated with the changes that were consecrated here," said one.

And Hungary's [József] Antall, whose own country had a reformist movement bloodily crushed by Soviet troops at the height of the Cold War in 1956, implicitly offered an explanation of the Kremlin chief's concern in his summit address.

Now that the East-West confrontation was over and freedom was sweeping Europe, he said, "We hope that there will be no countries where humiliated armies feel tempted to embark upon political adventures and disappointed military men attempt to bar the development of democracy."

NOTE
1.   The November 1990 CSCE summit in Paris.

STABILIZING EUROPE

102. *from* "Stabilizing Europe," *The Times* [London], November 22, 1990.

The signing of the Charter of Europe in Paris yesterday[1] was a moving celebration of the end of the Cold War. But there was anxiety present. At this week's Conference on Security and Cooperation in Europe, leader after leader from Eastern Europe warned Western governments not to start banking on the peace dividend yet. They do not feel confident of containing nationalism, ethnic tension and political extremism without a Western commitment to help them if things go badly wrong.

The West must take these warnings seriously, and must decide what emphasis to put on economic assistance and how far to be drawn into putting out small but potentially contagious brush-fires. Above all, Western governments must decide whether they view the maintenance of stability in Eastern Europe as a vital national as well as international interest. The answer must be yes, but the implications are costly.

Eastern Europe's own governments must bear the main responsibility for sorting out their problems. But the costs of repairing the economic and environmental ravages of communism far exceed these countries' means. The West has promised economic assistance, tied to political as well as economic reforms. The main vehicles are the IMF and the World Bank, institutions which—however hard these categories are to separate—take economic, not political, criteria into account.

Hence the West's creation of a new European Bank for Reconstruction and Development (EBRD), intended to give a distinctively political dimension to lending. In theory, the EBRD could use financial leverage to persuade governments to solve internal conflicts peacefully—where they are capable of doing so. The EBRD, however, is not yet operational and, with an initial capital base of only $14 billion, its leverage will be modest.

These countries, moreover, seek not only economic aid, closer political dialogue and economic integration with the West but some sort of cooperation on security. They want Western help to control ethnic conflicts. . . . The two possible vehicles for conciliation are the 34-nation CSCE and NATO.

Czechoslovakia and Hungary explicitly look to NATO, described by President Václav Havel as Europe's "guarantee of freedom and democracy," as the only available functioning security organization. NATO is not about to create peacekeeping forces to prise Czechs and Slovaks, or Bulgarians and Turks, apart. But Western leaders, as they rethink NATO's role, should keep the enthusiasm in Eastern Europe for its continued existence as an unequivocally military alliance firmly in mind.

For the first time, CSCE has been given a permanent secretariat in Prague and an office in Warsaw to help with free elections. In addition, states will be able to take disputes to a CSCE conflict prevention center in Vienna. The hope is that this could help prevent the outbreak of dangerous little wars over disputed frontiers, provided that workable voluntary conciliation procedures (a British idea) and dispute-settlement machinery are established. But will governments be prepared to accept external mediation of internal disputes, likely to be the commonest cause of instability?

Intervention in a nation's domestic affairs is untested, and justly sensitive, international ground, but even at the height of the Cold War, the CSCE made a start on this with human rights. Preparedness to accept arbitration might now be made a condition of economic aid. To qualify, Yugoslavia might for example have to accept independent mediation between Croats and Serbs. The costs of stability in Eastern Europe will have to be shared, even if the East's contribution involves some possible diminution of the independence its people have fought so hard to win.

NOTE
1.   At the November 1990 CSCE summit.

Slowdown After Euphoria

SOVIET DISARMAMENT EVASIONS

103. Quentin Peel, "Moscow Report Tells How Thousands of Tanks Avoided CFE Count," *Financial Times,* **January 10, 1991.**

Western claims that the Soviet Union moved thousands of tanks, armored cars and artillery pieces behind the Ural mountains last year, to escape counting in East-West arms cuts, have been given new credibility by the country's leading conservative newspaper.

Not only did the Soviet military carry out the massive operation, but it severely disrupted collection of the country's record harvest last summer by commandeering thousands of railway wagons, according to an interview published by *Sovietskaya Rossiya,* the Russian Communist party newspaper. The extraordinary claim was made by Mr. V. Litov, cited as an economist and leading critic of the CFE disarmament treaty signed in Paris last December.[1]

He described the military exercise, carried out "in the shortest possible time," as an essential operation to protect the Soviet military from the "miscalculations of our diplomacy," and called on the Soviet parliament to refuse to ratify the treaty.

At the same time, he confirmed the deep division between the Soviet military and the Ministry of Foreign Affairs, headed by Mr. Eduard Shevardnadze, over the whole disarmament debate.

Mr. Litov said the huge cuts in Soviet tanks required by the treaty—from 48,000 in Europe to just 13,000 in three years' time—amounted to virtual unilateral disarmament. Given the collapse of the Warsaw Pact, he said, there was now a big imbalance between NATO forces and those of the Soviet Union alone.

"This sharp reduction, unprecedented in history, is a very difficult and catastrophic process for our armed forces," he said. "It was caused by the desire of the Foreign Ministry, as soon as possible, and before the Paris summit[2] to prepare this treaty. A colossal amount of military equipment had to be destroyed, with corresponding tremendous expenditures which our economy simply could not stand.

"This is why the military, trying somehow to make up for the miscalculation of our diplomacy, organized this removal behind the Urals of thousands of tanks, artillery, and other equipment." Western estimates suggest that 20,694 Soviet tanks, some 25,000 artillery pieces, and 15,500 armored vehicles, vanished from eastern Europe in the months before the treaty signing.

Mr. Litov's claims fit with other reports that Mr. Shevardnadze's dramatic resignation before Christmas was precipitated by a fundamental clash with the Soviet military, and the failure of President Mikhail Gorbachev to support him.

Western diplomats in Moscow say that Soviet Foreign Ministry officials make no secret of their dismay at the military attitude to the CFE treaty. That includes not only the apparent removal of hardware behind the Urals, and therefore out of the Atlantic-to-the-Urals counting zone, but also to the last-minute reclassification of two divisions as "naval infantry," just days before the treaty was signed.

The issue is now seen as a threat to the US-Soviet summit in February, with US officials suggesting that a strategic arms limitation pact cannot be finalized without clarification on CFE. Moscow argues that there should be no linkage, and there is no reason to delay the summit.

NOTES
1. See Document 91.
2. See Documents 98–100.

VALLETTA: A SETTLEMENT OF DISPUTES

104. *from* "Report of the CSCE Meeting of Experts on Peaceful Settlement of Disputes, Valletta 1991," Valletta, February 8, 1991.

The participating States will endeavor in good faith and in a spirit of cooperation to reach a rapid and equitable solution of their disputes . . . and accept, in the context of the CSCE Procedure for Peaceful Settlement of Disputes . . . the mandatory involvement of a third party when a dispute cannot be settled by other peaceful means.

If the parties are unable . . . to settle the dispute in direct consultation or negotiation, . . . any party to the dispute may request the establishment of a CSCE Dispute Settlement Mechanism. . . .

A CSCE Dispute Settlement Mechanism consists of one or more members, selected by common agreement of the parties to a dispute from a register of qualified candidates maintained by the nominating institution. The register comprises the names of up to four persons nominated by each participating State desiring to do so.

The parties will consider in good faith and in a spirit of cooperation any comment or advice of the Mechanism. If, on the basis of the proceedings of the Mechanism and of any comment or advice offered, the parties are nevertheless unable . . . to settle the dispute . . . , any party to the dispute may so notify the Mechanism. . . .

Notwithstanding a request by a party, . . . the Mechanism will not be established or continued . . . if another party to the dispute considers that because the dispute raises issues concerning its territorial integrity, or national defense, title to sovereignty over land territory, or competing claims with regard to the jurisdiction over other areas, the Mechanism should not be established or continued. . . .

The representatives of the participating States noted that the Council of Ministers of Foreign Affairs will take into account the Report of the Valletta Meeting at its first meeting in Berlin. In this context, the representatives . . . recommend that the Council establish the necessary arrangements.

MADRID: A PARLIAMENTARY ASSEMBLY

105. *from* "Draft Final Resolution Concerning the Establishment of the CSCE Parliamentary Assembly," Madrid, April 3, 1991.

The delegations of the Parliaments of countries participating in the Conference on Security and Cooperation in Europe . . . agree to establish within the framework of the Conference . . . a Parliamentary Assembly. . . .

The CSCE's Parliamentary Assembly shall be composed of 245 parliamentarians representing . . . each country as follows:

Union of Soviet Socialist Republics and United States of America: 17,

Germany, France, Italy, and United Kingdom: 13,

Canada and Spain: 10,

Belgium, Netherlands, Poland, Sweden, and Turkey: 8,

Romania, Yugoslavia: 7,

Austria, Czech and Slovak Federative Republic, Denmark, Fin-

land, Greece, Hungary, Norway, Portugal, Switzerland, and Ireland: 6,
    Bulgaria, Luxembourg: 5,
    Cyprus, Iceland, and Malta: 3,
    Liechtenstein, Monaco, and San Marino: 2.
    The Holy See may send two representatives to the Assembly's meetings as guests of honor.
    The . . . Assembly will hold a plenary annual meeting for a period of not more than five days. . . .
    The purpose of the annual meeting . . . will be:

a.   To assess the implementation of the objectives of the CSCE.

b.   To discuss subjects addressed during the meetings of the Council of Ministers for Foreign Affairs and the biennial Summit of Heads of State or Government.

c.   To initiate and promote whatever measures may further cooperation and security in Europe.

GENEVA: THE INTRACTABLE MINORITIES

106. *from* Statement by Ambassador Lars Norberg, Swedish delegate. CSCE Meeting of Experts on National Minorities, Geneva, July 2, 1991.

At this meeting we should set as our task to identify and agree on ways and means to protect national minorities and to promote confidence and cooperation between them and all parts of the society in which they live. . . . We should focus on minority issues that carry security implications and thus concern us all.
    During the cold war minority issues were contained by an almost obsessive concern for military security. The totalitarian regimes suppressed systematically the aspirations of minority groups. We are again reminded that these problems can only be dealt with successfully by democratic means and in the spirit of tolerance.
    Hence, after the peaceful revolutions of 1989–90 minority issues have again come to the surface. On the whole this is a very positive development. Persons belonging to ethnic groups have begun to exercise their natural right to further their own interests, to safeguard their languages, culture and way of life. It is the obligation of our Governments to ensure the protection of national minorities. It

is also in our own interest to do so. Minorities provide rich contributions to our societies. . . .

. . . it is not the existence per se of a national minority that causes problems. In most cases the problems are a reflection of the conditions under which members of minorities live. . . .

Each minority situation has its own characteristics. It is therefore difficult to develop solutions that are generally applicable. Solutions must be designed to respond to the requirements of the specific situations. . . .

The CSCE is an appropriate forum for dealing with minority issues. The comprehensive nature of the CSCE concept—security and cooperation—is highly relevant when addressing problems involving national minorities.

The CSCE today faces a twofold challenge when it comes to national minorities. In a short-term perspective, the main task is to identify ways and means to defuse tension and prevent problems involving minorities from escalating to confrontational level. In the longer perspective the task is even more formidable. It should be to establish trusting relations between national minorities and the respective majorities as well as other parties concerned.

The structures of the CSCE that were established after the Paris Summit have further enhanced the capability of the CSCE to deal with minority issues. The new consultative political process, and maybe the Committee of Senior Officials in particular, constitutes a highly suitable forum for handling problems related to the situations of minorities. . . .

The CSCE Human Dimension Mechanism has proved to be a useful tool in implementing CSCE commitments as regards human rights. . . . My delegation will work for procedures that would add to the Mechanism the option of sending observers to the requested State. . . .

At this meeting we should not try to work out painstaking definitions of what constitutes a national minority. I believe that most of us have an intuitive and working understanding of the concept. Instead, our main effort must be directed towards devising ways and means of handling and alleviating problems involving minorities.

Confidence-building is a household word within the CSCE. Here truly is one area where confidence-building could be applied outside of the military realm. Its successful application would no doubt have positive effects on the security and stability in Europe.

Only cooperation over time can heal existing wounds. We should try to define concrete projects to promote inter-minority and majority-minority exchanges. Other organs, such as the Council of Europe, might be best suited for the implementation of projects of this kind.

FOR AND AGAINST REVERSE DISCRIMINATION

107. *from* Speech by Catherine Lalumière, secretary general of the Council of Europe. CSCE Meeting of Experts on National Minorities, Geneva, July 1, 1991.

The first thing to do, as those responsible for this meeting . . . have understood very well, is to delimit clearly the subject we are dealing with. We are concerned only with *national minorities,* not all minority problems.

In point of fact we must find solutions as quickly as we can to those painful cases inherited from history, especially from the wars of the 20th century, following which frontiers have been redrawn in such a way that persons belonging to one nation have found themselves included in another nation.

On the other hand, our meeting clearly has not to deal with cases of minorities resulting from recent immigration or from the temporary or permanent presence of persons who have freely chosen to live in a country which is not their country of origin.

The second remark before we come to solutions is that these solutions will be of two kinds: firstly a few common principles which derive their legitimacy from rights which are acknowledged as belonging to all, and secondly special arrangements for each particular case. Every national minority has its own history, frustrations, and aspirations, and every State, too, has its overriding needs, its necessary balances, and its responsibilities. It would be dangerous to try to impose a single mold which would not suit the case.

The third remark will not surprise you: it is that, in this field, we must be modest and cautious. The Council of Europe simply wants to be useful, but it knows that every step must be carefully measured.

Our work and experience can be presented in two groups. First of all there is what results in legal norms; these are our most ambitious contributions, but they are also the most difficult to achieve since we have to go beyond the principle of non-discrimination and acknowledge that [members of] a minority [and sometimes even a minority itself, have] certain specific rights. On the other hand, on a less ambitious level, but equally useful in practice, we can propose a series of practical measures to be taken on the spot. These can be described as confidence-building measures which make it possible to avoid or solve conflicts between a minority and the people around it.

When norms are concerned, . . . the aim is . . . to determine a minimum of principles that everyone can respect. . . .

. . . the standard-setting approach should not encounter too many problems when it is a matter of what I would call broadly *cultural rights.* . . .

Obviously, the standard-setting approach will be much more difficult in the case of *political rights,* that is to say effective participation by minorities as distinct groups in decisions concerning the towns, regions or countries where they live.

Here it will probably be impossible to go beyond guidelines, recommendations and commitments of a very general kind. . . .

Each state may have to ask itself if, in the light of its own special circumstances, recognition of certain forms of political expression, however bold this may seem, may not be necessary to safeguard the national community's future stability. In some cases the prudent course is not to deny all special political rights, but to know how best to "cut one's losses."

. . . I should like to draw your special attention to the idea of pilot projects, to the dynamic role which regional and local authorities should play, to widening opportunities for transfrontier cooperation, and to the principle of information exchanges against the backcloth of the quest for, or acceptance of, a harmonious multicultural society. . . .

To conclude, I should like to mention a third approach . . . the use of machinery involving intervention by third parties (visits for purposes of information, counsel, good offices, mediation, conciliation, or indeed arbitration, etc. . . .).

. . . such intervention may look like interference in the internal affairs of States. However, in certain circumstances it could be accepted, even requested, as a way of dealing with an insoluble crisis. . . .

For example, would it be out of the question to send a group of outstanding personalities or independent experts on fact-finding missions? Is it too early to think of sending such groups to use their good offices? . . .

We are looking for effective and acceptable solutions. It is far from easy. But I still remember what Bronisław Geremek[1] said recently: "Every country can be judged by how it treats its minorities."

And I would add: Europe will be judged on how it solves its

minority problems, for what is at stake is its humanist principles and also its stability and unity.

NOTE
1. Polish historian and Solidarity leader.

108. *from* Statement by Géza Entz, head of the Hungarian delegation. CSCE Meeting of Experts on National Minorities, Geneva, July 10, 1991.

The full and effective equality of rights of the persons belonging to national minorities with the members of the majority population is incomplete when conditions for the affirmation, expression, protection, and promotion of their identity are missing, when as a result of their disadvantageous position they are unable to enjoy all their rights in the political, economic, social, and cultural fields.

As we in the CSCE community establish our standards as common denominators for all of us, it is of vital importance that on the basis of those commitments specific solutions be found to the specific situations. . . .

It is in the common interest of Europe as a whole that existing tensions should be speedily allayed. Special efforts must be made to resolve specific problems in a constructive manner and through dialogue with a view to improving the conditions for the protection and the promotion of the identity of national minorities. In this spirit, particular attention should be given to national minorities created as a result of frontier changes in the course of the twentieth century. That fact should not be prejudicial in any field to the rights of persons belonging to such minorities or to their community life, and may justify the adoption of appropriate special provisions in their favor.

109. *from* Remarks by J. Kenneth Blackwell, US representative to the United Nations Commission on Human Rights. CSCE Meeting of Experts on National Minorities, Geneva, July 4, 1991.

National situations differ greatly. In each case, individual rights must be protected on a non-discriminatory basis. . . .

. . . I want to describe briefly our national experience and current debate concerning American minority groups and some of their civil and legal rights. . . .

The civil rights movement in the United States is under severe internal and external review and analysis as it adjusts to its need to develop a new agenda. Many, like me, are urging a new approach designed to define and promote policies that empower individuals to achieve their own potential through their own efforts, in a society which permits rewards for their work and their accomplishments. Empowerment does not mean control of others, but freedom to control one's own affairs. Minorities in America don't want paternalism, they want opportunity—they don't want the servitude of welfare, they want jobs and an opportunity to own private property. They don't want government dependency, they want a reaffirmation of our declaration of independence. . . .

Regrettably, there has been a tendency to face problems based on race with solutions based on race. Our objective must be to eliminate racism, not to perpetuate it.

Yet today, far too many of the policies and remedies being advanced by some in the traditional civil rights movement as solutions to the problems facing the United States African-American and Hispanic communities are race-based. These are remedies that are not race and gender neutral. Instead, they define people by race and sex. Often they result in preferential programs. . . .

. . . the civil rights movement risks losing the perception as a moral crusade for an even playing field and freedom. It risks coming to be seen as an advocacy movement for preferential treatment for minorities, at the expense of the majority.

110. from Statement by Elena Zamfirescu, Romanian delegate. CSCE Meeting of Experts on National Minorities, Geneva, July 11, 1991.

Another interesting paper was put forward by the "Pentagonale" group. . . .[1]

As far as the actual text of the paper is concerned, one of the most astonishing distortions of earlier CSCE documents consists in changing the approach to minorities' issues in the CSCE framework, namely, "to promote the rights of persons belonging to minorities as part of universally recognized human rights." The "Pentagonale" text puts emphasis on the minority as such—which is an abstract notion—rather than on the individual. Without exception, this emphasis prevails all through the paper, in a way that contradicts both the letter and the spirit of already agreed-upon documents. I will not dwell on the problem of "collective rights" and its irrelevance as a legal concept. . . . I would only like to add that a word like "collective" and its derivatives strike unpleasantly the ears of individuals who were fed up with collectivistic experiments more than four decades. . . .

. . . several other ideas are difficult to be accepted by us, as they have no relation to the problems of minorities. One of them is . . . transfrontier cooperation. . . . as far as minorities are concerned, even the premise the idea starts from is a wrong one, because it focuses on integrating minorities in societies other than the one they belong to. On the other hand, even if we were to accept such an approach, it would be irrelevant in the particular case of Romania. As you all probably know, the largest part of the minorities living in Romania can be found in the middle of the country, and not on its borders. . . . minority issues cannot form the object of transfrontier cooperation.

. . . the same observation applies to the idea to use the CSCE procedure for peaceful settlement of disputes between States. Such an idea seems to us out of place. Not being a part of the relations between States, minority issues cannot, in principle, represent an object of disputes between States.

NOTE
1.   Austria, Czechoslovakia, Hungary, Italy, and Yugoslavia.

A HOPEFUL OUTCOME

111. *from* "Report of the CSCE Meeting of Experts on National Minorities, Geneva 1991." Geneva, July 19, 1991. CSCE/REMN.20.

Reaffirming their deep conviction that friendly relations among their peoples, as well as peace, justice, stability and democracy, require that the ethnic, cultural, linguistic, and religious identity of national minorities be protected, and conditions for the promotion of that identity be created,

Convinced that . . . democracy requires that all persons . . . enjoy full and effective equality of rights and fundamental freedoms and benefit from the rule of law and democratic institutions, . . .

The representatives of the participating States took as the fundamental basis of their work the commitments undertaken by them with respect to national minorities as contained in the relevant adopted CSCE documents. . . .

Issues concerning national minorities, as well as compliance with international obligations and commitments concerning the rights of persons belonging to them, are matters of legitimate international concern and consequently do not constitute exclusively an internal affair of the respective State. . . .

. . . when issues relating to the situation of national minorities are discussed within their countries, they themselves should have the effective opportunity to be involved, in accordance with the decision-making procedures of each State. . . . appropriate democratic participation of persons belonging to national minorities or their representatives in decision-making or consultative bodies constitutes an important element of effective participation in public affairs. . . .

The participating States will create conditions for persons belonging to national minorities to have equal opportunity to be effectively involved in the public life, economic activities, and building of their societies. . . .

The participating States reconfirm the importance of adopting, where necessary, special measures for the purpose of ensuring to persons belonging to national minorities full equality with the other citizens in the exercise and enjoyment of human rights and fundamental freedoms. . . .

Aware of the diversity and varying constitutional systems among them, which make no single approach necessarily generally applicable, the participating States note with interest that positive results have been obtained by some of them in an appropriate democratic manner by, inter alia:

- advisory and decision-making bodies in which minorities are represented, in particular with regard to education, culture, and religion;

- elected bodies and assemblies of national minority affairs;

- local and autonomous administration, as well as autonomy on a territorial basis, including the existence of consultative, legislative, and executive bodies chosen through free and periodic elections;

- self-administration by a national minority of aspects concerning its identity in situations where autonomy on a territorial basis does not apply;

- decentralized or local forms of government;

- bilateral and multilateral agreements and other arrangements regarding national minorities;

- for persons belonging to national minorities, provision of adequate types and levels of education in their mother tongue with due regard to the number, geographic settlement patterns and cultural traditions of national minorities;

- funding the teaching of minority languages to the general public, as well as the inclusion of minority languages in teacher-training institutions . . . ;

- provision of financial and technical assistance to persons belonging to national minorities who so wish to exercise their right to establish and maintain their own educational, cultural and religious institutions . . . ;

- encouragement of grassroots community relations efforts between minority communities, between majority and minority communities, and between neighboring communities sharing borders, aimed at helping local tensions from arising . . . ; and

- encouragement of the establishment of permanent mixed commissions, either inter-State or regional, to facilitate continuing dialogue between the border regions concerned.

The participating States are of the view that these or other approaches . . . could be helpful in improving the situation of national minorities on their territories.

Testing the New Institutions

FROM VANCOUVER TO VLADIVOSTOK

112. *from* "The Euro-Atlantic Architecture: From East to West," Speech by James A. Baker, US secretary of state. CSCE Council of Foreign Ministers, Berlin, June 18, 1991.

We must begin to extend the trans-Atlantic community to Central and Eastern Europe, and the Soviet Union. These are the still incomplete pieces of our architecture. The revolutions of freedom in Central and Eastern Europe need our ongoing support to become lasting democracies. Perestroika needs our encouragement to move further toward a free society and free markets.

Our objective is both a Europe whole and free, and a Euro-Atlantic Community that extends east from Vancouver to Vladivostok. . . .

Our architecture needs to fulfill the long-established NATO goal, from the 1967 Harmel Report, of achieving "a just and lasting peaceful order in Europe." To do so, our structures need to promote Euro-Atlantic political and economic values, the ideals of the Enlightenment. They need to establish the components of cooperative security for a Europe whole and free. And we need to demonstrate how integration can cope with new dangers from old enmities. . . .

. . . We are seeing the beginnings of a Europe of Regions that may well be overlapping. Cooperation among Poland, Hungary, and Czechoslovakia; the Pentagonale; and the exploration of ties among northern states that rim the Baltic and of southern states on the Black Sea are examples of early efforts. Similarly, the Nine-plus-One accord within the Soviet Union is a first effort to reestablish the legitimacy of that multinational state on the basis of voluntary association among component parts. Furthermore, the interest of these states in associating themselves with Western institutions like the IMF, the EC, and the OECD is also evidence of this evolutionary tendency.

Evolution and devolution are not alternatives, but complementary, and indeed interdependent developments. The building of a Euro-Atlantic Community can only be achieved on a democratic basis if there is grassroots involvement in the process. Thus, the architects of a united Europe have adopted the principle of "subsidiarity," something like American "federalism"—that is, the devolution of responsibility to the lowest level of government capable of performing it effectively. By the same token, the process of devolution in the East will lead to fragmentation, conflict, and ultimately threaten democracy if it is not accompanied by the voluntary delegation of powers to national and even supranational levels for basic matters such as defense, trade, currency, and the protection of basic human rights—particularly minority rights. . . .

CSCE, the Helsinki process, remains the one group that brings together all the countries of Europe and North America on the basis of a common commitment to human rights and democratic principles. These rights and principles are the foundation for a Euro-Atlantic Community already reaching beyond Berlin to the East.

We need to build a practical record of success for CSCE, with appropriate capabilities in all three baskets in a mutually supportive fashion, and thus support the process of reform that will allow CSCE to become a true community of values. . . .

. . . We should adopt a procedure for calling emergency meetings of CSCE officials at the sub-ministerial level. We can strengthen the Conflict Prevention Center. And I hope we can also develop procedures under which ministers could direct the establishment of fact-finding missions.

We also need to entertain other ideas. Minister Bessmertnykh[1] has made a proposal for a standing CSCE human rights body. This merits serious attention. It might be complemented by adding fact-finding missions as a fifth step in the Human Dimension mechanism.

I propose we consider convoking a specialized CSCE meeting on support for free media. We might also expand the mandate of the Office of Free Elections to become an Office of Democratic Institutions so that voting day will be matched by 364 other days of liberty in the year.

In the economic area, I propose we establish new CSCE Chambers of Commerce in countries moving to market economies to organize and speak for the interests of private businesses. We might also organize a seminar on the social and financial implications of defense conversion and budget cuts.

CSCE is also an appropriate forum to address the issues of

migration within Europe. An experts' meeting could seek to develop humanitarian principles for handling massive immigration and refugees within the CSCE region and cooperative arrangements to anticipate and address the causes and benefits of such population movements.

In sum, I envisage CSCE developing an agenda that can foster the sharing of ideas and cooperation on issues of common concern. That is a prerequisite to more complex integration.

It is also important that we view CSCE as a framework, not a unitary body for the Euro-Atlantic agenda. Indeed, as we extend the Euro-Atlantic architecture to the East, we need to be creative about employing multiple methods and institutions—including NATO, the EC, the OECD, the Council of Europe, and others—to address common concerns.

Take the issue of security. We have in fact been developing arrangements for cooperative security to meet the needs of the newly emerging democracies and to engage a reformed Soviet Union.

One, CSCE will contribute by creating the political, economic, and security conditions that may defuse conflict. CSCE will also have systems to warn of potential dangers, mechanisms to attempt to mediate them, and ways to engage others to help resolve them. In this way, the structure would help avoid the conditions and bias toward escalation that characterized Europe in August 1914.

Two, NATO would provide a complementary role. A strong defensive Alliance allows for lower levels of military forces and provides a foundation of stability within Europe as a whole. The arms control agenda pursued by NATO will augment this security. NATO's liaison missions will communicate the Alliance's peaceful intentions, encourage civil-military relations, and contribute to a climate discouraging intimidation and aggression.

Three, such other integrating institutions of the Euro-Atlantic community as the EC, the Council of Europe, and the OECD are creating a network of political and economic support. This support both strengthens the new market democracies internally and signals to any would-be threat that these nations are part of a larger community with a stake in their success.

Finally, it is also important to shape the future security agenda in Europe to meet changing challenges, including the special needs of the East. The time has come to set new goals, which go beyond the concept of balance, and begin to establish the basis for a real cooperative security. To this end, I propose a three-tier agenda for future CSCE activities in the arms control and security area.

First, we need to institutionalize openness and transparency in our military affairs. We should intensify our efforts to reach an Open Skies treaty. We should establish a regular dialogue about military forces, budgets, defense plans, and doctrines.

And to address the possible regeneration of forces within the Atlantic to the Urals region, we should consider measures that would provide early and clear indications of rebuilding efforts—not simply to avoid surprise but also to inhibit such moves.

The second part of our agenda is conflict prevention. Such milestone measures as the CFE Treaty and the CSBMs agreement will all but eliminate the threat of a short-warning, massive war in Europe. But we also need to address more discrete localized problems within the CSCE area with the potential to lead to conflict between CSCE members.

These might include new measures to address some of the security concerns of particular regions. They might include new measures to cope with the problems of the Balkans or other areas where stability could be at risk. Some of these measures could be along the lines of arms control and confidence-building measures. They might also involve a broader, political approach, such as supplying CSCE fact-finding, mediation, and peace-keeping capabilities when requested by nations immediately concerned.

Third is the challenge of proliferation: stopping the spread of chemical, biological, and nuclear weapons—as well as the missiles that deliver them—and cooperating in the development of national policies to exercise restraint in the sale of conventional weapons. President Bush has called for a concentrated global effort to meet this challenge. We in the CSCE can contribute by building a partnership of responsibility and restraint.

CSCE members are some of the most important arms suppliers in the world. As an offshoot of East-West confrontation, some CSCE economies have become heavily dependent on exporting weaponry. This is a problem we must address together to find innovative approaches to the problems of defense industry conversion.

Taken as a set—the CFE Treaty and the manpower declarations being negotiated in CFE 1A; CSCE, including this new agenda for arms control; the continued vitality of NATO, including its liaison missions; the EC and other European institutions—we are building the basis for a cooperative security in Europe.

NOTE
1.   Aleksandr Bessmertnykh, USSR Foreign Minister.

KEEP YUGOSLAVIA TOGETHER

113. *from* Statement by the CSCE Ministers of Foreign Affairs. Berlin, June 19, 1991. RFE/RL B-Wire, FF075.

The Foreign Ministers expressed their concern and friendly support for democratic development, unity, and territorial integrity of Yugoslavia, based on economic reforms, full application of human rights in all parts of Yugoslavia, including the rights of minorities and the peaceful solution of the current crisis in the country.

The Ministers stressed that it is only for the peoples of Yugoslavia themselves to decide the country's future. They therefore called for a continued dialogue among all the parties concerned, and confirmed their view that the possibilities for such a dialogue were not yet exhausted.

They expressed their belief that the existing constitutional disputes should be remedied and that a way out of the present difficult impasse should be found without recourse to the use of force and in conformity with legal and constitutional procedures.

They urged all parties concerned to redouble their efforts to resolve their differences peacefully through negotiations.

The Foreign Ministers expressed their confidence that on this basis the international community will stand ready to assist Yugoslavia's efforts to transform itself economically and politically.

THE EMERGENCY MECHANISM

114. *from* Summary of Conclusions by the First CSCE Council of Foreign Ministers. Berlin, June 20, 1991. Associated Press.

Participating States will, in accordance with the following provisions, consult and cooperate with each other concerning a serious emergency situation which may arise from a violation of one of the Principles of the Final Act or as the result of major disruptions endangering peace, security, or stability. ... .

If any participating State concludes that an emergency situation, as described above, is developing, it may seek clarification from the State or States involved. The request will state the cause, or causes, of the concern.

The requested State or States will provide within 48 hours all relevant information in order to clarify the situation giving rise to the request. . . .

Should the situation remain unresolved, any of the States involved in the procedure described . . . above may address to the Chairman-in-Office of the Committee of Senior Officials a request that an emergency meeting of the Committee be held. . . .

As soon as 12 or more of the participating States have seconded the request within a maximum of 48 hours by addressing their support to the Chairman, he will immediately notify all participating States of the date and time of the meeting, which will be held at the earliest 48 hours and the latest three days after this notification. . . .

The meeting will be held at the seat of the Secretariat and last no more than two days, unless otherwise agreed.

The agenda of the emergency meeting will consist of a single item. . . .

The proceedings will be introduced by a short statement by the Chairman recalling the facts and stages of development of the situation. He will then indicate the number of speakers who have asked for the floor and will open the debate.

In light of its assessment of the situation, the meeting may agree on recommendations or conclusions to arrive at a solution. It may also decide to convene a meeting at the ministerial level.

The procedures for convening meetings under this mechanism do not affect the rule of consensus in other circumstances.

LOFTY GOALS BUT LITTLE ELSE?

115. *from* Marc Fisher, "New European Peace Institute Has Lofty Goals, Little Else," *The Washington Post,* June 20, 1991.

Bent Rosenthal, a ghostly figure in a black suit, sits alone amid four empty rooms of a drab office building in the old city.[1] The letters "CSCE" are taped to the front door of the suite.

This is the . . . Conflict Prevention Center of the CSCE, an impressive mouthful for an office that as yet has no shades to ease the late-afternoon glare, no files in which to store important documents, no staff with which to prevent conflicts.

Rosenthal, a Dane who . . . speaks in the soft, careful tones of a successful diplomat, is the harbinger of a new international bureaucracy intended to nip wars and other national conflict in the bud by giving European countries a way to quickly settle suspicions about one another's military moves.

Modest of size but bold of goal, the . . . Center is a $1-million experiment by the CSCE . . . to put some teeth into the "New World Order" idealism. . . .

The center has "a very loosely worded mandate," said Ambassador John Maresca, who represents the United States at the organization. The original idea was to make it "more difficult for nations to prepare hostile actions" by creating a place where all member states would file plans for military exercises, he said.

If any nation suspects another of military action outside such announced exercises and gets no satisfaction from that government within 48 hours, it could call a meeting of CSCE ambassadors at the Vienna center. The CSCE members could then "focus the light of public opinion on the problem," Maresca said.

If that sounds a bit vague, it is, Rosenthal and Maresca agree. In the seven months since the center was created, military movements in the Baltics and Yugoslavia have raised concerns among CSCE members. But in both cases, the Vienna center has received no call for help.

"It's not clear if the provisions setting up the Center apply to internal use of force," Rosenthal said. . . .

"This will never be a European security council," Rosenthal said. But "the real question is, can we live up to this impressive name?"

NOTE
1. Vienna.

TEST BARELY PASSED

116. *from* Robert Mauthner, "CSCE Crisis-Management Mechanism Scrapes Through," *Financial Times,* July 6, 1991.

Europe's new emergency crisis-management mechanism barely passed its first test . . . at a meeting of senior officials from 35 countries that frequently threatened to descend into pure farce.[1]

Much of the 16 hours of talks during the . . . meeting . . . was spent waiting for the phone to ring from Belgrade. It was there that the federal and military Yugoslav authorities were trying to agree on a reply to the CSCE offers to send "good offices" and observer missions to Yugoslavia.

As a result of the Yugoslavs' sensitivities about the precarious military and political situation in their country, several of the CSCE's original proposals were rejected by Belgrade. The word "observers" was finally dropped from the text backing the European Community's intention to organize a mission to Yugoslavia.

It was nevertheless made clear that such a mission would be sent "to help stabilize a cease-fire" and to monitor the return of troops to their barracks. The CSCE's other offer, to send a "good offices" mission to facilitate a political dialogue among the parties concerned in Yugoslavia, was shorn of one of its essential elements as a result of Yugoslav objections.

The federal authorities refused to accept a phrase which said one of the tasks of the "good offices" mission would be "the establishment of a new constitutional order" in Yugoslavia. The implied threat to the unitary state was clearly too much for the federal and military authorities in Belgrade to swallow at this delicate juncture in their relations with the two breakaway republics of Slovenia and Croatia.

The Soviet Union, though adopting a generally constructive attitude, also found it difficult to endorse a text permitting an international "good offices" mission to intervene in the internal political disputes of a member nation.

It finally did so. But, with an eye on its own troubles with the Baltic and other Soviet republics, Moscow insisted on making a unilateral declaration that such a procedure should not be considered a precedent. In other words, what may be all right for Yugoslavia, is not necessarily acceptable for the Soviet Union.

The talks underlined the shortcomings of the CSCE, which can be paralyzed by the veto of a single member country. The rule that all decisions must be taken by consensus and that the 1975 Helsinki agreement principle of non-intervention in the internal affairs of member states can be invoked at any time, have been shown to be serious obstacles to effective decision-making and the adoption of practical measures.

The final text on the "good offices" mission still left doubt about its acceptability to Yugoslavia. "If and when accepted by Yugoslavia," it said, though the Yugoslav delegate at the meeting had apparently signalled his oral approval after hours of telephone conversations with Belgrade.

However, the most significant indication of the relative impotence of the CSCE was the frank recognition in the final texts of the

European Community's leading role as a mediator in the Yugoslav crisis.

The EC acted much more quickly and flexibly than the CSCE in sending its "troika" of foreign ministers to Yugoslavia after Slovenia and Croatia had declared themselves independent.

Moreover, its plan for defusing the crisis—acceptance of a cease-fire, return of troops to their barracks, restoration of constitutional rules for the rotation of the presidency and suspension for three months of the implementation of independence declarations—formed the basis of all the CSCE's proposals.

The CSCE can derive some satisfaction from the fact that its emergency crisis-management mechanism, adopted in Berlin amid much self-congratulation only two weeks ago, has at least functioned, if belatedly. But, to the extent that international mediation can help to solve Yugoslavia's internal crisis, it is the EC that will be at the sharp end.

NOTE
1. CSCE Senior Officials meeting, Prague, July 5, 1991.

The CSCE in Another World

SOVIET DECLARATION
OF HUMAN RIGHTS AND FREEDOMS

117. *from* Declaration of Human Rights and Freedoms, Congress of
USSR People's Deputies. Moscow, September 6, 1991. TASS.

The freedom of the individual, his or her honor and dignity are of
supreme value in our society. Everyone is guaranteed the realization
of his or her aptitude for work and creative potential, active participation in public and state affairs. No group, party or state interests
may be placed above the interests of the individual.

Guided by the common principles of democracy, humanism,
social justice and proceeding from the lessons of the Soviet Union's
history, the Congress of USSR People's Deputies adopts this declaration.

Article 1. Every person possesses natural, inalienable and inviolable rights and freedoms. They are sealed in laws that must correspond to the Universal Declaration of Human Rights, the international covenants on human rights and other international norms and
this declaration.

All state agencies are obliged to ensure and protect human rights
and freedoms as supreme social values.

The exercise of the rights by the citizen should not run counter
to the rights of other people.

Every person bears constitutional duties, the discharge of which
is essential for the normal development of society.

Article 2. The provisions of the declaration are directly effective
and must be enacted by all state agencies, officials, public organizations and citizens. . . .

Article 5. No one may be deprived of one's citizenship or the
right to change citizenship.

Every citizen who is outside his state is guaranteed legal protection.

Article 6. Every person has the right to the freedom of speech and to an unimpeded expression of opinions and convictions and to their dissemination orally or in a written form. Mass media are free. Censorship is not allowed.

The ideological, religious and cultural freedom is guaranteed. There should be no state ideology made incumbent upon citizens. . . .

. . . Citizens have the right to unite into political parties, trade unions and other public organizations and participate in mass movements. . . .

Article 12. Every person has the right to receive full and true information on the state of affairs in all spheres of state, economic, social and international life, and on issues of rights, legal interests and duties.

Publication of laws and other normative enactments is a necessary condition for applying them.

Article 13. The right to live is an inalienable right of every person. Nobody can be arbitrarily deprived of life.

The state protects people from illegal encroachments on life, health, personal freedom and security.

Article 14. Every person has the right for protection of his honor and reputation and defense against any arbitrary interference in personal life.

Article 15. Inviolability of a person is guaranteed. Nobody can be arrested or illegally kept in custody, except on the basis of a court decision or a prosecutor's sanction. In case of arrest or custody, every citizen has the right for a court examination or taking an appeal against such actions.

Every person made answerable for violating the law, shall be considered not guilty, until his guilt is ascertained by the court within the framework of a proper legal action. . . .

Article 21. Every person has the right to move freely inside the country, choose residence and location. The right can be limited only by the law.

Citizens have the right to leave their country and return to it, and they cannot be expelled from the country.

Article 22. Every person has the right to appeal to court against illegal actions by officials, state bodies and public organizations and the right for redress of moral and material damages.

Article 23. Every person has the right to labor and its results, including the possibility to use personal abilities to productive and creative labor, the right to freely choose a job and reject it, to favorable working conditions, guaranteed minimum payment and protection against unemployment. Every person has the right to equal remuneration for equal labor.

Workers have the right to defend their economic and social interests, to collective bargaining and to strike. Forced labor is forbidden under the law.

Article 24. Every person enjoys property rights, including the right to own, use and dispose of property, both individually and jointly with other individuals. Ownership rights are guaranteed by law. The inalienable right to own property guarantees personal individual interests and freedoms.

Article 25. Every person has the right to sufficient and dignified living standard, to improve living standards and to social welfare. Everyone is granted the right to leisure, social benefits in old age, in case of illness, disability, loss of the breadwinner and after having a child.

Article 26. Every person has the right to education. Primary education is compulsory. Vocational, secondary special and higher education shall be available for all in accordance with every person's ability. Education at state schools is free.

Article 27. Every person has the right to state support in receiving and permanently utilizing an apartment with basic amenities in state or publicly-owned buildings or in building houses individually. A person cannot be dispossessed of housing arbitrarily, unless on grounds established by law.

Article 28. Every person has the right to health protection, including free use of a broad network of state health care facilities.

Article 29. A person has the right to favorable natural environment and to compensation of damage incurred to his health or property by ecological violations.

Article 30. The execution of rights and freedoms is incompatible with actions harming state and public security, public order, public health and moral integrity, human rights and freedoms.

Article 31. The right of nations to self-determination should not contradict individual rights and freedoms declared by this declaration.

EUROPE'S DUTY TO INTRUDE

118. *from* Speech by Hans-Dietrich Genscher, FRG minister of foreign affairs. CSCE Conference on the Human Dimension, Moscow, September 10, 1991.

Observance of the principles of the Charter of Paris[1] is not an internal matter for the signatory States; rather, it is an internal matter for the community of nations. Now the important point is for us to agree to counter contraventions of the principles of the Helsinki Final Act and the Charter of Paris with sanctions. This applies not only to violations of human and minority rights, but also to attempts to undermine the rule of law, to the suspension of constitutional order and to breaches of the harmonious coexistence of nations. To protect these individual and collective legal assets, we should agree on a system right here in Moscow which permits the sending of monitor missions also in cases where the country concerned does not grant its consent. In this way the CSCE would become one of the reliable guarantors of stability and security in Europe.

The cooperative organization of security in Europe and the protection of human and minority rights, democracy and the rule of law are the fundamental issues of our time. The emergency mechanism established in Berlin still has to prove itself. The joint response of the CSCE states to the developments in Yugoslavia demonstrated that:

- The use of force in one of the CSCE participating States concerns all of us.

- The democratic solidarity of the community of CSCE States calls necessarily for the solution of all disputes in Yugoslavia exclusively by peaceful means.

- Responsibility is defined as European responsibility towards each other.

- The CSCE principles apply everywhere—both beyond and within national boundaries. . . .

. . . We will never accept the threat or use of force in Yugoslavia, and we will never recognize boundaries changed by force. . . .

Like human rights, democracy and the rule of law, too, need to be protected and safeguarded internally and secured within the CSCE framework. In the event of an attempted coup d'état or putsch we must firmly support the legitimate constitutional organs committed to human rights, democracy and the rule of law. Should such a coup d'état or putsch succeed, we must take all possible steps to ensure that a participating State represented by such a regime returns to compliance with the obligations undertaken in the Helsinki Final Act and the Charter of Paris, and reestablishes its constitutional order. I propose the inclusion of the following principles in the Document to come from this Moscow meeting:

1. The enforcement of CSCE obligations by the CSCE participating States vis-à-vis another State cannot be construed as intervention in internal affairs.

2. Activities within a State in contravention of assumed CSCE obligations will not be recognized by the community of CSCE States. Insurgents cannot count on recognition. We insist on the reestablishment of the constitutional order.

3. The regime of a CSCE participating State which commits or permits serious violations of the Charter of Paris, particularly regarding human rights, national rights to self-determination and the democratic order of public life will run the risk of isolation by the community of CSCE States.

4. Isolation also means that all other CSCE States may agree on the measures they deem necessary to reinforce the system of values of the Charter of Paris, without being hindered by the need to achieve consensus with the regime involved.

5. The sending of CSCE observers to report on the conflict in a CSCE country at the suggestion of another CSCE State must be possible, even without the agreement of the country concerned. . . .

We are in favor of the introduction of a rapporteur procedure in the sphere of the Human Dimension. I support the remarks made by the Foreign Minister of the Netherlands on behalf of the European Community and its member States. It must be possible to conduct such monitor missions even without the agreement of any State concerned, since in the case of human rights violations, the objection of intervention in internal affairs must no longer be allowed to apply. But a voluntary procedure would also be useful which gave the participating States the opportunity to help in diverse ways to solve internal problems of other member States at their invitation. This could extend from fact-finding via good offices to the settlement of disputes. . . .

I should like to call for a new-style debate on implementation. In the past, we have concentrated heavily on poor human rights records on the part of governments. That was important and will remain so. Proceeding on the conviction that we wish to realize our community of shared values throughout our countries, there must be more cooperation and support among us. We need practical cooperation between those participating States which are in the process of building up their state as a democracy under the rule of law, and those which have firmly anchored, proven structures in these areas.

The European legal area must have the same standards as regards:

- legal protection for the individual vis-à-vis administrative acts,

- constitutional jurisdiction, and

- criminal, civil and commercial law.

In this context, the diversity of legal systems in Europe is not an obstacle. It is an expression of historical developments, but must not become a reason for varying quality. I propose the abolition of the death penalty throughout Europe. Our partners who are in the development phase should turn specifically for support and cooperation to individual participating States or groups of States.

NOTE
1.   Document 98.

HUMAN RIGHTS IN PUBLIC EMERGENCY

119. *from* "Human Rights and Fundamental Freedoms During a State of Public Emergency," Proposal submitted by the Estonian and Soviet delegations. CSCE Conference on the Human Dimension, Moscow, September 25, 1991. CSCE/CHDM.1/Rev.1.

The participating States will ensure that a public emergency is not proclaimed except in exceptional and grave circumstances threatening the life of the nation. The objective of the state of public emergency can be the defense of a State in time of war, protection of the democratic constitutional order, the rule of law and human rights and fundamental freedoms. The use of force must be avoided to the maximum extent possible. . . .

A state of emergency may only be proclaimed by a constitutionally lawful body duly empowered to do so. In cases where the decision to impose a state of public emergency may be lawfully taken by the executive authorities, that decision should be subject to approval (and control) by the legislature in the shortest possible time. . . .

The decision to impose a state of public emergency must be proclaimed officially, publicly, and in accordance with the provisions laid down by law. The state of public emergency only comes into force once such a proclamation has been made. . . .

A *de facto* imposition of a state of public emergency, i.e., the adoption of emergency measures without an official proclamation or the continuation of emergency measures after the state of public emergency has been lifted, is not permissible. . . .

. . . the activities of the legislative bodies cannot be interfered in during a state of public emergency.

The participating States will endeavor to refrain from making any derogations from obligations relating to human rights and fundamental freedoms during a state of public emergency. If undertaken, such derogations must remain strictly within the limits provided for by international law. . . .

. . . Persons who have been arrested or detained by the authorities will retain at all times the right to a hearing in the shortest possible time before a judicial or similarly competent body established by law. They will endeavor to maintain the freedom of expression and freedom of information, with a view to enabling a public and informed discussion on the observance of human rights and fundamental freedoms and a lifting of a state of public emergency.

The participating States will inform the other CSCE States without delay of all cases of the imposition or lifting of a state of public emergency, indicating the reasons for such a decision, as well as of any measures which derogate from their obligations in the field of human rights, through the CSCE Secretariat or another body appointed for that purpose.

A participating State in which a state of public emergency has been proclaimed will, at the request of other participating States, admit CSCE observers into the areas covered by the state of public emergency for the duration of its application.

THE MOSCOW FINAL DOCUMENT

120. *from* **Edith M. Lederer, "Delegates Consider Strengthening Rights Monitoring." Report by Associated Press correspondent, Moscow, October 3, 1991. RFE/RL B-Wire, FF0092.**

Delegates from 38 nations . . . considered a final document that would strengthen human rights monitoring. . . .

The document establishes both voluntary and mandatory procedures to investigate alleged human rights violations and creates a pool of 114 experts, three from each member state, who would be called on to conduct fact-finding missions. . . .

Under the mandatory procedure, three-member fact-finding teams would be sent to investigate alleged abuses in a member nation without its consent if 10 countries demand an inquiry or if a Committee of Senior CSCE Officials authorizes it.[1]

Reports from the mission would be submitted to the Committee of Senior Officials which could decide on follow-up action.

NOTE
1. See Document 99.

121. *from* **Edith M. Lederer, "Rights Conference Split over Effectiveness of Investigations." Report by Associated Press correspondent, Moscow, October 4, 1991. RFE/RL B-Wire, FF0093.**

The Final Document adopted . . . by the . . . CSCE[1] . . . for the first time authorizes investigations of member countries without their consent.

The United States, Canada and all European nations also agreed to abandon the long-cherished principle of not interfering in the affairs of other states and declared human rights to be the "legitimate concern" of all countries.

US Ambassador Max M. Kampelman called the new mechanism "the most important, even historic, contribution" of the meeting. "For the first time in the history of the CSCE process the CSCE is now equipped to apply its resources directly to help a fellow member deal constructively" with its human rights, Kampelman said.

But Sergei Kovalev, co-chairman of the Soviet delegation and a former political prisoner, said the 24-page document leaves "a certain bitter aftertaste" because it does not include an effective mechanism for automatic and compulsory monitoring of human rights violations.

"The whole CSCE process proves completely ineffective and helpless," he said, blaming the organization's rule that all decisions must be adopted by consensus.

The Soviets backed a German proposal to impose unspecified sanctions against any violating country. Diplomatic sources, speaking anonymously, said Britain, France and the United States were among nations opposing the German proposal.

Britain, apparently worried about the impact of mandatory investigations on Northern Ireland, held up approval of the final document for four hours while the cabinet met in London.

A senior Western diplomat, speaking on condition he was not identified, backed the Soviet position. He called the new mechanism "a pussycat" that can't deal with the problem of minority rights.

During a final round of speeches Friday, Polish ambassador Roman Kuzinar, who backed tougher measures to rapidly redress violations, said many states were afraid that mandatory procedures "might be used against them as well."

"It is a paradox that among them are states with longstanding traditions of pluralist democracy and the rule of law, states which eventually had enabled democratic transformations in Europe to come true," he said.

German ambassador Ernst von Studnitz said his country would continue to press for tougher mechanisms to allow CSCE to recommend peaceful solutions of rights violations "to impel the state that is in breach of its obligations once again to fulfill them". . . .

Von Studnitz and Swedish ambassador Henrik Amneus noted the conference's failure to take any new action on the rights of national minorities.

"In our further work in CSCE and elsewhere, we have a responsibility to see to it that the question of national minorities is dealt with in an appropriate manner," Amneus said. "If we do not live up to this, the problem will continue to destabilize our common security for years to come."

Bulgarian ambassador Atanas Nastev said member nations should wait to see how the new procedure is used before judging its effectiveness.

Delegates met against the backdrop of the Yugoslav civil war, the demise of the Soviet Communist Party following the August coup, and rising ethnic tensions as long-repressed nationalist sentiments are unleashed in former communist countries.

Another Western diplomat, speaking anonymously, said the conference was spurred to action by its impotence in dealing with Yugoslavia. CSCE's repeated appeals for Yugoslavia to end hostilities and seek a peaceful solution have gone unheeded.

The Final Document said new procedures for investigating alleged human rights violations would protect the rights of minorities. But it wasn't clear how this would be done. . . .

Ambassador Max van der Stoel of the Netherlands, speaking on behalf of the 12-nation European Community, said the Final Document "constitutes a significant step forward."

In other actions, the 38 nations agreed to protect human rights during a state of emergency, a key Soviet demand following the coup. The nations also recognized the need for CSCE nations "to make democratic advances irreversible."

The Final Document also calls for protection of journalists, equality of women and men, equal rights for the disabled and migrant workers, improved conditions for prisoners, and freedom of movement— a key human rights issue in the Soviet Union.

NOTE
1.   At the end of the third meeting of the Conference on the Human Dimension, Moscow, October 3, 1991.

THE NEED TO CHANGE DIRECTION

122. *from* Roland Eggleston, "Helsinki Process to Change Direction." Report by RFE/RL correspondent, Moscow, September 30, 1991. RFE/ RL B-Wire, FF0051.

Diplomats in the US and Europe are working on a new concept for the Helsinki process following the political transformations in Europe. . . .

The change in direction is expected to be approved at a summit meeting in Helsinki in March next year which will be attended by President Bush and leaders of the other 37 governments.

A special meeting on democratic institutions will be held in Norway in November to prepare the way. The 10-day meeting will discuss constitutional reform, the need for independent courts, the importance of free trade unions and the organization of democratic elections and political parties.

The change in direction, expected to be approved at a summit in

Helsinki in March [1992], is already apparent at the human rights conference in Moscow. There's been no discussion at all on political prisoners or other traditional causes. Instead most of the debates have focussed on how to defuse internal tensions and ensure respect for the rule of law.

Hungary believes the new-model Helsinki process can also play an important role in stabilizing democracy in states declaring independence. The leader of the Hungarian delegation in Moscow, Zsuzsanna Hargitai, has been very active in promoting this idea.

"The Helsinki process should be a permanent forum to discuss the problems associated with the birth or rebirth of states," she told delegates. "The Helsinki process could send missions to monitor referendums on declaring sovereignty; it could act as mediators in case of conflicting interests." She said the Helsinki process could also help new states draw up democratic laws.

Hungary also wants the new-model Helsinki process to take a strong role in protecting Europe's minorities. It believes more minorities will appear as new states are born.

Some diplomats believe the change in direction will bring an end to some of the traditions of the current Helsinki process. In particular it seems possible that the Helsinki process will modify the rule requiring the consensus of all 38 states for every decision. At present the rule is so rigid that even a decision to take a coffee break requires the agreement of all 38 states.

The chief Soviet delegate, Deputy Foreign Minister Yuri Deryabin, is among those who believe the consensus rule should be abolished in at least some situations.

"It is the only way to allow action to be taken," he told reporters recently. "It is difficult to get 38 states to reach unanimous agreement on decisive action. It will be even harder if the process grows to 45 or more states." Several of the Soviet republics are expected to join in coming years. That is another issue for the summit meeting in Helsinki next March. . . .

Some governments also want a reduction in the number of public meetings, like the current Human Rights Conference in Moscow. Germany in particular believes that more problems should be discussed at private meetings between officials rather than at the present large-scale events.

A start has already been made on this with the regular meetings of Senior Officials in Prague. These are highly-restricted gatherings which give the press and non-government organizations virtually no access to the officials. The main source of information is a communiqué read after the meeting is over. This means the public gets little information about the positions taken by individual governments or the disputes which arise.

Both the United States and Britain say they will resist any trend towards secrecy in the Helsinki process. They would prefer more openness.

The US says it is worried that private meetings will limit the effectiveness of non-governmental organizations, such as human rights groups, minority organizations or associations of independent lawyers. Such groups have an important role in bringing problems and causes to the attention of governments. . . .

Whether they continue to play a role will depend on how the new-model Helsinki process evolves. Diplomats say the most important thing is that the Helsinki process will survive and will continue to push for the observance of human rights in all the states of Europe.

APPENDIX

CHRONOLOGY OF CSCE MEETINGS, 1986–1991

Date	*Location*	*Meeting*
1986		
April 2–11	Bern	Preparatory meeting to the Meeting of Experts on Human Contacts
April 15–May 27	Bern	Meeting of Experts on Human Contacts
Sept. 23–Oct. 6	Vienna	Preparatory meeting to the Vienna CSCE Review Meeting
Nov. 4, 1986– Jan. 19, 1989	Vienna	Vienna CSCE Review Meeting
1989		
March 6–9	Vienna	3-day mtg. of foreign ministers from the 35 CSCE countries to open negotiations on a) Confidence- and Security-Building Measures (CSBM), and b) Conventional Armed Forces in Europe (CFE) (Vienna Talks)
March 9, 1989–	Vienna	Negotiations on Confidence- and Security-Building Measures (CSBM)
March 9, 1989– Nov. 21, 1990	Vienna	Negotiations on Conventional Armed Forces in Europe (CFE)
April 18–May 12	London	London Information Forum
May 30–June 23	Paris	First Meeting of the Conference on the Human Dimension
Oct. 16–Nov. 3	Sofia	Meeting on the Protection of the Environment

1990

March 19–April 11	Bonn	Conference on Economic Cooperation
June 5–29	Copenhagen	Second Meeting of the Conference on the Human Dimension
Sept. 24–Oct. 19	Palma de Mallorca	Meeting on the Mediterranean
July 10–Nov. 17	Vienna	Preparatory Committee for CSCE Summit
Oct. 1–2	New York	Meeting of CSCE Foreign Ministers
Nov. 19–21	Paris	CSCE Summit
Nov. 29, 1990–	Vienna	CFE 1A Negotiations

1991

Jan. 15–Feb. 8	Valletta	Meeting of Experts on Peaceful Settlement of Disputes
Jan. 28–29	Vienna	Committee of Senior Officials
Feb. 25	Vienna	Meeting of the Consultative Committee to the CPC
May 23–24	Prague	Committee of Senior Officials
May 28–June 7	Cracow	Symposium on Cultural Heritage
June 16–17	Berlin	Committee of Senior Officials
June 19–20	Berlin	Council of Foreign Ministers
July 1–19	Geneva	Meeting of Experts on National Minorities
Sept. 10–Oct. 4	Moscow	Third Meeting of the Conference on the Human Dimension
Oct. 8–18	Vienna	Second Seminar on Military Doctrine
Nov. 4–15	Oslo	Seminar on Democratic Institutions

ACKNOWLEDGMENTS

Generous permission to reprint the articles and book extracts contained in this volume has been granted by the following publishers:
The American Enterprise Institute for Public Policy Research, Washington, DC [2, 5, 6]; Reuters [10, 83, 89, 91, 101]; The Baltimore Sun [16]; Frankfurter Allgemeine Zeitung [17]; The Carnegie Council on Ethics and International Affairs [22]; International Affairs [23]; City News Publishing Co. [29]; Associated Press [33, 114, 120, 121]; Los Angeles Times [34]; Knight-Ridder Tribune News [36]; The Independent [44, 57, 94]; John Maresca/IHT (distribution by New York Times Syndication Sales) [53]; Süddeutsche Zeitung [54]; The Washington Post [60, 86, 115]; Le Monde [61]; The New York Times Company [67, 95]; NP Engel Verlag (for the Human Rights Law Journal) [85]; NATO Review [87]; Circolo di Studi Diplomatici [88]; Agence France-Presse [92]; The Economist Newspaper Ltd. [93]; The Boston Globe [100]; The Times [102]; Financial Times Syndication [103, 116].

INDEX

Afghanistan, 5, 53, 123
Akhromeev, Sergei, 10, 72–74
Albania: CSCE observer status of, 31, 233; and final report of Geneva minorities meeting, 43; Greek minority in, 233; refugees from, 42
Albanian minority in Yugoslavia, 43
Amneus, Henrik, 325
Andersson, Sten, 264
Andreeva, Nina, 122
Antall, József, 275, 288, 291
Anti-Semitism, 251
Arbitration. *See* Dispute-settlement mechanism
Armellini, Antonio, 174–77
Armenians in USSR, 121
Arms Control Association, 152
Arms race, 6
Arms trade, 310
Assembly, freedom of, 247, 279
Austria, 22, 184–85

Bahr, Egon, 147
Baker, James A.: on Baltic republics, 263–64; at Berlin foreign ministers meeting, 40, 307–10; and CFE treaty, 38–39; and CSCE institutionalization, 40; on new European architecture, 25–26, 196–97, 287–88, 307–10
Baltic republics, 39, 121, 187–89, 278–79; CSCE membership of, 44; CSCE observer status for, 34, 263–65, 290
Barry, Robert, 75–76
Baryshnikov, Mikhail, 96
Basket One, 109–10, 196
Basket Three, 2, 4, 45, 109–10, 187–88
Basket Two, 25, 29, 45, 109, 196, 218
Bauer, William E., 171–74
BBC, 97

Belgrade Review Meeting (1977–1978), 6
Berlin Meeting of Council of Foreign Ministers (1991), 40–41, 307–12
Bern Meeting of Experts on Human Contacts (1986), 7–9, 61–70, 105; draft final documents of, 8, 63–67, 92; and family reunification, 64; final document of, vetoed by US, 8, 67–69, 108; and freedom of information, 63, 66; and freedom of religion, 64; and freedom of travel, 63–65, 66; and human contacts, 63–66; statements by US at, 61–63, 68–69; statement by USSR at, 69–70
Bessmertnykh, Aleksandr, 39, 40, 308
Biological weapons, 310
Blackwell, J. Kenneth, 302–3
Blechman, Barry M., 152
Bondevik, Kjell Magne, 264
Bonn Conference on Economic Cooperation (1990), 29–30, 217–28; draft final document of, 30, 219–22; and environmental protection, 227; final document of, 222–28; and forced labor, 220, 223; and free elections, 220, 223; and free trade, 220, 224; and industrial cooperation, 225–26; and job discrimination, 220, 223; and market economies, 220, 223–24; preparations for, 217–18; and private property, 220, 222, 223–24; and rule of law, 220, 223; and ten principles proposed by US, 220–22; and trade unions, 220, 223
Bozer, Ali, 237
Brandt, Willy, 263
Brezhnev, Leonid, 3, 121
Brezhnev doctrine, 10
Budapest Appeal, 13, 75, 91, 109–10

and jamming of foreign broadcasts, 16–17, 97, 124, 126–29, 137; and Jewish emigration, 97; and Jewish minority in USSR, 106; and labor camps, 124–25; and Mediterranean region, 90; and migrant workers, 242; and minority rights, 106, 136, 177, 249–50; and political prisoners, 96, 124–26; proposal by EC and NATO member states at, 101–2; proposal by USSR at, 102–3; proposals submitted at, 103–6; and proposed Moscow meeting, 11–12; and protection of journalists, 137; and psychiatric abuse, 124–25, 135; and reservation by Romania to concluding document of, 18, 24, 141–42, 192–93; and right to education, 92–93, 141; and right to employment, 92, 93, 141; and right to equal pay for equal work, 141; and right to housing, 92, 93, 141; and right to medical care, 92; and right to peace, 93; and scientific exchange, 138–39; and standard of living, 141; statement by Romania at, 141–42; statement by US at, 95–97; statements by USSR at, 88–93, 93–95, 149–51; and terrorism, 137; and

torture, 136; and tourism, 139; and trade, 138; and Turkish minority in Bulgaria, 182–84; US strategy at, 12, 85–87
Voice of America, 97, 131
von Studnitz, Ernst, 325

Warsaw Pact: at Bern meeting, 65–67; Budapest Appeal issued by, 13, 75, 91, 109–10; and CFE talks, 27, 148–49; dissolution of, 26–28, 35, 40, 193, 209–10, 275, 288; future of in new Europe, 201–3; internal divisions in, 142–44, 157
Williams, Anthony, 64
World Bank, 292

Yazov, Dmitrii, 290–91
Yeltsin, Boris, 121
Yılmaz, A. Mesut, 182–83
Yugoslav crisis, 39–40, 41–42, 311, 313–15, 320, 325–26
Yugoslavia, 33, 41, 43, 239–42

Zamfirescu, Elena, 303–4
Die Zeit, 263
Zhivkov, Todor, 22–23, 183, 191–92
Zimmermann, Warren, 12, 95–97, 111–12, 140

ABOUT THE AUTHOR

Vojtech Mastny is Professor of International Relations and Director of the Research Institute at the Paul H. Nitze School of Advanced International Studies of the Johns Hopkins University in Bologna, Italy. He is also a visiting professor at Charles University in Prague. His most recent positions include Professor of International Relations at Boston University and Fulbright Senior Professor at the University of Bonn. Professor Mastny was also a 1990–1991 Research Adjunct at the Institute for East-West Security Studies.

Professor Mastny has taught and written about the history of international relations, European security, Soviet foreign policy, and Central European politics. His publications include *The Czechs Under Nazi Rule: The Failure of National Resistance, 1939–42* (New York: Columbia University Press, 1971) and *Russia's Road to the Cold War: Diplomacy, Warfare, and the Politics of Communism, 1941–45* (New York: Columbia University Press, 1979). His previous book on the CSCE, *Helsinki, Human Rights, and European Security: Analysis and Documentation,* was published in 1986 by Duke University Press.